The World at 15mph...ish

Naomi Johnson

Published in 2023 by Bold Font Publishing

ISBN Paperback: 978-1-7393811-0-3
Ebook: 978-1-7393811-1-0

A CIP catalogue copy of this book can be found in the British Library.

Published with the help of Indie Authors World
www.indieauthorsworld.com

IndieAuthors
World

To all those who helped to make this adventure happen. Friends, family, and strangers.

Your support, challenge and kindness will never be forgotten.

Table of Contents

INTRODUCTION

I hope you will find this an enjoyable and informative read. The book sets out to provide an overview of a long cycle tour taking in various parts so the world.

For those of you planning similar routes there are detailed tables highlighting miles travelled, metres ascended and descended and stop over points. However, data gathering varied and where we rode following a company organised route, I have not given a breakdown in this way, though distances are noted within the main narrative.

There are some key achievements in the book, most notably riding over the Thorong-la mountain pass in Nepal and going from Cairo to Capetown, but this is an attempt by a non-athlete, and someone determined to be a tourist as much as a cyclist.

I hope the story that follows offers inspiration whatever your dream.

1.

THE JOURNEY

"All journeys can have their own individual meaning and motivation.

However, every journey is a journey to connect with people, to connect with the planet, and to connect with oneself."

Satish Kumar, Earth Pilgrim

The human quest for knowledge and experience has been with us throughout history. Despite everything we know already, it seems there is always something new to discover. Another journey yet to travel – another diverging road. There is always more we can learn about ourselves.

Maybe we can leave ourselves behind a little when we simply go on holiday or take a short break. When we travel, we take every part of us along too. Satish Kumar, in writing of pilgrimage says that "we make the outer journey in order to make an inner journey."

I can't pretend my trip was a pilgrimage and, perhaps on a bicycle, I was still going too fast, but this is a book about a journey. This is a book that tells the tale of a cycle trip around the world, but it's also more than that. Travel tells a story of human nature; in the people we meet and our reactions to the world around us. It's also about what we leave at home. It gives us real time to think – an exploration of oneself out from the usual constraints. Freedom to do, freedom to be, and freedom to change.

In July 2012, I set out on a near 20,000-mile cycle trip around the world. Travelling with a man I'd met just three times prior; this would be the adventure of a lifetime. There are many things I love about riding my bike: I love the speed, the environment, the freedom, the achievement. I love the people I meet, the food I can eat. I love the planning, as well as the ride. I also love coming home, even if it would never be the same again.

2.

SPEED

"Slow down and enjoy life. It is not only the scenery you miss by going too fast. You also miss the sense of where you are going and why."

Unknown

Like many people, I'd probably been going too fast for some time. Long work hours, lots of interests, friends, and subsequent socialising. I was tired, suffering with shingles and yet still burning the candle at both ends. Sometimes, life has a way of telling us what we need to do, and life was about to do just that.

According to physics, speed=time/distance. Used as a verb, it means "going quickly" and when people talk of speed, it is often in this context. There are 168 hours in a week, and given we spend around a third of this sleeping we are left with around 112 hours of waking time. Incredibly, many people watch television for around 28 hours. By contrast, while some pass time watching the real and fictional lives of others, others race through with their "to-do" lists. According to recent reports, while average working hours have reduced in the past few decades, 20% of people still work over 45 hours a week. I was most certainly in this latter category. Constantly setting new goals I was speeding through life. It was time to reassess.

In his book, *In Praise of Slow*, Carl Honoré takes time, literally, to describe a new movement and pace, noting that the slow movement is more a philosophy for how we live our lives than a strict description of its speed. As efficiency increases, so too do expectations. Stress has replaced backache as the key cause of absenteeism from the workplace, and as fast thinking (rational, analytical) takes precedence, we leave less time for creativity. Increasingly, we see surges in approaches such as mindfulness, yet "slow" still seems to be a dirty word and being mindful still needs to be diarised.

While rushing around, I'd lost my mojo. I moved to Edinburgh, slightly arrogant, proud of achievements and more than ready for my new post. My previous life had become steady. It was predictable. I was surrounded by many amazing friends, but with no time to meet new people. It was routine, full of regular habits and activities. Life was stagnant, and I was tired. Five years later, I found myself in the same position: busy, stagnant, and tired. I was also struggling. While passionate about the work we did, I was far removed from the real activity. I'd become stressed, anxious, and caught up in politics. I was starting to take note of what I didn't want to do. What was I looking for? What would I do next? I'd worked hard to be in this position, and while I didn't want to go backwards, I wanted other aspects of my life back.

I'd started to consider my next options. There was one great new role coming up that would enable me to follow my dream of building my own home further north, and an interest in establishing my own business at some point in the future. The job application was complete, and I would sell my house in Bristol, putting money towards either a self-build or in-part investment in a new enterprise. The idea of a big cycle trip wasn't even on the radar yet. It wasn't until Friday, 27th October 2011 that I started considering a cycle tour. I hadn't always been a keen cyclist, or at least, not consistently. I remember being a little girl and setting off from my gran's house in the summer holidays. Always home for tea, I would head out on my bike, never too far and always with a project in mind. However, as teenage years hit and vanity struck, the bike was out. I was 21 before I would ride a bike again – just short rides with lots of moaning on all the hills. I drank, smoked, and – all in all – was pretty unfit.

In 2004, aged 29 I needed a holiday. I had money, time due from work, and yet no one to travel with. Many of my friends were either skint, coupled up, or simply interested in different holidays to me. Eventually, I signed up for a cycle trip through

Vietnam, despite a 30-mile return trip along the Bristol to Bath cycle path being my longest ride to date. Every morning before work, I would get going on my exercise bike, I'd head out on a weekend and would even persuade people for rides after work, which in February/March was not always easy. I still remember the night a friend accidentally cycled into the river on the way home!

It was the trip to Vietnam that brought back my love for the road. A love of going not at 70mph but much, much slower, feeling the contours, working up a sweat and being a part of the environment around me. Despite being the least fit and last to arrive, I felt so proud the day I reached the top of the Hai Van pass. One of the guys on that trip had cycled Land's End to John O'Groats, and on talking to my friends on my return, I announced this was to be my next big bike adventure. And it was – the following year. That year, I hit 30, and the countdown was on. I gave up smoking, ran my first half-marathon, and cycled 1100 miles – a camping trip, mostly very wet, with my good friend Tom. Then, I just became too busy again. I was going too fast, and the treadmill just kept rolling.

Since moving to Scotland, ironically, given the scenery and my love for the outdoors my cycling here had reduced. Fewer friends were interested in riding, and I was not great at getting out without company. A lack of familiarity with routes and a somewhat irrational fear of just being out on my own (oh, to be that fearless 12-year-old again!) meant my rides were dependent on others and were therefore much less frequent. But what of that day in October? It was my colleague Kim who mentioned it first...

In 2007, Mark Beaumont, a Scottish cyclist and adventurer, smashed the Guinness World Record for circumnavigating the world on his bike. Through promotion at various cycle clubs, an event had been organised where he would be doing a free talk about his record attempt. One of these talks was in Edinburgh. Kim and her husband were already booked, and on October 27th 2011 she received an email notifying her that more tickets were still available. That email was forwarded to me. However, while the talk was of interest, it was the reason behind the event that then made me desperate for a spot. Mark was also launching the opportunity to join a supported trip cycling the globe. I was now in a unique position in my life where I could join this World Cycle Challenge. However, my job application had also been successful, and I was invited to a first-round interview. Of 71 applications, I had made it to the top 11.

My parents were anxious at this time, and news that I had an interview was a big relief to them. They were keen to see me settle again. I remember telling my father he would need to really hope I got the job, as he wouldn't like plan B! Plan B would be a tough sell to both my parents, and on that basis, I chose not to reveal what I had in mind.

The day of Mark's talk coincided with my father's birthday, and as I headed up to the Royal College of Physicians, I phoned my dad to wish him many happy returns. Naturally, he asked where I was going, and on telling him of my destination, he put two and two together. The call finished with "I really hope you get that job." I came home that night knowing I really wanted to cycle the world, and my great friend, Jim, helped me pay a deposit for the trip, given it was cheaper if I committed by the end of November. Even if I couldn't do it all, I was going to ride a significant section. Life was passing by, and I was determined to enjoy the scenery.

Work ended on the 30th of November, and while incredibly nervous as to what would happen next, I was excited about the year ahead. I had a second interview for the job in the Highlands, and on the 3rd of December, I was flying out to Sri Lanka for a two-week cycle trip, having already booked this break some time ago. Friends were all behind me with my interview; it was a great position and one I would accept should the offer come my way. I was in Kandy, Sri Lanka, when a text came through saying I had been unsuccessful. Naturally, I was disappointed not to get the job, but I was also overjoyed. My global tour was on. I would be doing the World Cycle Challenge.

A Facebook group was established for the riders who had committed, and we were soon discussing our motivations, reservations, and training plans. The tour would average around 100 miles per day and while our gear would be carried, flights and visas sorted on our behalf, the training and sheer bloody mindedness required to complete this journey would be down to us.

I was lucky. Having finished work, I had all the time needed to train before leaving in September for what would be the toughest challenge I had ever signed up for. Circumstances had given me this opportunity to have time for myself, and I went to spin classes ten times a week alongside a gym routine designed to build my core. My house was put up for sale, and all were informed. Family and friends were of course nervous, but equally knew that once I set my mind on something, that's usually it – just the mental state required to contemplate such a task, I thought! Little did I know just how much this determination and mindset would be needed.

I was at the Post Office when the call came through. It was January 14th, 2012, around 3pm. The World Cycle Challenge had just been cancelled. I was gutted and, in a rare moment, speechless. Now what would I do? I met friends later that evening to share this updated news. A few hours had passed, and while I wasn't sure exactly what would happen next, I was confident that things would work out. The commitment had been made. I'd told others of my plans; I would be cycling. I just had to work out where, when, and with whom.

The solution came just a few days later. John, another rider who had signed up for the challenge, posted on the Facebook group. While upset the trip was cancelled, he noted he still had the time, money, and inclination, and wanted to know if anyone else was interested. I didn't need to think about it. The answer was yes. We'd never met, had chatted only briefly through a Facebook group, but this was my chance to live a dream. Once again, I was going to cycle the world. The challenge would now just be slightly different.

John and I chatted regularly as we made our assessments on whether we would make suitable ride and travel partners. I hadn't met John, but soon we were sharing not just our dreams but also our hopes and fears regarding the forthcoming trip. I guess it was hard for either of us to know whether this may work, when also feeling this may be our only opportunity. Building trust required honesty, and with that a sharing of the traits we both had that really could wind each other up. Having never been married or lived long-term with a partner, deciding to spend a full year in John's company when I covet my independence so much was a big move. But it was my chance, and I was taking it. Fortunately, he too was keen to seize the opportunity.

With the organised tour cancelled, we no longer had a designated route, and so we started to talk about the places we wanted to see, ride, and experience. Pretty soon, I had routes and flights mapped, a bike designed, and cycle jerseys ordered. My blog was registered, and I started posting my plans of a 15mph adventure. Given we were both itching to do the trip but couldn't guarantee we would get on, we decided to ride some sections with other people too. I had always wanted to ride Lhasa to Kathmandu, so we signed up for an organised three-week tour. We were also looking to join a trip covering the length of Africa with the Canadian company Tour d'Afrique. I didn't feel ready for my first time in Africa to be just the two of us on our bikes.

It seemed great minds think alike and while there were slight differences in our bikes of choice, we had both chosen a Koga Signature. Also, both opting for the Rohloff hub gears, I had also made the decision to use a belt drive rather than a chain. I'd booked a bike maintenance course but as someone not particularly comfortable with mechanics I was trying to minimise potential problems we may encounter on route. I hoped John wouldn't feel like he would be travelling with a complete numpty though! We were both excited to chat through equipment and items we were planning to take with us and of course (my idea) the bikes would need a name and after much deliberation The Captain and Kylie were born. You'll just have to guess whose bike was who!

Planning was going well, the excitement was building, and it felt like nothing could now hold us back... and then the next call came through. Just like last time, it was unexpected news, but while the last update on the proposed trip left me feeling gutted, this one was truly devastating. My mother's cancer was back, and this time it was terminal. Her prognosis: a mere two months to two years. This would change everything. This was not a case of slowing down; I was automatically stopped in my tracks.

I called John, and his response over the next few days made me more and more confident I had found a great travel buddy. However, I was now unsure the trip would ever come to be. I felt guilty for being upset that my trip was on hold; my mother felt awful to have put me in this position. For John, I sense this was even more frustrating, though he only ever showed compassion. Fortunately, the initial appointments with the consultant gave a more promising outcome. The cancer, while there, did not appear too aggressive. The relief was huge. I was overjoyed for me and my mom, and I know we were both keen to make sure that this would not disrupt either her plans or mine.

Following much discussion, we decided we would still embark on our cycle, but the trip would change. Not being home for Christmas was now a no-no. The trip would be divided into five-month sections. I would always be ready to return to the UK, if needed. Once more, we consulted maps, flight paths, climate charts, and dates of organised tours to develop a new schedule.

To plan routes, one needs a sense of speed – from this, we can estimate destination points and book flights and accommodation, as appropriate. According to Yahoo! forums, bike speed ranged from 13-22 mph depending on bike set-up and tyres. On this basis, I opted for 15mph. It made a good strapline for the blog, despite turning out to be a little optimistic for a fully loaded tourer. I would later discover 10mph was a more common average for this kind of riding.

It was cheaper to book the Africa tour by a designated date, and with my house sale waiting to go through, John said he would pay for me. The trust between us had built very quickly, and I think the fact that he was willing to transfer such a significant sum to cover the costs for us both into my bank account really did set some of my friends' and family's minds at ease. Despite this, they remained nervous. John and I arranged to meet and go for a ride in Bristol, and we would each make the effort to introduce ourselves to parents and pals.

By now, it was April, and we would be leaving in just a couple of months. Life had certainly slowed down. I'd spent many years racing through life. I had no regrets, yet knew I was ready for this change of pace. Honoré notes that "When bicycles first became popular in the 1890s, some feared that riding into the wind at high speed would cause permanent disfigurement, or 'bicycle face'." I'm happy to say that other than a mostly permanent smile, no disfigurement was apparent. My trip of a lifetime was about to begin.

3.

NATURE

"Thousands of tired, nerve-shaken, over-civilised people are beginning to find out that going to the mountains is going home; that wilderness is a necessity; and that mountain parks and reservations are useful not only as foundations of timber, of irrigating rivers, but as foundations of life!"

John Muir

Of all the cities to leave behind, Edinburgh was not a bad one. Aesthetically pleasing, a showcase of both classic and contemporary culture and surrounded by stunning countryside, it's no wonder Edinburgh is listed as one of the top cities to live in or visit in the UK. However, with most of my time spent in the office, bars and restaurants, the gym or my basement flat, I was missing something – nature.

The view that the outdoors is critical for the soul is one shared by many, from poets to environmentalists and health professionals.

"The world is too much with us; late and soon,

Getting and spending, we lay waste our powers:

Little we see in nature that is ours;

We have given our hearts away, a sordid boom."

Wordsworth wrote often of nature, of the need to take a break from cities and urbanisation, to learn from it, to feel it. Increasing studies show how critical nature is to recuperation, noting even how just a window from a hospital bed can make a key difference. We cannot afford to take it for granted. We cannot afford to forget our connection with it. Whether plants or animals, we need the air around us, the sunlight, the minerals. Nature is a precious resource, and we are its users, observers, and protectors. My break from urbanisation was long overdue.

As cyclists, we are certainly part of that environment. The thrill of riding with a tailwind versus the gruelling push of wind in your face certainly puts you right there. The distance covered, as opposed to shorter journeys by foot, enables the rider to truly get a sense of the geography. You see the shape of the land change and, while gradients on the road are perhaps most visible, it's about more than that. It's about the birds and other animals; about recognising how land is used, be it agricultural, barren or industrial. You see plants, learn to love the silhouettes of trees against the horizon. You observe the colours in the sky, the cloud formations, the onset of new weather. You feel the change in temperature, get wet in the pouring rain, and boy, you really do know when it's hot and humid. It's not always pleasant, yet the sound of raindrops clattering on your tent, of the bird call in the morning, and the feeling when the sun finally gets its hat on really is bliss.

It was July 7th, 2012, when we set off on our first trip. We would start our tour with a ride down the West Coast of America from Seattle to San Francisco. To date, John and I had met just three times: once to introduce ourselves, a second time to meet respective family and friends and finally when John visited Edinburgh to run the marathon. Now, we were here at the airport, about to embark on the trip of a lifetime. It was late when we arrived at Tacoma International Airport. We'd booked a room here for our first night, and after a beer and food, we caught up on rest before we would wake the next day to ride into the city. Bikes assembled and panniers loaded, we set off to Greg and Patricia's house – these friends of friends had agreed to put us up for a few nights. Neither of us had been to Seattle before, and we were both clear that, as cycle-tourists, it was about both the bike and exploration of new places.

Months in the planning, holding off while waiting on consultant reports regarding my ma and then the slow withdrawal from life as it was, we were ready – now. Despite recognising a need to slow down, I was still impatient. We were in Seattle. It was a great city, and there were several things to go see, but we just wanted to ride. We were invited to stay for longer but were desperate to get going. Consequently, we

The World at 15mph...ish

decided to add in few more miles. We would now catch a ferry across to Bainbridge before joining route 101, as previously planned. It was time to leave the city behind.

Given we still had a lot to learn about each other our choice to start in America was a very conscious one. This was a well-established route, and we were following the details set out in "Bicycling the Pacific Coast". The book highlighted distances, gradients, camping spots, shops, hotels, and restaurants, as well as sites worth visiting and small detours. We had needed to work out much of this before booking flights, but the guidebook meant that we could concentrate on getting to know each other rather than spending time researching or worrying about these day-to-day details.

Our first day was overcast, and the views from the ferry were very misty. We were planning to stay in Quilcene that night – it should have been a 57-mile day, yet by the time we stopped, we had done just under seventy miles. We were also much, much slower than the anticipated 15mph. The camp pitch in Quilcene was just on the edge of town, and the guidebook provided great directions. It would not, of course, have been able to tell us that folks were just hanging out there having drunk too much beer and that we just wouldn't feel like pitching up there with bikes and belongings in tow. We decided to continue to the next camping possibility. The book indicated the next site was just over 3 miles, though it also noted that the steep climb by Mount Walker begins just after crossing the bridge out of town. We were so ready to stop. Unfortunately, the next camp had no water; the next site was closed, and so we had no choice but to continue our ascent. We reached the summit, and eventually pulled in at Dosewallips State Park. We were shattered, having ridden much longer than planned, but at least this one had hot showers and a hiker-biker area.

Hiker-biker sites can be found in various state parks throughout America, and they certainly make exploring the outdoors a pleasurable and relatively easy thing to do. They refer to the principle that those arriving by self-supported means will not be turned away from a camp pitch, recognising that walking and cycle tours are not always predictable, just as traveling a further 5 to 10 miles may not be possible, either. The sites are areas set aside in national parks and provide basic facilities. We would also discover that the advantages, of course, go beyond just this guarantee, and on popular routes such as the one we were embarking on, they also create temporary communities for those on multi-day trips. In Dosewallips, we were on our own. It was perhaps just as well. John was about to inform me he had never put up a tent or cycle-toured before! Tents eventually up, we cooked a dinner far too ambitious on our small Trangia stove, ate late, yet slept well. Before we knew it, we were back on the road, though I'm still not sure if the magnitude of what we were doing had set in. It still just felt like a short holiday.

Route 101 is apparently known as the scenic highway, as our photographs would also demonstrate. The proof at this stage, however, was not based on the great views and stunning landscapes. We knew merely from the signage as our ride took us past numerous fireworks stands and the cooling towers of the abandoned Satsop nuclear plant. As we took off for Potlatch the following day, even the guidebook noted that "very little of the area's abundant scenery is visible from the road". We continued over the next few days through Lake Sylvia national park, the place of my first tent repair. The Lake Sylvie camp can be found one mile above the town of Monsesanto. There was a fabulous descent to the park, where our pitch, next to the lake, was surrounded by beautiful wood-lands. We were relieved to see a poster showing that the local pizza parlour would deliver to site. Not only did this mean we had a scrummy dinner, but we were also able to wait until the next morning before having to climb back out of the park. Our route then crossed a few rivers, and we ended on a privately-run campsite at Westport. This time, we had stopped for food in the local town before heading out to camp. We were so pleased to have made this decision. The site was rife with mosquitoes. Thankfully, we were both now much quicker at putting up our tents. Given we had laundry to do and wanted to avoid bites, we spent the evening in the laundry block, using the electric to charge up phones and watching the machines go round. I'd also managed to get my first puncture a few miles from camp. It turned out that, despite all my planning, I had the wrong-size inner tubes, rendering all my spares as excess weight. Fortunately, our bikes were virtually the same, and so John was able to find me a spare once we got to camp. In the meantime, I just pumped tyres every mile or so. I guess it's good to get the basics wrong at the early stages. Still, our fish and chips had been lovely, and the following night we would tuck into local oysters at Willepa Bay. Life was not too bad. We rented a cabin and enjoyed a walk on the beach. It was also time for my second tent repair, though the puncture fix had thankfully been successful. The site was very sociable, and it was here we first met Kevin and Stephanie, who were doing the same journey as us, accompanied by their two small children.

Till now, our additional detour had not overwhelmed us, though I was still happy just to have started. Our hopes were raised as we crossed over the Columbia River, which would take us from Washington State into Oregon. According to the guidebook, it was excellent both for bike touring and sightseeing. Oregon comes with promises of 378 miles of spectacular ocean views and rugged headlands. We just needed to cycle over the 4.2-mile Astoria Bridge first. It was daunting, given our heavy bikes and the short, sharp climb at the far end. But thanks to roadworks and a kind lolly-pop man giving us a head start, we were soon safely over. I was happy to get to the bottom of the sweeping curves that wound down from the top of the bridge to street level. We found a great cafe, right next door to the 'Bikes and Beyond' cycle store. I called in to buy inner tubes, also getting a new bell as mine had snapped off the day I left Birmingham. I'm not sure I had full approval for my choice of a dinosaur shaped squeezy, but I was very happy with my new addition. Dino had just joined the journey. We pulled into camp that night and were told to camp between two massive RVs (super huge American camper vans). It made us smile, especially given the owner, Tim, came out with a cold beer. The next morning, there were 'all you can eat' pancakes. Happy days.

As soon as we crossed into Oregon, it felt like the trip had really started. We had got into a rhythm, and the scenery had now changed. We were also about to feel nature. It was going to get very wet. It rained and rained all morning as we cycled just 25 miles from Warrenton, our previous night's camp, into Cannon Beach. A popular tourist spot along the coast, we were surrounded by hotels, pubs, galleries, bakeries, and other eateries. It didn't take much discussion to decide that we would have our first rest day here. It was our seventh day on the road, and we were just over 300 miles in. We decided it was time to check into a hotel for the night. After some lunch and a mooch, we headed back to the pub later where I was also able to indulge in another love of mine – real ale. For John, it would be an introduction into the tastes and flavours of pale ales, ruby ales, porters and stouts.

We woke early the next morning, and before heading off fully loaded, pedalled up the tough climb through the lush spruce forest to the top of Ecola State Park. Once reaching the top, the views were outstanding – some of the best on this American trip. It was clear why the vista was often chosen as the key photograph for the Oregon coastline. Ecola State Park stretches along 9 miles of coastline around the Tillamook headland, and we stood for some time watching the waves roll in, crashing against the rocks which themselves were covered in mist. It was well worth the additional workout, though we were glad we had left the panniers back at the hotel to collect on our way out. For a few days now, we would follow the coast. I love riding by the sea. The sense of openness one gets is comparable only with being in the mountains.

Hundreds cycle the Pacific Coast Highway (PCH) each year, and now that we were on the main drag, we would meet a few more folk like ourselves. We waved to Tom as we left Cannon Beach, and he would arrive at the same camp we were at later that day. We all walked to watch the sunset together and arranged to ride with him the next morning. We would continue to ride with Tom all the way to San Francisco. The road had followed the coast from Nehalem with one of our big highlights. Tillamook cheese factory was on our route, and they were also famous for making other dairy products, like ice-cream. Numerous flavours were on offer, and so I had no choice but to get two scoops. The lady serving was a little surprised, as was I, when she presented me with a gargantuan pile. Forty-five minutes later, I was ready to continue. It would take another double scoop order a few days later before I was reminded again about American portions. That night, we stopped at Cape Lookout where Kevin and Stephanie also arrived later, and it would be a first introduction to Paul and Jeanne. We were enjoying seeing familiar faces. The weather was filthy that night and the morning brought more rain, so we all decamped to the picnic gazebo to cook breakfast and dry our tents. It may have been wet, but morale and camaraderie were at an all-time high.

The road climbed to Beverly with three major ascents in a day. At this stage in our world cycle, a 2.7-mile steep climb was still very tough-going. Thankfully, the ride was still very rewarding, as the coastline was stunning the next day. Rocky headlands, natural coves, and the accompanying clam chowder really made this an incredible ride. While we didn't stop at the Sea Lion caves, we did take a few photos at the world's largest collection of chainsaw woodcarvings. We'd also needed to find time for jobs. We had that touring cyclist smell and desperately needed a laundry. We found one right next to the Newport café, which John will always remember for serving the best breakfast burritos of the American leg.

The next night saw us stay at Jessie B Honeymann national park. There were a few riders on the hiker-biker site when we arrived, but the rain that night was so heavy that we all trooped off to our tents and listened to the thunder and lightning. Consequently, the next day our gear was very damp, so we hatched a plan. It was just an excuse for a motel and a night-out given it was a Friday. We headed to the town of Charleston to see what was on offer, and we all felt like we needed a beer after crossing the busy Coos Bay bridge. I'm not sure we found too much entertainment, to be honest, which was perhaps as well given the ride out of Charleston starts hard with a road called the 7 Devils - seven hills each over 120 metres and the biggest topping out at 158. There was no coast road today; we were following routes by forests and fields. A strong tailwind blew us to Bandon for our coffee stop. In addition to the delicious peanut butter cookies, Tom was also reunited with his lost shoe as two brothers who were on the same route had seen it left at camp. Knowing they would catch us at some point, they brought it along, having spotted our bikes from the road. However, while Tom had carried his odd Croc for one day, he had now thrown it away. It was great to see the guys, but sadly it was not quite the happy reunion they had hoped for. The search for a new pair had already begun.

On pulling into Port Orford, the road signalled that there was great 'ocean views' to be had. It was a fabulous bay known as Battle Rock Park. We were not disappointed and went out to admire the views again before dinner. I was really chuffed to see a piano available in the restaurant we ate in that evening. I had a few pieces of music hidden away in my panniers. Over the past few years, I'd started to play my piano much more, though, sadly, that was something I could obviously not carry! So, while the wine chilled and the waves rolled in, I amused myself with Satie's Gnossienne pieces and a little Mozart before joining the guys for dinner. Our community was building, the sun was shining, and all was good with the world. There was no sense of racing against other riders we constantly passed by or who overtook us as we made our way South. It still didn't feel like an epic adventure though.

From here, Tom was riding inland to meet up with a few friends, Maggie, and Shaun, who were camping at Kimble Creek. We were invited to join him, and given we were ahead of schedule, free from diary dates, and with an agenda purely to explore, we decided we had nothing to lose. It was a hot ride, and we didn't take much persuasion to cool down in the river for a swim before sharing beers and a barbie. It was a long climb out of the valley the next morning, and just as the road climbed, so did the temperature. It was another landmark day as we ended the ride in a new state. The guidebook had noted that we may get checked for an agricultural inspection as we passed the border. Perhaps we're just not so cautious in the UK, or it's simply that fact that we are geographically much smaller, but this was new to us. We ensured all fruit was eaten, though had little else to worry about. This was a practice we would become a little more familiar with as we pushed bikes through troughs of chemicals in Africa and scrubbed all outdoor gear to perfection before entering New Zealand and Australia. As it turned out, the inspection was somewhat insignificant, though we did take time to pose for pictures under the "Welcome to California" sign. Tom kissed the tarmac as he entered his home state, pitching up at Crescent City. It was another site with eat-all-you-can pancakes and we, the hungry cyclists, were happy to oblige. The fuel would see us good as we had a 5-mile climb. Staying on an inland route, the road would follow farm fields, cattle ranches, and forests as we pushed ahead. I guess we shouldn't have been surprised then to find a few lumberjacks hanging out in the local bar, "The Country Club" as we stopped for lunch in Klamath. Desperate for the loo, I arrived first at the bar while John waited for Tom out on the main road. The windows were covered over and all I could hear were a few male voices. I opted to cross my legs till the boys got there. As it turned out, it was just a few guys drinking cocktails under what was labelled as the biggest chainsaw in the USA. I can't believe I'd held on to use the toilet for so long.

We continued South, and soon we were riding through the Redwood National Park. We pulled up on the bikes to go and explore, laughing and joking as we made our way through the paths leading us round to what is claimed to be the world's biggest tree. We didn't get there first off. Tom and I seemed to wind John up, he lost it, and that was that. I didn't know what to do. Dynamics often change as groups themselves do, and at one point I thought the tour was over despite having only just started. I'm not very good with arguments and try to avoid confrontation, but if we wanted to continue, we had to get this sorted. Camp was just a mile or so down the road, so Tom continued ahead as John and I talked about what had happened. We did take the obligatory photo at the world's biggest tree, though I think it may be one of the few shots from our tour where I really wasn't smiling. We arrived at camp and, following apologies and a beer, set up for the night. It was going to be okay.

The camp was called Elk Prairie, and roaming elk could apparently be seen in the mornings and late afternoon. There were also notices pointing out the dangers of bears and raccoons. I didn't want to catch glimpses of all the wildlife on offer, and we were diligent in moving all our food and toiletries to the bear box before going to sleep that night. Alas, it was not restful for me. I woke to find my cherry lip-balm at the bottom of my handlebar bag and, whether stupid or not, I lay in bed, desperate for the loo, unable to clear my mind of the sweet smell of cherries. I was paranoid the smell would lead the bears directly to my tent. The next morning, we started the myth about bears fearing orange nylon, the colour of my tent. It became one of our running jokes throughout the tour. It was wet and drizzly as we left the following day, but after about 13 miles, we were rewarded when we spotted elk on the beach. The rest of the ride was fairly uneventful as we ended it on the busy highway at Eureka. We opted to stay on a privately-run campsite that night, and since it was very hot on arrival, we treated ourselves to ice-cream. I was looking forward to dumping the bike and sitting in the sun. Alas, our pitch was in the forest. I was so grumpy. It was cold in the shade, and this camp pitch was falling way short of my expectations. Tom was happy, though. He'd finally found some new Crocs.

To date, we had passed through a variety of towns that we had felt looked closed. Empty shops and abandoned buildings, and sadly, the people we bumped into were just hanging out, drinking on the streets. There just hadn't been much going on to us, and they seemed a little run-down. The same was not true of Ferndale. An old Victorian town, its buildings were newly painted, there was an abundance of restaurants, cafés, and delis, and it seemed to be thriving. We stopped for lunch and indeed shared our observations with the café owner. He talked to me and John broadly about the growth of the economy, leaving out the more direct response he gave Tom, our Californian friend. Tom told us as we left that it was the legalisation of cannabis (for medical purposes) that has transformed the town.

Our detour had meant we had a welcome break off the busy section of Highway 101, though there was a point when we thought we would simply have to turn around. The road ahead was closed, though it was unclear why. The temporary signs gave no indication as to the reason. We decided to risk it, and thankfully, we were in luck. They were cutting the hedges along the road, and while too narrow for a car, we were able to pass by. Not being able to would have added around 20 miles to our day's ride, and because we were due to head through the Avenue of the Giants, we didn't want to feel tired to enjoy this coastal highlight.

Avenue of the Giants is a world-famous scenic drive, a 31-mile portion of old Highway 101. Running parallel to Freeway

101, the road is lined with over 51,000 acres of redwood groves - the largest remaining stand of virgin redwoods in the world. Redwoods average as much as 20 feet in diameter with a height of over 300 feet. While they were once found worldwide, their natural range is now restricted to 3 main areas - Sierra Nevada, China, and the coast of Northern California. In California, the coast is often foggy and it's this and the average temperatures here that enable them to thrive. John got a puncture as we cycled through, causing us to stop. While John was busy with patches and glue, I took the opportunity to get some photos. The trees were much wider than the length of the bike, a brilliant shot. Our camp site that night was at Burlington. It was more basic than other hiker-bikers, but the setting amongst the trees was fabulous and it was a pleasure to start riding again the next morning.

We were heading to Standish Hickey, and our ride that day would see us cycle through the 'drive-through tree', an obligatory tourist stop, of course. It was, however, the night we all remember with great affection. The local bar, The Peg House, had a live band on, served great beer, and had won awards for their burgers. My mom had also just been to her first appointment with the consultant since I left. Anxious for news, I called home, and thankfully, the update was positive. I had a few beers that night, and we all walked back to camp with much laughter. The following morning, we had our biggest climb to date, and I had a hangover. Whoops! John and Tom went on ahead as I steadily climbed. Lugget Hill stands at over 600 metres and is the highest point on the Pacific Coast route. Sadly now, we were still among the trees, and so there was little to no view, and therefore, no excuse to stop before we had a further 200 metre climb over Rockport Hill. Thankfully, the nine-mile descent was smooth, gently winding, and a thrill to ride. The boys reached the bottom first, though I was happy with my speed. I was on a day with much slower reactions, so it felt the safer option for a girl with a sore head. My headache lasted all day, and while Standish Hickey was a brilliant night, I'm not sure I could have done those nights too often throughout the trip. As we pitched up at Russian Gultch national park that evening, I was ready to rest.

Despite a climb-out from our camp pitch, I was in a much better state for a climb the next morning and glad to be feeling better. The ride today would be one of my favourites on this trip through America. We were back on the coast and heading to Gualala. The road climbed up above the clouds, offering glimpses of the coast way below. The shoulder was narrow and the drop at the side of the road was steep at times, but I had the biggest smile on my face. We posed for photos, and as the road dropped, it continued to loop around the coast, with sharp twists and turns at the inlets of water. I loved it. It was also the day I remember for its overwhelming hospitality. There were a number of cyclists out, since it was a Sunday, and while our first café stop was shut, we found a great alternative, "Queenie's" just up the road. I got chatting to a couple of female riders before tucking into my coffee and cakes. We watched them leave, completely unaware that they had settled our bill. It was incredible and not the only kindness we came across that day. Jenifer and Ed kindly shared their wine with us as we arrived that evening too. We'd checked into the Surf Motel in Gualala, having been enticed by the owner. Apparently, he did the best breakfast around, and we were not disappointed. The coffee woke us up by the smell alone, and along with cereal, eggs and sausages, there were also the traditional American biscuits and gravy available. Yum!

We had just three more days of riding until we reached San Francisco. It had been a relatively easy introduction to our first tour, and we had met many great people on route, particularly other riders staying on the biker camps. Given the route was well-used, we didn't always ride together, even though we would wait at regular intervals. As we pedalled towards Bodega Bay, I was riding alone. John was going faster, and Tom was somewhere behind. An older guy with a big beard stopped to say hi. He seemed friendly, though as he went on to ask if I was alone, I was very quick to let him know that John and Tom were around. It freaked me out a bit, and I felt a little on edge until the next meet point. As it turned out, big beardy Bob was both harmless and great fun. We were all set up on the camp pitch when he arrived. Bodega Bay was a busy camp though, despite there being 16 of us there that night. I couldn't help noticing they were all guys apart from me. John and I got some wood for the communal fire, and we all stayed up chatting about our experience to date. A couple of beers later, I retired to bed.

The next morning, John and Tom were talking routes. John and I had the book on cycling the Pacific coast; Tom was using the printed maps produced by the American Adventure Cycling Organisation. They differed occasionally and offered various side trip options. I kept out of the way as the debate on the day's ride was discussed. On leaving camp, it was confirmed that we were going pretty much straight-on. With no turns to remember and feeling good, I pedalled hard. Again, John was a little ahead and Tom behind. I didn't see the right turn John took and continued to speed ahead. Thankfully, he saw me race on, though. With full panniers, it takes a while to build up speed, and therefore, it took John a few miles to catch me. Apparently, he'd been shouting at me to stop for quite some time! Back on the right track, we continued to camp. The hiker-biker Samuel P Taylor site was right inside the national park, and it was a pitch away from major roads. Bob turned up again, and we were also joined by Serge and Cameron - two other riders we had gotten to know over the past few weeks. As in previous camps, we were warned about raccoons, though I don't think Bob managed to avoid them entirely, as they came looking for food during the night.

The next day would be the last ride day for a few of the riders who were also due to end in San Francisco. For me and John, it was our first major milestone on this global tour. We were excited to be approaching our final destination, and of course, to ride over the Golden Gate bridge. While I had done this before using a hire bike on a previous trip, this was a brand-new experience for John. It also represented a key target, and John still lists this as one of his key highlights, given the sense of achievement it represented. He was keen to arrive, and despite holding up the journey a little as I found another local store hosting a public piano, we were soon on our way. The roads got busier, and the area was becoming increasingly built up. We stopped for lunch in Sausalito before glimpsing the views of San Francisco in the distance. Despite being a frustrating ride due to the vast number of hire bikes on the compulsory cycle path, it did have the advantage of making it easy for us to stop for photos. We were saying goodbye to Tom here as he headed home, though we did arrange to meet him for dinner to share some final beers that night. John was a confirmed real-aler now, so we opted for a local brew pub.

The ride into the city followed the cycle path before we then made our way to Freewheelers, where we had both booked our bikes in for a service. Cycling here was new to us, and so, without the local knowledge, we found ourselves riding up and down the steep hills of San Francisco, taking in the city sights with the biggest smiles on our faces. After a few days of sightseeing, we would leave for the airport. Our bikes were now in boxes and getting to the airport required planning. We ordered a pickup van, having been assured all would be okay for our 5:30am pick up. I was confident it was sorted, and it was only when the driver arrived to take us that we realised we had a problem. Despite checking several times when booking, he couldn't fit us and our bikes in after all. One cab passed, and I hailed him over, though I wasn't sure how two adults, two bikes in boxes, and two large holdalls would ever fit. However, our flight wouldn't wait and there was little traffic around. We couldn't thank the cab driver who squeezed us and all our bikes and gear into his big yellow taxi enough. What a relief! We were heading to Japan.

It wasn't really till we reached San Francisco that we really realised we had left the day-to-day city life behind. Yes, we were staying in one of America's great cities, yet we were free of the usual rat race ties. It was here I think both of us knew we were on a much bigger adventure. We were not flying home. We were not heading back to work. We were not in a rush. While I still hold that one needs to get away from the urban environment to fully immerse oneself in nature and take that break from urbanisation, I also can't help feeling that we can be in a city without being nerve-shaken. We just need to be less busy.

The Stats; Seattle to San Francisco
1,126 miles

Destination	Total Distance	Average Speed	Metres Up	Metres Down
Dosewallips	69.3	6	998	1100
Potlatch	29.4	6.3	463	431
Lake Sylvie	49.5	-	495	455
Westport	36.8	6.2	304	318
Willepa Bay	53.7	8.8	263	252
Warrenton	54	-	375	363
Cannon Beach	21.7	-	191	207
Nehalem Bay	18.4	5	455	459
Cape Lookout	48.4	8.4	569	584
Beverly	56.7	8.2	1061	1070
Honeymann	-	-	-	-
Charleston	51.7	-	774	781
Port Orford	49.4	-	780	753
Kimble Creek	28.3	-	473	484
Crescent City	60.9	9	906	871
Elk Prairie	41.1	7.5	819	806
Eureka	48.1	7.7	634	657
Burlington	60.7	8.1	728	648
Standish Hickey	46.7	7.8	927	680
Russian Gultch	54.4	8	1282	1454
Gualala	51.3	8.3	1105	1097
Bodega Beach	47.3	7.9	942	927
Samuel P Taylor	43.5	8.3	814	772
San Francisco	32.5	6.4	518	446

Notes

- Places often align with Hiker-biker site names

- Data taken from my diary notes – recorded in miles in USA

- As km this was a total of 1,812km

The world at 7.5 mph (averaged from averages)

4.

DISCOVERY

"Humanity's interest in the heavens has been universal and enduring. Humans are driven to explore the unknown, discover new worlds, push the boundaries of our scientific and technical limits, and then push further. The intangible desire to explore and challenge the boundaries of what we know and where we have been has provided benefits to our society for centuries."

NASA website

Prior to starting this adventure, I had been fortunate enough to do a little backpacking and a few shorter cycle tours. I'd loved the freedom of the rucksack, the evolving itinerary, and when cycling, the chance to be outdoors in new places too. To date, the ride through America had been a gentle introduction both to longer tours and to each other. For John it had been a whole new experience. In America, we had the advantages of a common language, similar food, and mostly familiar culture. Landing in Japan would be completely different. We would enter an environment with much greater challenges.

I had wanted to visit Japan for some time, mostly because it was a country I knew very little about. In fact, had I been more thorough in my research on both the topography, climate, and exchange rates we may never have put Japan on our itinerary. I didn't know Japan was 90% hills, was quite unaware how humid it would be in August and had no idea an apple would cost the equivalent of a fiver. Needless to say, we were here. I knew only how to say hello - Konnichiwa - and pronunciation as well as an ability to recognise the writing using traditional kanji/characters would be a major challenge.

We arrived in Tokyo, and after a little research, I had booked us into a small hotel in Shinjuku near the airport drop. It was around a 10-minute walk to our accommodation, but with two large holdalls containing all our panniers, tents, etc., and two large bike boxes, this was not a single journey. Looking bewildered, the coach porter indicated that we could leave our bikes with him, on the pavement. They were our prized possessions - unlocked and abandoned under the occasional eye of a complete stranger. They were completely safe. Japan ranks incredibly low in global crime statistics, and where I would never leave a good bike unlocked and unwatched in UK cities, in Japan we had no worries. Having checked in, we warned the hotel we were returning with bicycles and given the size of our room and would require the use of the luggage store.

Again, given we were just as keen to be tourists as cyclists, we explored Tokyo for a few days, taking in night-time viewpoints, eating sushi and sashimi at the fish market, as well as the palace, temples, and markets. Trust me, being a mad dash tourist can be just as tiring as riding the bikes.

The region of Tokyo and Yokohama is home to 37.8 million people - the largest urban population ever recorded. Its streets and suburbs stretch out for miles and because of limited time and a slight fear regarding navigation, we decided to take a bus again. Avoiding busy roads and miles of suburbs, we would start near Mount Fuji. Despite the challenges, we wanted to see more of Japan than just towns and cities. However, we were about to hit a major problem - an issue which had never crossed our minds.

The bus dropped us off in Kawaguchiko, and we had planned to camp that night at Lake Motasuko, just 10 miles away. With bikes still unpacked, we would first need to reassemble them. We had a routine with this now, and John would usually take the lead as I performed the role of handy assistant and waste disposal. This time, getting rid of our cardboard boxes would prove to be the most difficult part of the reassembly. Fortunately, I'm stubborn, persistent, and polite. I fear, were any of these characteristics lacking, we may have ended up back on a bus to Tokyo. Apparently, being in the national park meant that disposal of our cardboard was impossible. There was nowhere we could leave it, the local hotel/restaurant would not take it even if we paid them, and tourist information were insistent we could not leave it there. The boxes were large, and it was precisely because of their size that we were unable to ride away with them, despite considering the option. In the end, after a number of those persistent and polite requests to tourist information, they conceded. We just needed to make the package as small as possible. It was a pain, but John quickly set to work with his Stanley knife to reduce the package to A4 size. We couldn't afford for them to change their minds. While I was relieved, we had a solution, I have to say I also admired them for their environmental policy. Campaigning for better recycling facilities was something I had been involved in for many years.

The ride to Lake Motasuko was a gentle one, and while the campsite seemed very expensive and basic as we pitched up on wood chippings and paid yet more money for our hot shower, little did we know how much we would later wish to find similar places at these affordable prices! Our accommodation throughout Japan was incredibly varied - the only common thread being the cost. Wherever we stayed was pretty pricey.

A new time zone meant we woke very early the next morning, and the heat and humidity further accelerated our departure from camp. We were fed, watered, packed up, and on the road before 7am. It would be 630 pm before we eventually came to a stop. Our route was a roller-coaster, constantly rising and falling. It was very hilly, and even the optimistic description of undulating was way off the mark. Further, Mount Fuji was surrounded by mist and our detour to see this "must do" seemed somewhat futile. While missing this top site, our first visits to Japanese temples and surrounding gardens gave us great pleasure - nearly as much as the bakery van that pulled up just as we stopped for lunch. High humidity, hill climbs, and hours in the saddle meant that by the end of the day, I had a very, very sore bottom. In fact, it was sore well before the day ended.

We planned to end our day at a youth hostel in Miho. This would put us on the coast, positioned well for this first section of our journey. Despite a red raw bum and the overwhelming draw of hotels about 6 miles before Miho, we were determined to push on. We did not want to be defeated on this, our first full ride day in Japan. As it turned out, the failure came in finding anywhere to stay. Having searched and then asked in another local hotel where the youth hostel was, we would find out it had closed the previous year. The hotel that was left was hosting a school football contest and was full. There was not even a chance to camp in the garden or sleep in the lobby. Trust me, we did ask. While we had tents with us, neither of us were keen on just pitching up when we didn't know what's allowable. I was about to cry. The very thought of getting back on the saddle brought tears to my eyes, something that was obvious to both John and the hotel proprietor. Taking pity on us, they decided to help us find an alternative. The question was - did we want to go 6 miles back or continue for II miles. While a reservation was possible should we head backwards, it was not possible to book in advance if we pushed on. Despite this, we opted for the latter. By now, the female owner had persuaded her husband to drive us. We were to load our bikes and luggage in their small coach. It was dark now, and as we unloaded our gear forty minutes later; we were relieved to find three hotels in front of us.

Japan was proving very expensive, and we each set off to investigate prices - or at least we tried to. Lights were on, cars were there. The hotels were definitely open, yet we could not find a reception area for any of them. Hmmm. We had to work it out. There were TV screens showing photos, price, and availability, though despite trying the phone handset in the reception, the language barrier meant we were no further ahead. We would have to wait until someone else checked in. After around 20 minutes, our luck was in, and a middle-aged couple guided us through the process. Soon, we had selected a room from the screen and carried all our luggage, having been informed we were not able to keep going in and out of the room given you paid on exit.

Designed for discretion, the Japanese love hotel is probably less frequented by European tourists. Not listed in the tourist guides, this is certainly one of those moments of discovery one may not have had were we not on our bikes. It's often said that the world has become smaller, and while earlier travellers found new foods, new cultures and even undiscovered land, there is little these days that the modern traveller can't find out in advance: travel guides and writing, television programmes, blogs, Google Maps, and even individual restaurant reviews. However, it was through some of our accommodation that we would discover elements of Japan that one simply has to experience. Far from sleazy, love hotels exist to offer couples time and space. You pay by the hour and peak times, as one may expect, are before and after work. Overnight stays were not common, and therefore the non-peak hours were priced accordingly. It was our cheapest night so far. The facilities were exceptional. A huge bed, spa bath and robes, and a massive TV and karaoke system. Given we are just friends, we found little use for the sex toy vending machines or dressing up catalogue. We were pleased, however, that we had already bought two cans of beer and a couple of pot noodles. Eating out in Japan can be exquisite, but on our budget, we needed to temper this with take-outs from the 7-11!

We were back on the coast, and while less picturesque, it was certainly much easier terrain to navigate. Following routes became much easier, though finding somewhere to stay remained a challenge. Still sore, we set off the next day at the later time of 9 am. It took us a while to get out of the room with its automated pay system, though eventually I had pressed the right combination of buttons and inserted the correct money. The day saw us visit temples and do a short detour past some waterfalls. The tourist attractions were well signposted, and it was good to get a break from the sweaty riding. We would learn different skills and etiquette at our hotel later that day - a typical Japanese Ryokan. Again, we would have cycled straight past this pit stop had the guy in the electric shop in the small town not taken such time to interpret my drawings and attempts at asking where the nearest hotel was.

The ryokan is listed as a must-do while touring Japan. Originating in the Japanese Edo period as rest stops for travellers situated along highways, they are traditionally built from wood and comprised of tatami-matted flooring, and communal bathing and dining areas. Food is included and ryokans pride themselves on the dinner provided. While a fabulous experience, we still describe it as the most expensive hotel we have ever stayed in while we sleep on the floor and have a shared bathroom. Further, we were constantly changing shoes to slippers or bare foot depending on whether we were outdoors, indoors, in the room, or going to the toilet. That would be okay, but with the average height of a Japanese man being 5 ft 7.5 inches, there were no size 13 slippers around for John.

We left the following morning, continuing our coastal route. While in a different country, the signs noted that we were, once again, on the Pacific Coast cycle route. The temperature was still high and the humidity unbearable. I have never sweated so much, and even trying to get dry after a shower was virtually impossible. We'd hoped the cycle path would help us with navigation, but sadly, sections of it would suddenly close for repair and we would then have to find our way back to the roads. Finding routes was sometimes as hard as finding hotels and campsites. Given our difficulties in finding accommodation, we decided to head to the tourist office in Hammamatsu to see what was on offer. It was only mid-afternoon, but we had become nervous about finding somewhere to stay until too late in the day. I'm not sure too many foreign tourists called in to ask for advice, and they were excited to post a photo of us with the bikes on their website. Unfortunately, there was a big conference in the town, and accommodation was scarce. We ended up in a somewhat uninspiring business hotel about a ten-minute ride out of town. I think it had a leisure floor, though sadly this was for men only. Given this, we opted to head back into the city to view the castle and find some dinner.

We'd hoped to camp throughout Japan due to the cost of hotels, but so far, we'd had little success, and the month in Japan was very costly. Our wallets soon became empty, and the cash-point machines seemed very selective about recognising our cards. When successful, we cheered, noting we were "winners" and then proceeded to max out all the cards we had. While we had emergency travellers' cheques, the dollars we had wouldn't last long here. Thankfully, we found a campsite for our next night. We were at Cape Irago from where we would leave early the next morning for the ferry. We were heading to Tsu, where, at the end of another long, hot day, we faced another challenging accommodation search. We had no idea where the campsite was and could see only one hotel which looked way beyond budget. The sun was starting to go down, and so we decided to ask them if they knew of any cheaper hotels nearby. We were overjoyed when they quoted us a very cheap room price. I think they just felt sorry for us, and even though we were tucked away on the top floor, we were so happy to come down the escalators past gleaming chandeliers as we went in search of dinner. Unable to read the menu, our selection was made simply by pointing to the choices of other diners. Fortunately, we had a bit less trouble ordering a large beer. Strange, that.

The sky was grey as we left, and the day that followed was very tough, with a few steep inclines. and our first climb was around 15 miles. I don't normally enjoy riding in a thunderstorm, but the heavy rain was so welcome. I'm not sure I'd have made it to the top of the hills in the heat and humidity of the previous days. The air-trailer that had been converted into a burger van was such a delight as we stopped for lunch. Heavy rain and steep climbs continued in the afternoon, and of all the days to find a campsite, it was today. At least there was large shelter we could pitch the tent under and cook dinner. We were really getting to know our favourite noodle brands at the 7-11 shop now.

*

The morning saw us up and away by 7 am with a short ride to Uji to see the Byodin Temple. Too early to get a ticket, we went for coffee before starting the queue for entry. Built in 998, Byodin was first built as a countryside villa for powerful politician Fujiwara no Michinaga. It was his son who transformed the building into a temple and, in 1053, added on what is now known as its most spectacular feature - the Phoenix Hall. The hall, named after the two phoenix statues on its roof, is now featured on the back of the Japanese 10-yen coin. While Byodin's buildings were repeatedly lost to fires and other calamities over the centuries, the Phoenix Hall was never destroyed, making it one of the few original wooden structures to survive from the Heian Period. Still regarded as one of the finest buildings in Japan, a national treasure, we were not disappointed.

This sense of history continued in Kyoto - our next stop. Kyoto served as Japan's capital from 794 until 1868. It is now the country's seventh largest city with a population of 1.4 million people. Given its historic value, Kyoto was dropped from the list of target cities for the atomic bomb and spared from air raids during World War II. Our hotel in Kyoto had been booked in advance - we wanted to compare cost as well as know where we were heading. Because finding a very particular building can be difficult in a bigger town or city, we would often choose somewhere near to another significant landmark. That way, our route would be signposted. Our hotel was close to the station, and so we had soon unloaded and checked in. Unfortunately, we were unable to store our bikes there, and so we had to go and leave them in a bike park just around the corner. Normally, we'd be nervous, yet our experience in Japan so far had taught us not to worry. Further, the bike park was manned, and entry was not allowed unless to park or collect your bike. Racks filled the warehouse, and John helped me lift my bike to the second tier. I wish we had secure parks for bikes like this back home. That way, I wouldn't need a separate city bike chosen specifically to be unattractive to the bike thieves.

Japan was unravelling. It was still such an alien culture to me. I was slowly getting used to the politeness, getting nowhere with the language, and thoroughly enjoying the discovery. I was always struck seeing the old traditional building styles next to some of the most modern architecture; watching barefoot rickshaw guys in a country with some of the fastest trains in the world and observing the manga comic trends alongside ancient calligraphy techniques. Nowhere was this more obvious than in Kyoto, and on our first day we wondered round the ultra-modern station with its never-ending escalators and skywalks, visited Ni-Jo castle, and then headed over to the manga museum.

Kyoto is how I perhaps most imagined and thought of Japan. Narrow streets in the Gion area were busy with tourists, restaurants and shops, and traditional temples. I loved wandering around this old district, spotting bright kimonos and Geisha girls, and we booked in to enjoy some kaiseki dining in the evening, consisting of multiple courses of small, precise dishes. As when trying most new foods, it had a mixed response from us, though we were both in agreement that despite 11 courses we were still absolutely starving. We called in at a cheapo chicken eatery on our way back to the hotel. It was fabulous, and we certainly felt like we had eaten now. We would head back to Gion the next day, see the Shorenin temple, and walk round the Maruyama-Koen Gardens. However, for dinner we would leave tourist-ville. The cheapo eatery was, once again, our destination of choice. We were back on our bikes the next morning and needed a good feed.

The roads were busier now. We were riding between some of the bigger cities and towns and as we left Kyoto in the direction of Kobe, we were in the middle of a rainstorm. Despite being very wet, it was quite a relief given the first part of the journey was fairly hilly. However, just as the hills ended and a more urban and industrial landscape became the norm, the sun once again began to shine. With it, the humidity rose! We'd settled into a fairly uninteresting ride and were content to just get to Kobe, when up ahead we spotted a lone cyclist on a road bike. As we drew nearer, we managed to strike up a conversation and soon realised we were heading for the same area. It was fortunate for us that Hajime, our lone cyclist, knew the area as some of the bike paths were hard to follow, and without him we would have struggled. A few miles passed, and we continued our broken conversation enough to invite him to join us for lunch. He told us he knew of a decent place about a 15-minute ride away, and we finally stopped at an Italian Cafe just a few kilometres from our destination. We were all set to buy Hajime lunch, but he was insistent that the treat would be given in reverse, and we felt awful now that we'd gone for dessert too.

Leaving Hajime at the restaurant, we carried on to Kobe to find the campsite we had listed. It was getting late and dark and had started to rain. We realised that our hopes of finding the campsite were fading fast. The local hotel was fully booked, and we were once again stuck. We were in a very built-up area, and even emergency camping would be tough. There was an information centre inside the station, and so we decided to try and enlist their help. However, while we had now taught ourselves to recognise the sign for hotel in Japanese, we still had very little in terms of language skills. They were unable to help us, but we couldn't give up. Thankfully, the Japanese were not only some of the politest people we had met, they were also incredibly helpful, and just as our hotelier had gone out of his way when we were stuck in Miho, so too another random stranger would go way beyond what one may expect to help us out here. This time, our helper offered to make calls to hotels in the area and check out availability. While places could be found, they were so expensive and we were lucky he persevered, until 45 minutes later he came up with an option we could afford.

So far in Japan we had camped, stayed in a love hotel, a ryokan and business and tourist hotels, and while we didn't yet know it, we were about to have another overnight experience.

It's hard to share fully the details of the kind of place we stayed at, because we still don't really know despite research since. We followed our new friend on his scooter from the station, and at this stage, all we knew was that we were heading to something that offered us a night's sleep, was in our budget, yet was not really a hotel. As we weaved around traffic and pedalled hard to keep up, we were soon unloading and locking up our bikes outside what looked like an office block-come-shopping centre. Happily, there was a coffee shop on the ground floor, so we knew we would be okay for caffeine in the morning. We exited the lift on the third floor where we removed our shoes, as is always custom, and struggled to get all our panniers, water bottles and camp gear through the automatic barriers. Our friend told us we would need to just take our overnight bag with us - everything else would be left at reception till the following morning. He checked us in, and we selected kimonos from the options available, and were given a locker key and number on a band to be worn around the wrist. We said goodbye to our scooter man and stood there blankly as we tried to work out what was next.

Smelly and dirty from our ride and far from inconspicuous, we stared at the options on the buttons inside the lift. There were bathing, accommodation, and restaurant floors. Desperately in need of a shower, we headed to bathing where the doors were very clearly marked male and female. Whatever we had to discover next, we would be doing so on our own. Apprehensively, we both went our separate ways. Japanese sentō, or public baths, came about given that in the past, many Japanese homes were not equipped with their own bathtubs. Public baths then became places not only to wash but also to socialise. While there are perhaps now fewer smaller bath-houses of the past, a new type of bathing house has developed due to home improvements in more recent decades, and I guess this was what we were now experiencing. These larger facilities now come with a range of pools, saunas, fitness facilities and restaurants, yet while the complexes have moved with the times, on one level the same rules and etiquette still apply. We had no idea what they were. We'd had no chance to check a guidebook with tips on how to behave because we didn't know where we would be heading. We'd not visited a Japanese bathing house before, and of course, as rules dictate, we were on our own trying to interpret the expectations. We couldn't read signs or ask advice since we spoke no Japanese, and even watching people is much harder when everyone is naked. Faced with a roomful of lockers, I stripped off, put my gear in my locker, and opted for walking into the baths with a towel.

I passed quickly through the changing room door into the bathing zone. Near the entrance area were two showers and a long row of sinks, all supplied with a small stool and bucket. Three large pools, all labelled at a different temperature, lay behind, and outside was a jacuzzi. The facilities were immaculate, and if they were ever to be found in the UK would most certainly be top end. There was no one else using the baths as I entered, giving me a few minutes to try and work out the rules. I was aware of how much I stood out, since I was obviously not Japanese, but also because I was sporting very distinctive tan lines!

As mentioned above, the Japanese public bath is one area where the uninitiated can upset regular customers by not following correct bathing etiquette designed to respect others. *Sentō* commonly display a poster describing bathing etiquette and procedures in Japanese or occasionally in other languages for international customers. This one certainly had no instructions for foreign visitors, and so I went first for a shower and to wash my hair. Thankfully I only found out the following morning that I was not supposed to use the shower for this because of the risk of introducing soap to the baths. I think there was probably a preferred order to enter the differing temperature baths, but despite having no idea, I thoroughly enjoyed my soak. Apparently, it's common to hear people say, "gokuraku, gokuraku" when they get into the bath. It's a way of expressing pleasure; and I certainly felt it was a good feeling for the body and the soul. I was worried how John was getting on, though, given he doesn't like getting things wrong, and with that on my mind, I dried off and went to wait for John. Ten minutes later, John arrived in his kimono. He also wore a big smile. Despite sharing my nervousness, he too marvelled in the experience. We headed to the restaurant floor, feeling relaxed in our "pyjamas" before working out what the sleeping arrangements were. While individual rooms were available, they were way beyond our budget, and we were quite literally in the cheap seats. We slept that night in reclining chairs, having opted for the mixed room accommodation. We may not have had a proper bed, but we had certainly rested and enjoyed this experience. If only we could find more places like this, we would have stayed in them again. Alas, internet searches even after our return have still not revealed exactly where we were.

The next morning, after a large coffee, we set off again. John has a keen interest in engineering, and we were hoping to ride over the Akashi bridge. The Akashi Kaikyo Bridge is, with a length of almost 2.5 miles, one of the world's longest suspension bridges. It opened in 1998 and spans the Akashi Strait between Kobe and Awaji Island. What we didn't realise was that it is part of the Kobe-Awaji-Naruto Expressway, one of three expressways which connect Honshu with Shikoku. As such, it was not open to cyclists, and we would have to plan an alternative route. While unable to ride, we stopped for photos and looked round the Bridge Exhibition Centre before continuing our way. We would now ride to Himejji that day. Himejji is around 38 miles from Kobe, and we still had 28 miles to go. This was a fairly easy day, though given sightseeing and humidity, we finally pulled into central Himejji in the late afternoon. The local tourist office told us of a campsite just out of town, and since this was a much cheaper option, we set off straight away. They closed at 5pm, were 4 miles away, and up a very, very steep hill. We just made it. The climb had been hot, and I was very sore. My period had started, and I came out of the toilet crying. It had hurt to pee and was way too painful to use a tampon. All I could do was apply cream and wait for the burning sensation to calm down. Travel is certainly not always glamorous!

After a good night's sleep, we set out to be tourists, stopping in at Himejji Castle. It was listed in the guidebook and meant to be stunning. We weren't disappointed, and after a wonderful few hours wandering round, we set off for the ferry to Shodashima, a small island only about an hour's ferry ride away. The island is not huge but does have a few good hills - on a road bike with no baggage, you'd get round the island in a day. We took it slightly more gently and covered about two-thirds before finding the campsite we had in mind. It was beautifully presented, clean and tidy, and with stunning views to boot. This was probably the best campsite we'd had since we started our trip, and we were in no great rush to leave in the morning. While we planned to ride to another camp the following night, we were first going on the cable car up Mt Kan Ka Kei. The view cleared once we were up there, and it was brilliant to get this helicopter view of Japan and its islands. We were back at our next camp late afternoon, where we spent an hour or so on the private beach before showering and looking for dinner. There was a restaurant nearby, but they were having a family BBQ. Dinner that night was just crisps and nuts, with the carb intake coming from a couple of beers as we watched the sunset. At least we weren't riding far the next day.

In previous times, many explorers would plant flags and sometimes new islands/towns would be named after their discoverer. While there are still some far reaches and communities, we still know little about, there isn't much of this true discovery left - as far as we are aware. Consequently, we were now looking for places that had already taken our names. Naoshima, our next small island, had been in my sights since leaving Kobe. There are still few things called Naomi, and given I often shorten my name in texts and emails to its first three letters, Naoshima was close enough for me. As well as having such a prestigious name, it also sounded like an interesting place to visit. While pleased it was not just an ugly industrial town, I was not aware it was so popular that accommodation was scarce! Despite having caught the ferry from Takamatsu that morning, we would need to return to find a bed for the night, repeating the journey the next day to finish our sightseeing. The island housed some fabulous traditional baths (always closed when we had a chance to go) and a series of 'artist houses' to cycle round and view. This new plan also meant we had more time in Takamatsu and we wasted no time there either, taking in an extra visit of Ritsurin traditional gardens, reputed to be some of the best in Japan.

We had a 47-mile ride to Tokushima next. It wasn't far but came, as usual in Japan, with a few good hills. Thankfully, the road then levelled, and a few tunnels saved us from significant climbs, even if we were putting our life in our hands! We arrived at 1pm and had the chance to relax before enjoying our best and rather accidental night-out in Japan. We only called in to a wee street stall called Miyabi for dinner that evening, but after numerous shots of sake and some of the best sashimi I have ever tasted, we left having enjoyed stilted, though fun, banter with staff and other customers.

We had another ferry to catch the next morning, this time to Wakayama, where we'd booked a hotel about 15 miles from the port. We wanted to cut down the last day's cycle to Osaka and knew we'd be off the ferry about 1:30 and needed to do some riding. The day was roasting, and the ride started well with some great bridges, though as the afternoon went on, the scenery deteriorated into a more industrial landscape. The roads were busy, and with lots of junctions, we were constantly stopping and starting. By the time we got to our hotel in Izumisano, we were both shattered and ready for a cold shower and much-needed beer and food. We had just 25 miles to Osaka, though again the whole route was busy, and it took much longer than we expected - traffic lights every 400m stopped you from gaining any rhythm or momentum.

Our home for the next four nights was the Sheraton Miyako Hotel. It seemed like a crazy luxury, but this had been the cheapest central option I could find since we wanted to be near the airport bus stop. In this case, it was right outside the hotel door. I like it when a plan comes together. Having reassured the very nice young man on the door that these two scruffily dressed urchins with bicycles and 14 pieces of luggage did indeed have a reservation, our bikes were duly locked away and luggage taken to our room. What a treat. We had a lot to sort as we prepared to leave Japan, and it was good to have enough space to get organised.

Before packing could commence, we really needed to do some laundry, or unpacking again would be a very unpleasant experience. Given our plush hotel, we couldn't afford the in-house service, so we went out to find a laundrette and hunt for bike boxes. An internet search led us to a nearby bike shop less than a mile away, and we took a stroll only to find it shut. In the end, it was a local road cyclist who pointed us in the direction of "Bici Termini" and the very helpful man running it called Koji. Boxes secured we returned to collect clean washing. We always liked to get things sorted, ready to leave, quite promptly. While I was perhaps more relaxed and last-minute, John certainly liked to know all was ready so he could truly relax and enjoy sightseeing. The early prep was certainly helpful here - taxis were nowhere near the size of American cabs and we would soon find out that the airport bus would not take our bikes at the time we needed to for our flight. It seemed getting to the airport with all our stuff was never that simple.

The next morning, we (the royal we that is) would start dismantling and packing up the bikes. It was still very hot and humid, and we were very happy that the hotel didn't mind us doing our bike packing in the air-conditioned foyer - keeping bikes in the luggage room until we had worked out an airport plan. Fortunately, just as we were buying the tickets for our pre-run, I had a brain wave. The only challenge with the bus had been that for the time we were flying, they were too busy for us and all our luggage. We could however take the bikes on a quiet bus and leave them in left luggage. We had a solution, and so we were able to stop worrying and enjoy our final days in Japan.

Our month of exploring Japan was coming to an end, but we still had time to sample street food delights we had not tried yet while taking in the neon signs around Dotomburi. The

Takoyaki (octopus dumplings) were delicious, though the real food highlight came on our last night as we sampled Kobe beef, cooked in hot broth on the table, with some of the finest sushi and sashimi I've ever tasted. We were done with temple, shrines, and castles, and so we enjoyed a bullet train ride back to Kobe as we had only passed by before. We decided to go and look at The Great Hanshin-Awaji Earthquake Memorial, Disaster Reduction and Human Renovation Institution. A very formal and Japanese name for what was a memorial to the Kobe earthquake of 1995. The exhibition details the before, during, and after of one of Japan's worst disasters, and most of the info is from people who survived, plus footage from security cameras, private individuals, and some footage from news agencies. The most amazing bit for us was the incredible way that Kobe has bounced back and how quickly it seemed to do it. Such an organised country.

Japan was like nowhere else I have ever been, and our journey had simply teetered around the edges. We'd found language and navigation a huge challenge outside key cities, and while we had slowly picked up knowledge regarding etiquette and culture, perhaps one of the most valuable things we learnt on this trip was how to read "hotel" in Japanese script.

The Stats; A Tour of Japan
457.4 Miles

Destination	Total Distance
Kawaguchiko	10
Lake Motosu	16.1
Ryokan in unknown place	(Inc. below)
Hammamatsu	95.1
Cape Irago	45.4
Tsu (from Toba)	(Inc. below)
Joho	(Inc. below)
Kyoto	69
Kobe (via Hyago)	45.4
Himejji	37.3
Shodo-Shima circular	(Unknown)
Takamatsu	(Inc. below)
Tokushima	47.8
Unknown	(Inc. below)
Osaka	91.3

Notes

• No bike computer was used for this section of our tour; therefore, data is based on subsequent estimations.

Given a lack of data I am unable to say whether 15mph was achieved. However, I suspect it's safe to assume given the hills and the heat that this was unlikely!

5.

CONTOURS

"It is by riding a bicycle that you learn the contours of a country best, since you have to sweat up the hills and coast down them.

Thus you remember them as they actually are, while in a motor car only a high hill impresses you, and you have no such accurate remembrance of country you have driven through as you gain by riding a bicycle."

Ernest Hemingway

Mountains have long been a thing to "go conquer". Since Mallory first noted he wanted to climb Everest simply "because it's there", the queue to reach one of the world's biggest peaks has been getting longer. Whether it be the balance of risk and reward, whether our achievement comes from the fact that we now seem to live in an ever-competitive world, or where we are searching to find meaning, I know I am not unique in my draw of the mountains. While the goal is of reaching the top, there is still more to the environment than this perhaps more macho take. Closer to home, Nan Shepherd, talking of the Cairngorms gave a different perspective. Rather than seeing a mountain as something to be cracked, she spoke of the mountain in terms of the plateaus, not just the peak, of what she termed its totality. For me, there are a number of reasons why I find this such an appealing environment. I love working towards a goal, love the views and the sense of perspective they provide, both physically and metaphorically, and I love the space they provide. The wind, the wildness, the baroness. I love that sense of being in a place which seems to have changed little over the course of time. It really is all about the totality.

We arrived in Kathmandu in the early hours on 2nd September 2012. It was pitch-black, and as our taxi driver took us through deserted streets, we were somewhat nervous. There was no one around and it just didn't look like an approach into a major city. The roads were narrow and lined with rubble. It was residential, yet there were no people or lights anywhere to be seen. We were tired and unsure of where we were. Eventually, despite shutters all being down on the surrounding stores and restaurants, we pulled up in front of the hotel. Given we knew we were arriving in the middle of the night, we had pre-booked for our first accommodation. The next morning, we woke, overwhelmed by the noise of the back streets of Thamel

- the main backpacker area. The Kathmandu Guest House is famous here, and rightly so. Previously a Rana Palace, the hotel retains a stately air. It was the first hotel to open in Thamel and although we liked it very much, it was expensive for our budget, and so we'd already made arrangements for a cheaper guest house. Our next room was far more basic - dingy and in need of a good clean. We'd get used to places like this over the next few months.

Our original plan in Nepal had been to join an organised tour, riding from Lhasa to Kathmandu. Unfortunately, due to difficulties with British tourists getting a VISA into Tibet at that time, our trip had been cancelled. Consequently, I had done no research for our time here. All we knew was that we had a month or so before we could enter India, and we didn't just want to ride the main highways. As I read the guidebook, John contacted the guys who ran his local pub - a strange thing to do were it not for the fact that they were former Gurkhas still very much connected with Nepal and its tourist industry. Within five minutes, two local agents came to our hotel and. I suggested I'd quite like to ride the Annapurna circuit. Why? Well, because it's pretty! While unaware of exactly what this would go on to involve, I knew we wouldn't just be able to head onto mountain tracks without local help. Ten minutes later, Rosan arrived. He was an accomplished walking and mountain bike guide. A plan was coming together, and in 3 days' time, having explored Kathmandu, we would set off on an initial short cycle tour around Kathmandhu.

For the next few days, we made daily trips to the cash point, every time retrieving our daily allowances in order to pay for food and accommodation while in the mountains. We also paired down our luggage, reducing to just two rear panniers having arranged to leave excess gear in Kathmandu. All other cycle tours round Annapurna were generally completed on mountain bikes and, like trekkers, utilized the services of local porters to carry all the gear.

Rosan had split our trip into two sections. We would only start our journey around Annapurna having completed a shorter three-day trip East first. Looking back, we came to see he was testing our future capability and fitness. We were still completely ignorant of what cycling the Annapurna circuit would involve.

Eight of the world's highest fourteen peaks (over 8,000 metres) lie in the Nepalese Himalaya. Altitude sickness can kick in at anything above 3,000 metres. We were on our way to ride over Thorong-la - one of the world's highest mountain passes at 5,416 metres high. There was little tarmac and few roads on what is essentially a trekking route and boy, do we have an accurate memory of the contours on this trip.

Despite some big climbs on our initial trip out to Nagarkot and Dulikhel - a 600 m climb over one pass that reached 1900 metres - Rosan seemed happy with our progress, and we were all set to start the main tour. We would leave at 7 am, following the busy road out past the airport. Our first day would consist of a relatively gentle 45 miles on what were mainly paved roads. Riding out past Bhaktapur, the scenery would quickly change as we headed into rural areas. Heavy traffic was replaced with views of the hills and decorated with trickling waterfalls, and we arrived at our hotel in Trisuli mid-afternoon. Having secured our bikes, the local children were soon amusing themselves playing with Dino - the bicycle bell I'd purchased in America. Despite the ongoing hooting, it was a great way to know the bikes were still safe, and it was good to see the kids being even more excited by my squeaky toy than I had been.

Unaware of what lay ahead, we would only have to wait until tomorrow to get a taste of what we had somewhat unknowingly signed up for. The next day came quickly as we rose with the sun, and after a hearty breakfast with plenty of coffee, we set off for Katunje. Distance-wise, the day was much shorter, though the terrain made this a much, much harder day. A steep climb started the day leading up and over a bridge, providing great views of Trisuli below. Smiling and admiring the view, we were still blissfully unaware. The paved road disappeared, replaced by loose stone. We were still going on an upwards trend, and to add further interest, we crossed through rivers and over a few dodgy bridges. We were still smiling at this stage amused by the adventure. We really had no idea just how tough the day was about to become.

The route took a very sharp upward turn. It was impossible to cycle and both John and I resorted to pushing our bikes up the stony track. We had a way to go, and the road continued its ascent. We pretty much pushed our bikes the rest of the day, and while I had some help from a local man heading our way, even the walk was tough when you only have a pair of cycle shoes. The metal clips designed to fit into the pedals of the bike for easier riding were not necessarily fit for purpose on dirt tracks and wet stones. We were so relieved to reach our accommodation that night. Despite being just 16 miles in distance terms, we had climbed 1500 metres on mountain biking terrain, and we were certainly not going 15mph!

It was one of those days where you could have just about got over it with a hot bath and comfy bed. Alas, we were in a very small Nepalese village called Katunge. There were no hotels here and we were to stay with a local family. It would be our most basic accommodation of the whole cycle tour. Our room was dug out of the earth under the main house. There was no lock on the door and no glass on the windows. The rich earth room smelt of damp and the only toilet in the village was a few minutes' walk up the hill behind a neighbour's house. There were no locks on the toilet door, and each time I made a visit, the local kids waited patiently outside until I was finished. Though I wasn't used to being followed in this way, it wasn't the only reason why I'll always remember those children. As we arrived in the village (a small row of houses on either side of the continuing track) they were playing with a simple hoop and stick, running up the road. Once again, they loved the dinosaur bell, and we spent quite some time showing and taking their photographs. They were such a pleasure to be around, and I can still recall their faces.

As the sun set, we headed for bed. We were shattered, and while I thought nothing would be able to wake me from my sleep that night, I was woken by heavy storms and wailing dogs. They were taking shelter just outside the glass-less window, and as I looked around, I noticed the door had also been blown open. I didn't even want to alert John given I was conscious not to draw any attention from the wild dogs outside. I'd not slept well, and who knew what we would face the next day. We already knew we would start with another steep push on the track that continued past the village. Luckily, despite a lack of sleep, when the time came to set off, we were well fuelled-up. The ladies in the village made money selling homemade donuts to passers-by, and we were more than happy to be their first customers. However, this was not the only reward of our early start. As we reached the top of the road, we saw our first glimpses of the snow on distant mountains. The view was a great morale boost and a small hint of the scenery we would soon be a part of.

We'd become used to the idea of there being no more paved roads; getting into our accommodation wet, muddy, and absolutely shattered, but we didn't expect that it could get worse. All roads led uphill, we were at the close of the monsoon season and what little roads there were quickly turned to muddy tracks. Progress slowed to a crawl as we pushed and carried our way ahead. Local children would often run alongside me or help push my bike as I followed behind John and Rosan. At times, I felt like a real pied piper, and I think the boys were amused as I appeared around the corner with my entourage in tow. Our third night would be in Arughat, again around 15 miles down the road, but before we got there, we would have several long metal suspension bridges to cross first. It was here John found out I had a fear of heights though thankfully he didn't say that the children following me on one of the bridges were deliberately jumping up and down behind me. Had I known, I think I would have found crossing these rivers even harder.

The paths were very muddy, and we were filthy as we arrived at our hotel that night. Shangri-La, or at least that's what we called it, was a completely out-of-character building with its surroundings. As plastic penguins met us in the garden, we were delighted to see the air conditioning, ensuite with hot shower, and a western toilet in our room. We only had two sets of cycle gear with us, and so with time to spare and an attached bathroom we decided it was time to do some washing. Sadly, it poured with rain all night and most of the next day. While our riding gear was clean, we would have to start out in wet clothes - not great for chaffing.

Gorkha was our destination for the day. It's a larger town and we'd been promised paved roads as we got nearer but, as we were finding every day, we had a few challenges to overcome first. Having made reasonable progress, we soon came across a serious problem. Apparently, heavy rain and a gushing river had swept away the main river crossing just three days before. Rosan was busy talking to the locals to find out more information. It seems a temporary bridge had been erected, though it's fair to say this was still not looking to be the perfect solution. The wooden bridge was weak and was missing a few slats. The water was gushing below, and we had heavy bikes and panniers. Soon Rosan had enlisted the locals to help us...for a small fee. All John and I needed to do was get ourselves across as others went ahead with all our gear. Despite the help I was still finding this incredibly difficult. The bridge led round to a very precarious, narrow, and high cliff edge. It was now Rosan's turn to find out about my fear of heights. One of the guys was then asked to get me across. I gripped his hand tightly as we edged our way across the wet, slippery rock. The ledge was too short to stand tall, so looking down at every footstep was the only thing you could do anyway. My heart was pumping when we touched solid ground again. That blissful lack of awareness was soon slipping away as we became more and more aware of the trip we were embarking on.

Heart rate reduced, we paid the locals and continued with our journey. We were just making progress when we were halted again. There had been a substantial landslide. Now not only was there no tarmac, but the rugged path had also disappeared. Undeterred, Rosan lifted his lightweight mountain bike, and John followed. There was no way I could follow quite so easily. Despite reducing my luggage substantially, my bike and panniers still amounted to 36kg, and I did not have the strength to carry it across the distance on uneven and sliding terrain. Thankfully, Rosan came to help as John also went back to help two guys with their motorbike. We were beginning to wonder what our next challenge would be, and it wasn't long before progress was, once again, halted. Rough wet tracks were taking their toll on my brake pads, and while I carried spares, they had already been changed, and so John offered me his even though he was also requiring a new set. We always carry spares but did not anticipate needing to change them more than once while on a 17-day tour. Maintenance complete, we moved on and we would soon be approaching a downhill ride into Gorkha. Ordinarily it would have been great, especially after working so hard to date, but with John now having no brakes, he couldn't even ride the downhill, his frustration made worse by the fact that this section was also tarmac!

Gorkha was our guide's hometown, and he was pleased we were going this way. His familiarity with the area and contacts for cycling in Nepal would also prove necessary. We were desperate for more brake blocks and knowing we were generally changing them every three days meant we may need a few sets yet to complete this course. There were no bike shops around - after all, you'd be a fool to cycle in these hills. Our bike blocks would be brought in from Kathmandu as one of Rosan's business partners was dispatched to buy 12 sets of brake blocks, catching the overnight bus to dispatch them to us ASAP. They would be the most expensive and worst-quality brake blocks I have ever bought, yet they were priceless. Our trip would have been over had we not managed to get any.

The paved road continued out of Gorkha, and our bikes made small work of the first few miles, though, as we were coming to expect with this tour, it didn't last, and our first obstacle didn't take long to manifest. We had another river to cross, and as this one had no bridge, we were destined to get wet feet. The boys removed their shoes and socks and headed across before looking back to see how I was getting on. It seemed it was my lucky day, and my feet were preserved for a short while longer - I was getting a lift over in a pick-up truck! Smiling, we carried on, at least until the next hurdle...thick, clay mud. The earth was rich, red, claggy, and about 18 inches thick. It stuck to everything, the tyres collecting it as they pushed ahead. Soon, the wheels stopped as mudguards were the last thing we needed right now, and while sticks were useful at the declogging, it was never long before the process needed to be repeated. John was particularly frustrated, and soon he resorted to carrying his bike, but I just couldn't manage this. Walking in cycle shoes in the mud was not easy, either. It took ages to get through this very short stretch, and as we passed by the next stretch of water, both the bikes and our legs had a full wash down. We were filthy.

Our stop that day was at Paundi. It was another home stay, and while there was no shower - just a water tap in the middle of the village - the house did at least have its own loo. We were well-fed and welcomed by the locals and as was becoming the norm after such exhausting days, we retreated to bed as it went dark. The nest morning, filled up on potato curry and Tibetan bread, we had a comparatively easy ride to our next stop.

So far, this trip had been a massive test, and while we had now become accustomed to our adventure, we were still blinded to the fact that it was about to get even harder. We were about to join up with the trekking route around the Anna-purna circuit. Every year around 5,000 people are estimated to walk the route from Bhulbhule to Jomson, crossing the mountain pass called Thorong-la at 5,416m. According to the guidebook the route should take 15-20 days, and as this is a well-known trek, there are a various lodges and places to eat on the way. Over the past few days, we had been far from any western treats, and we were excited to see chocolate bars available in Bhulbhule that night. Being on a designated route also meant we now needed our permits to continue, which Rosan sorted for us. We would need to get them stamped at the various checkpoints along the way. Not only did the TIMS (Trekker Information Management System) give us permission to enter the national park, but it also meant people would know where to search for us should the worst happen. Yikes.

So far, we had not met any other travellers since leaving Kathmandu, but as we were now joined by walkers and their associated porters, not only were there more options for places to stay, but they were also much busier. Our first lodge on the route was quiet when we first arrived, and John took the chance to do some much needed bike maintenance - swapping over his worn tyres from front to back. The Nepalese "roads" had taken their toll.

They were also taking their toll on us. Wearing cold wet socks and cycle shoes meant our feet were raw. Wet cycle shorts led to the requirement of very liberal applications of nappy rash cream, and the mental challenge of such difficult riding was exhausting. The scenery was incredible, though, and each time John and Rosan waited to see how I was doing, I always managed a smile despite my huffing and puffing. Many of the paths were next to sheer drops, and as the riding was technical and beyond my capability, I pushed more than them. Thankfully, they managed the perfect balance of helping me when I really needed it without doing too much such that it would have made me feel my achievement had been diminished.

We pushed on, though I struggled to move my bike up the final steep incline into Chamie, and Rosan was, once again, at hand. This was the last stop on the ride that any vehicle could get to. After this point, everything we found up the mountain had been carried there by porters or mules. From now on in, we could only carry on or turn around. The roads were increasing in gradient and stones, and it seemed that the following morning would be a particularly difficult section. Our bikes and luggage would need to travel separately, and so our guide had enlisted help. As John and I carried our panniers, two local guys carried our bikes, and about an hour later, we arrived at a fabulous tea stop for a much-needed break. The guys helped us just a short section more before heading home as we continued, but it wouldn't be the last bit of help I would need that day. In fact, I would need the boys for a few obstacles that followed.

I'd become accustomed to the metal suspension bridges now and had even laughed at myself as an older lady breezed past carrying a heavy load, while wearing flip-flops, on a bridge I'd just crossed on my hands and knees. However, even with this experience, I still didn't have the confidence to push my bike and all my gear across the three tree trunks laid above another fast-flowing river. I may not have always had the ability, but I hope I added good cheer and morale to our merry troop as we persevered.

So far, most of our obstacles had come from going over water, but as a full-flowing waterfall was coming down onto the road ahead, this time it was more than our socks and shoes that would be getting wet. The road was covered in loose rock, and while I had set out to follow the guys, it didn't take long before the fear set in, and I tentatively retreated. The power of the water was pushing me close to the edge of the cliff, and once again I would need help. This time, as Rosan took my bike and gear, John would help me get through. What an adventure. I was so happy to reward myself with chocolate pancakes when we stopped for lunch. My feet were now feeling every bit sore as the cycling to walking ratio has been decreasing. This is a tough walk but imagine doing it in the wrong shoes while pushing or carrying 36kg. I was so relived to reach our trekking lodge in Bhagachap that night, and as I peeled back my shoes, it was apparent why my feet were so painful - they were red raw. The lodge owner, a former soldier, ran me a hot salt bath to soak my tootsies, and after dinner I applied liberal applications of antiseptic cream before going to bed.

Anticipating another early start, I headed for bed, but as the night progressed, I started to feel unwell. I had a dodgy tummy, and while I could barely walk, I spent much of the night squatting over the loo. If only there had been a western toilet here! I woke for breakfast and got ready to go but felt unable to eat or move. There was little else we could do, and despite being on a tight schedule, given we had only hired Rosan for a set number of days, we would have to wait. It was 10:30 that morning before I felt able to get going. Given my lurgy, Rosan had cut the day short, and we would just head to Temang. Yet again, Rosan enlisted some local help for me, and the lodge owners' son would also now come with us. John went on ahead as Rosan stayed back with me and my much-reduced pace. Unfortunately, John was also carrying the emergency loo roll. This challenge was just getting harder and harder, but because we had to walk whichever direction we went, we just wanted to continue with our original target. I went to bed on arrival that day, and while I wasn't 100% fine the next day, we still had to continue.

It was pouring with rain, and we were drenched and cold. While the scenery kept us going, it's certainly much harder in these conditions. Smiles were also found as we passed by a bank - the only one we would see until we were on the other side of the mountain pass. Every day when we were in Kathmandu, we had been visiting the cash point, but the need for additional porters as well as food and accommodation meant our wallets were empty. We were so happy that we were able to exchange some of our travellers' cheques, especially given we had now even borrowed some money from Rosan.

Happy to be in credit again financially, we were sadly very much depleted health-wise. It was now John's turn to fall ill too. We were slipping behind schedule, but still determined to carry on. As John slept, I joined Rosan and the lodge owner around the fire in his kitchen, more drenched souls started to arrive, and the lodge owner lit the fire burner in the main eating area of the hostel instead. I'm not sure his kitchen would have housed us all. Well-fed and warmed up on lemon tea - soon becoming our Nepal favourite - I sat around with the other guys as we dried our socks on the fire. The next morning, we woke to sunshine and John was feeling a little better. I was proud not to have burnt our socks as the others had, though it seems that despite there being no visible holes, they had indeed perished. We now just had the pair we were wearing. Oh well - less weight in the panniers!

Our next stop would be Manang, and we were excited for several reasons. Firstly, this is the biggest place and a key stop before the final push for the pass, and as many stay here for a few nights there is also much more here in terms of facilities - hotels, shops, and restaurants. Secondly, my period had also now started, and I was running out of tampons. I desperately needed the chemist too and was hopeful of finding what I needed. Thirdly, and by far most importantly for me, our itinerary had the words REST DAY standing out from the page. I was so ready for some time off.

In the most part, our expectations were met. The place we would end up staying in was well known for its apple pie. More importantly, we had a room with its own toilet. Both of us still had the squits and with very, very frequent toilet needs, this was even better than the pudding choices on offer. Also, I finally found tampons in the very last shop I tried, much to my relief, as the more easily available padded towel was not just a great option inside already padded cycle shorts. Unfortunately, it was the rest day that had been most misleading. There was no such thing.

We were now at 3,500m and one of the reasons Manang was much busier than other places so far was because this is traditionally the stopover people use for a few nights for acclimatisation. I've said ignorance is bliss a few times in relation to this trip, and despite being very well-researched for most of our tour, this section had been a little more ad hoc given our complete change of plans. I'd had a brief chat with my doctor about altitude sickness. He's suggested some people prescribe Viagra given it can help in this situation, as well as the more well-known effects for which it is known. However, as I had been expecting to be riding with an organised tour, I'd not worried too much about this. Perhaps I should have done.

Altitude sickness, at its worst, is fatal, and it was this I had to focus on as we were told our day would start at 8am the next day. While two hours later than our more normal 6am start, I was still struggling, as rest day for me certainly meant a slightly longer lie-in. Acclimatisation means climbing and then returning to a lower height to sleep. For us, this involved taking just our bikes another 6 miles up the mountain on our day off before coming back to Manang before heading back up the same route the next day with our panniers. While I enjoyed walking out from Manang, taking the right turn to the now-signposted Thorong-la, the route was challenging. The narrow flagstone track out of the village led to a number of deep steps, hard enough without having a bike on your shoulder. It was all making the previous days seem easy. I had to keep reminding myself of the reward on offer, of the great feeling of achievement we would have on reaching the peak. With our bikes left in Yak Kharta 900 metres higher, we set off back down the hill. It started to drizzle with rain. Rarely grumpy, I was now. Our day off had been eight hours of tough climbing to end up back where we started. At least I had apple pie to cheer me up.

We joined another couple for dinner, though it's fair to say I didn't eat much. In fact, I'm not even sure I spoke to them overly. Unfortunately, I spent most of the night dashing back to the loo. John and I may not have known each other too well a few months ago, but we were certainly more familiar with each other now.

The next day, we set off to climb up to Yak Kharta again. Back down the narrow tracks, up the steps, and passing the prayer wheels. This time I stopped to turn them as was custom. John was finding it hard, and I was really struggling. The altitude takes all your strength and your breath. Wowsers. Progress was slow, but the views were so inspirational. We looked back down to Manang, over the glacier and up to where we were heading. The scenery a great excuse for regular rests! After a couple of hours, we knew we'd be able to stop, the previous day had shown us a great place at almost exactly halfway, and the second half we knew would be easier as most of the altitude had already been gained. We feasted on good coffee and fresh muffins and tried the local Seabuckthorn juice. The Israeli Trekkers who'd given us a cheer on the way into Manang stopped at the café, and this time we were able to cheer them in. It was another great moment followed by hugs all round and hearty congratulations for making it so far!

We left them at the café as we started the second part of our trek. The gradient reduced, and with our bodes adjusting, we were starting to breathe a little easier. Rosan's trick was beginning to pay off. We were soon back in Yak Kharka and checked into our room. Yet again, we had a private toilet. It was still an absolute necessity.

Our room at the lodge was clean, basic, and warm, and while the shower was just a bucket and jug affair, the water was warmed for us, and it felt lush. Dinner was great as we met up with quite a few people we'd been seeing enroute. We talked about the days to come, especially getting over the pass, though the whole conversation sprang from the news of a French trekker who'd sadly died of altitude sickness. The seriousness of our route was made even more clear. I went to bed all set for another early start, though I would be woken even earlier than I was expecting. John had risen earlier, and on seeing just how amazing the sunrise was, had woken me to take a look and share this magnificent experience. The sky was a hazy pink as the sun slowly rose to hit the peaks. Amazing.

*

This start to the day put us in great spirits for what would be the hardest day of the whole adventure. We would have lunch at Phedi (low camp) before continuing to High Camp to sleep for the last night before going over the pass the next day. The air was getting thinner and thinner. Given the difficulty, Rosan had decided that I would need another porter, and while stubborn, I absolutely trusted his judgment. This is no place for risks. John would take his own bike to Phedi - another 900-metre climb.

The route involved a number of long metal suspension bridges, one of which had such a steep slope down to it I was on all fours as I tried to stop my cycle shoes slipping fast in front of me. I don't know how John did it. I was so proud. He was there as I arrived, as were the other trekkers. They too had been finding it hard and recognising the extra work we were doing taking bikes and all our luggage (at least for the most part), they gave us a standing ovation. I cried. John cried. We were both so overwhelmed.

Having feasted on chocolate pancakes and coffee, we set off for the next 600m ascent to High Camp. We were on scree covered slopes and with all these loose stones our shoes kept slipping. In addition, there were signs warning you not to linger given the potential for landslides. It took a lot of concentration, but my mind was on other things. I had sharp stomach pains and desperately needed the loo. My tummy was still causing me problems. There was no cover, and as I saw a local man leading his mules up the hill just a short way back, I knew I just had to go before it was too late. Soon the other trekkers could catch us too. Business done, I tried to hide my doings under a few stones before continuing up towards John. We were just one sleep away from going over the pass.

The next morning, we would leave as the sun rose. Breakfast would be at 4:30am and the plan was to start walking at five am. Rooms at high camp were scattered across an open yard with the toilet and restaurant all in different buildings. There was only one loo, and I was now pleased my squit moment had occurred on the mountain rather than while in a queue - that would have been far worse. Dinner was an early affair, and we were in bed by eight. There had been snow as we arrived in the afternoon, and I was very happy to see I could buy a hot water bottle for the night. I was warm, though it was not necessarily restful. By the time I went to bed, I had a headache around my right eye. My chest felt heavy, and whether real or imagined, I was starting to feel like I was showing symptoms of altitude sickness. I knew I would have to take care, but I certainly didn't want to have to turn back now. I shared my concerns with John. Should things get worse, descending would be the only option.

Thankfully, I was OK. Who knows whether it was real or paranoia, either way, we were now setting off to the high point of our journey. Apparently, it takes about 3.5 to 4 hours for your average trekker to ascend the 600m to Thorong-la, and I was certainly finding it slow-going. I would need to stop every few steps just to catch my breath. John wasn't finding his breathing quite so tough and so went on ahead. Accordingly, he reached the top in one hour 40 minutes, and would have the privilege of being first to get to the top that morning. I would arrive about 20 minutes later.

The top of the mountain was adorned with prayer flags, covering the sign that would mark the 5416-metre mark. It was an obvious photo spot, and for me, it was time for triple star jumps, my usual top of monumental hills celebration. Such was this one that John said he too had partaken on his arrival. It was freezing at the top, and while we did stop at the tea shack and applaud in a few of the trekkers, we didn't hang around too long. John was shivering, having already been there a while longer, and we needed to warm up again. We were also very much looking forward to the downhill.

Having helped us to the top we said a final goodbye to our amazing porters and attached the panniers back to our bikes. We now had a 1,900-metre descent to Muktinath, and while it may sound like an exhilarating race back down the hill, the gradient and loose gravel made it completely unrideable. Such was the challenge of holding our bikes and gear back from rolling away from us that about halfway down, Rosan swapped my heavy tourer and bags for his much lighter mountain bike. Who knew a downhill could be this hard. Even a group of mountain bikers were carrying their gear on this section. We struggled down, the only consolation being the lunch stop at the bottom. We continued to Muktinath and thankfully, while a little technical for my riding skills, we were pleased we could at least attempt riding this section.

The town now lay just ahead, and the sun was shining. Famous for its temple and its distinctive colourful buildings, we were so happy to arrive and took time to wander around. Later that evening, we sat with Rosan both to celebrate getting over the mountain pass and to talk about the last few days. Having had no alcohol since leaving Kathmandu, given it is inadvisable when at altitude, I can say that the cold beer with dinner that night tasted even better. Cheers! We had just a couple of days left with Rosan and having been ill and therefore cut short two of our days, we had some time to make up. Ever resourceful, Rosan had a plan. We would ride to Jomson and then catch a bus to Tatopani.

The road continued downhill from Muktinath, and for me, was one of my favourite days for scenery. Unlike the lusher green and wet side of the mountain we had just climbed, this side of the pass was much drier and dustier - taking on the look of a more lunar landscape. I loved the sense of desolation, though sadly we were also informed that a large landslide the previous year had meant that many people had lost both homes and lives here. An hour or so later, we arrived in Jomson. This is the largest town on this side of the mountain, and once again we were very happy to see a bank. This one had a cash point, and we used every card we had to retrieve maximum withdrawals. We owed Rosan money once again, as well as still needing to pay for more food and accommodation.

While we were busy dealing with our finances, Rosan had been sorting out bus tickets for us, and after a small snack, our bikes were loaded onto the van roof, and we took our seats. It was bumpy, but we were making reasonable progress. It felt like the key challenges in our adventure had come to end. They had not.

The bus we were on did not go all the way to Tatopani, and we would have to change. The next bus was full, though we were squeezed on, and we ended up sharing the ride with both the Israeli trekkers we had met and an Irish and Australian couple who'd cheered us on as I rode right through puddles and streams earlier on in our journey. While there was less room, we were enjoying catching up with our new friends. Then this bus stopped too. There had been a landslide, and the bus was not able to continue. Bikes unloaded and panniers hooked on, we would head around a mile down the road before another vehicle was waiting for us all. This would be our third bus, and while the number of passengers remained constant, the number of seats were reducing with each change. There were no way too many of us to be on a small minibus, but in Nepal it seemed this was not a problem. We were squeezed on seats, surrounded by luggage, and with just as many people standing, it's perhaps as well we were going downhill, or I don't think the bus would have even moved. While the amount of personal space had significantly decreased, the speed of travel had gone the opposite way. The road was narrow, the driver had the music blaring, we were rammed in, and the bus was going way to fast. At times the road seemed to just disappear, and there was less than an inch - if that - between the side of the bus and the sheer drop to the river below. We joked, calling it the party bus, but this was quite the adrenaline ride, and we were all so relieved to finally reach Tatopani. Only now could we all really laugh about our ride down the mountain. Petrifying.

Tatopani is known for its hot springs, and I enjoyed dipping my toes. It was nice to get a chance to relax before we would come across another landslide. We saddled up and cycled in the direction of Lumle. Once again, to make up time, we would part-cycle as far as Beni and then get the bus. The road out of Tatopani was good, both in terms of surface and scenery, though just as we hit a nice rhythm, another landslide meant another detour. Once again, we utilized the support of local porters for our bikes as we carried our panniers. While it may seem like we "cheated" - the panniers were not light, and neither are they made to be comfortable on your shoulders. This was still no easy ride. With the panniers reattached to the bike, we were off again, but again not for long. A second landslide had the army out, and while I helped the guys with all the bags, I did also take a hand up from one of the soldiers. In my defence, cycle shoes are not made for climbing over mounds of loose earth! Soon enough, we were at Beni and stashing the gear for a three-hour bumpy ride to Lumle. The day would end with a nine mile climb back up and given the temperature had now risen dramatically as we had dropped in altitude, we were not upset to be on the bus. The last two weeks or so had been so exhausting.

We had a great meal and retired early, ready for our cycle ride to Pokhara the following day. We were met with bright blue skies, and after a great breakfast of Tibetan bread and potato curry, we set off. After a three-mile ascent, it was then downhill to Pokhara. We would have a couple of days here, giving us time both to rest, celebrate our achievement, and say goodbye to Rosan. We were both clear that we could not have managed this incredible experience without him.

We had paid for someone to bring the rest of our gear from Kathmandu to here. Our time in Nepal was coming to an end, and we still wanted to try a bit of rafting before finishing our journey here in Lumbini. Having completed a master's degree in Buddhist studies, I wanted to visit the place he was reputed to have been born. There were temples everywhere, all in the differing styles of their country's tradition, and I enjoyed seeing the contrasting architectural styles, as well as the trees awash with prayer flags. It made for a peaceful end to this incredible mountain journey.

The Stats; A Tour of Nepal
284 Miles and Lots of Climbing

Destination	Total Distance	Altitude (metres)
Bhaktapur	(Inc. below)	1401
Nagarkot	23.6	2175
Dulikhel	15.5	1550
Trisuli	45.4	-
Kutunge	15.5	-
Arughat	15.5	-
Gorka	21.8	862
Paundi	23	-
Bhulbhule	15.5	840
Chamie	18.6	2620
Bhagachap	12.4	-
Temang	-	-
Bardang	-	-
Manang	9.3 (Bike)	3519
Manang	12.4 (Bike carry and walk)	3519
Yak Kharta	6.2 (Walk)	4010
High Camp	7.5	4450
Muktinath (via Thorong-la)	13.7	2800 (Over 4516 pass)
Jomsom / Tatopani	-	-
Beni	21.8	-
Pokhara	21.8	822

Notes

• Bike computer was used sporadically for this section of our tour; therefore, some data is based on subsequent estimations or missing entirely given online map systems do not cover this area.

• Altitude data has been added to give a sense of the climbing involved.

• High altitude is classed as anything above 2,500m where the air is thinner, has less oxygen and therefore breathing is more difficult.

• If you prefer to think of height in feet than 4,516 metres is 14,816 feet.

Again, given a lack of data I am unable to say what our average speed was. However, I suspect it was certainly less than 5mph and once at altitude may even have been as low as 1.5mph!

6.

FOOD

Potato curry

- 1/2 tsp cumin seeds – put in oil till they splutter.

- Add large finely diced onion and cook till brown.

- Add 1 tsp each of garlic and ginger paste plus 2/3 tomatoes - soften.

- Add salt, ½ tsp turmeric, 1 tsp coriander powder, 1 tsp garam masala and red chilli powder to taste.

- ONLY once all spiced are cooked through for flavour, add diced potatoes, water, and cook through.

- SERVE with Indian paratha breads for the breakfast of champions! (I'd cheat and buy the frozen ones from a nearby Indian supermarket!)

They say India is like Marmite - you either love it or hate it. I love it. My fascination with its culture, history, religion, and people started at university while studying theology. I can't say why it has such a hold on me. It has a way to go in its treatment of women, the poverty is always a shock, and for many it can often seem like the filthiest place on earth. Yet, it can smell intoxicating and has a history and wackiness that draws me in. It makes me smile, is full of colour, varies incredibly from state to state, and quite frankly has the best food of any country. Other than reducing my meat intake - given a lack of refrigeration - I planned to lap it up. Truck stops for chai, street stalls for snacks, never ending thali and "curry" for breakfast, lunch, and dinner. Yumm.

We crossed the border into India at Sunauli, just South from Lumbini, and immediately the chaos began. Immigration was a scruffy hut, full of piles of paperwork which we duly completed, and not long after passing through the border gate, the roads were lined with trucks. They were all wondrously decorated, brightly painted, and often adorned with garlands and gifts for the gods throughout the cab. The roads in India are completely bonkers, and despite attempts to bring in a highway code of sorts, it seems more people follow the practice of prayer than the rules of the road. Our first day cycling through India would see us cover just under 60 miles, and while it was a relatively straightforward journey without too much undulation, we would navigate predominantly by asking directions than any other method. Our map covered all of India and given the land mass here is about 13 times larger than the UK, you can only imagine it was somewhat lacking in any detail. Fortunately, there were few turn-offs as we made our way to Gorakhpur, in the Eastern part of Uttar Pradesh. Despite being in the North, I would start this foodie journey with a masala dosa – a savoury rice pancake stuffed with potatoes served with both a tomato-based and coconut and chilli sauce - usually more associated with South Indian food. The food set us up well for the rest of the day and we arrived at the hotel following a young guy on his scooter who we had asked for directions.

We were followed by another young boy, scruffily dressed and with wild, wild eyes. Gorakhpur is described in Lonely Planet as "little to see but a well-connected transport hub" and it was the railway that we were heading for. We had two months in India, and in our attempt to both ride bikes and be tourists, we would do what some may consider cheating. To us it made perfect sense. Besides, travelling on one of the largest rail networks in the world and coming to grips with the bureaucracy involved was just another part of our Indian adventure.

India can be a tough place and, as a Westerner it's not easy to blend in. Add in the bicycles, Lycra, and blond hair, all we needed now was a public announcement. I remember feeling absolutely petrified the first time I visited India in 1998, eventually settling in after a few days.

Having considered where we wanted to ride prior to our arrival, we had opted for Rajasthan. It was a part of the country I had not been to, and for John it was all new, so he was fine with going there. I did however feel no first trip to India was complete without seeing the magnificence of the Taj Mahal, and so we would start the Northern part of our riding in Agra.

It had been some time since I'd last completed the train booking forms - dates, times, tourist allocations, seats and names of both trains and passengers. One often wonders how the system works yet, I'm always surprised by both the reservation system and the punctuality. We were ready to go and so, following a brief discussion, we opted for the cheaper seats in sleeper class. We still had a bunk and so assumed all would be good. Our bikes were taken to the station for booking in four hours before departure. Unfortunately, this now left us to carry our panniers, handlebar bags, helmets, etc. to the station later. Too far not to struggle, but too close for a cab. We arrived overheated and a little grumpy to then wait an hour on the platform. As we sat, there were both increasingly large sweat patches on our clothes and a growing crowd of spectators. You just have to get used to be stared at, though as perspiration literally pours, I only wished I was looking even a little closer to my best. I was relieved when the train finally pulled in. We collected our many bags and tried to find our place among the many others doing the same. The train was heaving, and our six-seater bunk ended up with nine people in the end. We had a bottom and middle bunk with the luggage stashed underneath. It was a tight squeeze and we had to push for the space we had booked. We were on the overnight train for 15.5 hours. We were getting the space we had paid for, even if we did have to climb over the extra travellers lying on the floor of our carriage.

I wasn't sure what food we would get in sleeper class, and we had packed a variety of crisps and fruit to keep us going. We needn't have worried. The supply of snack food and chai was plentiful. Far from either a dried-out or soggy sandwich, the food on Indian trains is superb.

Soon, I was ready for some sleep. I took the middle bunk, gently dozing until we pulled up into the station at Agra very early the next morning. I'd got up just once to climb over the bodies lying between my bunk and the toilet. John had stayed awake all night. Something had made him not trust the six other guys who made up our carriage, and perhaps the word of warning to keep an eye on all our possessions from the police chief who passed through the train had not helped. Throughout the night, one of the young guys seemed determined to persuade John to move to the top bunk. He wanted to stay close to our bags.

It was still dark in Agra as we left the station, though first light would soon be here, and people were starting to murmur. We'd already booked a hotel, and while having the advantage of having somewhere to aim for on arrival, it does of course mean we have to find it. We had booked a treat - while still reasonably cheap, it would have a little more than just the basics of Nepal and Gorakhpur. We were staying here for a few nights, taking the time to see one of the world's greatest monuments - the Taj Mahal. This ivory-white marble mausoleum lies on the south bank of the Yamuna River. It was commissioned in 1632 by the Mughal emperor, Shah Jahan, to house the tomb of his favourite wife, Mumtaz Mahal. Despite walking past the "Clean Agra, Green Agra" signs set amongst piles of rubbish and being enjoyed by the sacred cows on our way to "do the tourist thing", the Taj glistens in the sunlight, its majesty proud for all to see. It truly is one of the great wonders of the world.

Having done the tourist thing, it was time to eat again. Curry, beer, and a rooftop view of the Taj: perfect and worth the climb up the many steps. It was a more relaxing eating experience than dinner - proof that a good meal is not all about the food. We ate in the hotel and, accustomed as we were to eating out, we knew to ask for starters and mains to be delivered separately - not just in the order the kitchen had items ready. Sadly, they failed, and I think as tensions had been high from the train journey, John just found it too frustrating. He left, and I stayed behind, crying over diner. The food was lovely, I was really hungry, but I just couldn't face it. We didn't speak that night, though as apologies were shared the next morning, it became obvious that the tensions from our overnight train journey had not gone away. India can be tough on friendship, though as ever, we were determined to make our trip work. Our next stop was Fatehpur Sikri. It was only a short ride, and given the heat, we left early. It also gave us a full day to explore this long, mostly abandoned city.

From here we were heading to Jaipur, but it was 130 miles away, and so we knew we would need to break up the riding. There wasn't anything particular to see enroute. We were on a main road with a few villages, so the only thing to really watch out for was the traffic. We passed through a few busy junctions, and despite the many warning signs to be careful, it seems these are ignored by the vast majority. A motorbike pulled out, and John and I clipped bikes. Fortunately, the only thing to fall off was a pannier. We were slowly getting used to Indian roads - the sound of horns from passing trucks, the motorbikes slowing down to say hello and the buses that just stop right in front of you as pedestrians hail them down. We stayed in a small family-run hotel in Bilaji, leaving early the next morning. The food here was simple – home-cooked channa dal, rice and veg curry. It was different from the richer food on offer in tourist areas, but just as yummy. We only had one consistent dietary requirement - yogurt. We ate it with every meal when it was available, never losing the opportunity to add much-needed good bacteria into our digestive systems.

As we joined the Indian traffic again, I'd decided it was time for The Captain to take on an Indian persona. Much like the trucks and buses on the roads, he too needed decor. I'd been looking at the bright colours and garlands and decided that when I had the chance, my black framed bike would be transformed. It was John who spotted the truck adornment store on the side of the road, and I didn't need much persuading to stop. In a matter of minutes and much to the amusement of many young men around the stall, my bike soon had yellow "go faster" stickers on the mudguards and garlands of flowers hanging around my handlebar bag. The Captain looked fabulous, and I had a massive smile. We continued making our way to Jaipur. The road was uphill, and we were in the midday sun. I remember the pedal clearly for two key moments - neither of which was particularly pleasant. Not only was I tapped on the head by travellers on a passing bus, causing me to wobble, but I also managed to ride past a young lad doing a number two on the side of the road, just as peristalsis was taking place. Fortunately, the welcome at the "Pearl Palace" - a highly recommended travellers' hotel - was much nicer. We were staying here for a couple of nights and straightaway knew we would enjoy our time here. Real coffee, friendly hosts, and many sights to see. We had a long list of jobs to do here too, and thankfully, the tuk-tuk driver we enlisted spoke excellent English and helped us immensely as we organised shipment of our excess baggage to Mumbai. We had no plans to camp here and didn't need the levels of warm gear we'd required in Nepal. The chance to reduce our load and make daily rides much easier was too good an opportunity to miss. Hopefully, we would find the couriers' office in Mumbai and all our belongings would be safe. Only time would tell on that, though... We would collect our bags on the 4th of December - roughly two months' time.

Jobs done, we were tourists again and were taken to the Maharajah's cemetery, followed by the more well-known Amber Fort. The tuk-tuk approach to tourism feels a bit like being on a city sight-seeing bus but with a private driver and guide. The drivers, too, like being hired for a full day - guaranteed fare for the whole day and at a good price - it's no wonder the drivers are often desperate to get the tourists' attention! They pack the day and seem to have learnt the history and key points, and while you do have to watch out for being taken to the tourist shop, we still loved our tuk-tuk days, and true to form, we were packing in the sights today too as we continued to Nahargarh fort. The views from here were fabulous and we were lucky that this driver was also a pretty good photographer - this is one area where skills can certainly vary! Many camera clicks later, we went via the station to book numerous trains for the rest of our time in India. This time, it was second class upwards. We were not doing another train journey like the last.

*

The following morning, we set off for Tonk, back on the national highways, not picturesque but good Tarmac. The road was flat and there were plenty of chai stops. We made good progress and had covered about 50 miles when I spotted a problem. The sidewall of my rear tyre had split, and the tube was poking through enough to catch the mudguard supports. We had no spare tyres and so looked for a patch. Thankfully, India is one of the most resourceful countries I have ever visited, and it wasn't long before the truck repair guy over the road had a solution. He promptly provided us a with a spare piece of rubber. The crowd was growing as we made our repair - or should I say, John did the repair while I led on distraction - trying to stop everyone from "helping" is a job in itself. With the tyre repaired we decided to swap over the front and rear tyres, so the best tyre was the one taking all the weight. It was a good plan, though unfortunately for us it was this decision that meant my bike was soon unrideable as both our bike pumps failed. We still don't know if it was the heat, dust or cold in Nepal that was responsible but either way I was going nowhere. Thank goodness for the crowd - a third of it was made up of four guys from a passing truck. Five minutes later, our bikes and luggage we loaded, and John and I joined them in the cab. It was 14 miles to Tonk and would have been a long walk to the bike store.

With our bikes fixed and a new bike pump, we cycled back in the direction we had come. The hotel was three miles back and there was little else around. Having convinced the hotel owners we were married and would take no alcohol past their door, they checked us in. It was a great family-run place, and at the outdoor kitchen just five minutes' walk away, we enjoyed one of our favourite meals in India. Once again, we kept a growing crowd amused as we tucked into three veg curries, two salads, rice, chapatis, and the obligatory yogurt. Absolutely gorgeous and all for less than a fiver.

The next morning, we would continue our journey, and Devli would be our next stop. There was nothing really to see here, but we once again entertained the masses in the village chai stop. These moments were becoming one of our favourite parts of the day and being on the bike meant we could stop as often as we wished. With nothing much to stay for here, we left very early the next day and arrived in Bundi, our destination, in time for a late breakfast. We checked into to an amazing old raja palace with expansive rooms, antique furniture, and a beautiful garden. The light was stunning as we sat admiring the views of the old palace behind us and the river to the front. The guidebook said little of Bundi - it was certainly not one of the key tourist hot-spots - yet it was one of our favourite places to wonder around. The palace had long been deserted, and we were free to roam and explore. Apart from the monkeys - for which we had been provided a stick - we were the only people around, and it was lovely to find this space in a country that so often surrounded us. We clambered through this charming ruin, imagining just how it could have looked in its heyday. As we walked back from our walk towards the town, nervously passing a large group of monkeys and their young, John's flip-flop snapped. We would spend the rest of the day trying to find replacements, as the only other footwear John had were cycle shoes. It was to be a fruitless mission - the largest sizes available were size ten and it would be some time before we were in a tourist enough area to find the size required. Thankfully, the street cobbler soon had them fixed! We'd enjoyed our night in old time splendour, and I perused the guidebook looking out for our next opportunity. Determined and resourceful, we were soon booked into Castle Bijapur the following night.

The route to Bijapur was too far to ride in a day, and there was nowhere to stay in-between, but the hotel owner helped us work out a solution. Having cycled the first 40 miles to Bijolia, we would then catch the bus to Bassi before riding the final 16 miles. Details in hand, hotel reservations made, and our grateful thanks conveyed, we set off. A final glance back at Bundi in the sunrise gave us all the inspiration we needed, though it would not be quite as simple as it sounded. It was a lovely ride to Bijolia, and we were pleased to have something more interesting than flat and busy highways to ride. We arrived at the bus station, and after we promptly consumed various snacks and crisps, the locals assured us they would let us know when the bus we needed was ready to depart. They forgot, and it was not a regular route. Fortunately, in that ever-so resourceful Indian way, there was a solution. A different bus passed by the highway about two miles away, and one of the guys we were chatting with had the mobile number of the driver. It was not a usual stopping point, but he would look out for two cyclists desperate to get to Bassi!

The ride to the hotel was off the highway, and I was enjoying taking my time to absorb my surroundings. Castle Bijapur was a truly wonderful place, owned by Maharaja Rao Saheb Narendra Singh Ji, himself a keen cyclist, and he told us that the castle has been in his family for thirteen generations. He also seems to know how to run a hotel, the staff were attentive, the food excellent, especially the breakfast. It had been worth the detour. As we only had a short ride to Chittorgarh in the morning, we decided not to check out until midday. We just wanted to indulge in the luxury for a while longer. Just as we were getting the bikes ready to leave, Rao Saheb came to see us off. Once again, we were on a glorious back road - gentle rolling hills with fabulous views.

Chittorgarh is dominated by one of the largest forts in India - its walls stretching out some ten miles. Ordinarily, we would have been right there, taking pictures and exploring, but we were a bit 'forted' out and decided we would give this one a miss. Instead, we sent off to check into a hotel. We'd had a couple of nights of relative luxury now, and in reigning in the budget, we settled down in our cheaper digs, spent some time wandering around, eating street food, drinking chai, and chatting with people. We were back to the hotel early, bikes locked and off to bed. The next day's ride to Udaipur would be a long one!

Despite being back on the highway with a fairly flat terrain, we had 85 miles to cover. The sun was almost down as we navigated our way through the maze of narrow streets to Jagdish Temple. According to the guidebook, this was hotel central, and it didn't take us long to find suitable accommodation. As always, we conducted our search with three key criteria in mind: first, is it safe for our bikes; second, is the price okay; and third, is it clean? All too often, we had to compromise on the latter!

The receptionist was good enough to care of bike security and gave us a map and basic directions to some of the sights. Udaipur was one of the key tourist destinations in Rajasthan and there was plenty to see. After settling in, we headed out for a wander in search of proper Indian food, not the bland tourist rubbish on offer. We'd started to become fussy after such amazing flavours on our journey so far. Soon, a local tuk-tuk driver suggested Ronji's - that was where they all ate, apparently. Our Gujarati-style thali was amazing, and we piled down copious amounts of food at this all-you-can-eat establishment.

By the next morning, our stomachs had settled, and we were all set to sightsee, spending hours at the palace before embarking on a boat trip out to Jagmandir island. The island housed a stunning hotel and spa but given we could have eaten many times over at Ronji's for the price of a coffee, we just took some photos before heading back to the quirky museum I'd read about in the guidebook. It may not be on every tourist list, but I thoroughly enjoyed seeing the world's largest turban and a collection of various models of iconic world sites made from polystyrene. I always love seeing something a bit different and it was a nice change before we headed to Kumbhalgarh the next day for another more traditional fort visit.

It was a 56-mile ride uphill to Kumbhalgarh, and because we thought the fort would be surrounded by hotels and restaurants, we slowly pedalled our way up the steep hill to the top. It was a mistake, and we were unsure whether to leave our fully laden bikes while we explored. The hotels were two miles back down the hill, and we didn't really want to leave all our gear with our bikes while we explored. The views from the fort were amazing, and our bikes were completely safe. Sometimes I think Western city upbringing has removed our sense of trust.

Having visited the fort, there was little else to do now other than eat and sleep. Fully rested, we left at 7am the next morning, and having arrived at our intended destination, Beawar, by 12pm, we decided to push on to Ajmer. Despite having started the day on country roads with good views, we would arrive in Ajmer on the national highway. We stayed in a small haveli with fabulous home cooking and a breakfast the following morning that would include chapatis with curd and chilli powder, a spicy omelette, and strong, sweet coffee. While we only had 15 miles to ride now in to Pushkar, everyone had warned us that it was a tough climb. The breakfast was not luxury but necessity! As it turned out, we found the climb quite easy and wondered what all the fuss had been about.

Pushkar is well known in India for being religiously significant and amongst tourists for being a place to get stoned. The latter had never really interested me and in fact, if anything, put me off staying longer. Just not my thing. Instead, we just wandered through the market stalls, down by the ghats, and John visited the barber. While wandering around, we noticed that there was the option to go on a sunset camel trek and decided it would make a nice change from the bikes. Despite having to pass through the local rubbish dump on the edge of the town, we were first taken, along with an American couple, to a beautiful spot to watch the sun set over the surrounding hills. The other woman's trip was unfortunately hampered by a rather sick and therefore smelly camel who threw up all over her, and while perhaps it was another "to do" item crossed off on the list, we both agreed to stick to the bikes in the future! We headed back into town for dinner, and despite being offered various Ganga to eat, we opted for a more traditional curry, washed down with a cold beer, carefully concealed by wrapping the beer can in foil and drinking from a mug. While getting completely stoned here is fine, you're not really supposed to drink alcohol.

We passed various hippies, gap year students and pilgrims on our walk up the monkey temple the next morning. It was baking hot, and the temple stood outside the town up a nearby hill. It was a very sweaty experience, but the views were phenomenal despite the heat haze. It had been worth the climb. Our tour through Rajasthan was coming to an end, with only Jodhpur now left to visit. We had originally planned to ride there, but in talking with locals it became clear that we may struggle to find anywhere to stay on route, and we didn't fancy a 130-mile day. Instead, we rode just 40 miles before completing that day on the bus.

The Govind hotel was, as with most hotels in India, very accommodating for our bicycles (they were stowed on an internal roof) and we took time to use the Wi-Fi and do some washing in preparation for our time in Delhi. We also decided to treat ourselves and headed to one of Jodhpur's most expensive and best-situated restaurants, Pal Haveli's Indique Restaurant. The restaurant was recommended in the guidebook, and rightly so. I enjoyed a chilled white wine with delicious food while overlooking the best views of the Fort and Clock Tower. Some treats were well worth the expense. It also gave me the opportunity to wear my silk dress - one of my luxury items I'd squeezed in the panniers. It was great to make an effort for a change.

I dressed down again the following morning as we were heading out on a jeep safari in the desert. It wasn't quite off-roading on the dunes, but we enjoyed a camel fair and home cooking. Sadly, I woke the next morning feeling ill. I'm not sure the home cooking agreed with me. Not wanting to ruin our next day's sightseeing out to Umaid Palace, I set off in the rickshaw with John. The palace, part-museum and part-hotel was full of interesting artefacts and history, but I was not up for much, and soon our sightseeing was abandoned.

Throughout India, I ate raita (yogurt) with every meal I could. A natural probiotic, my theory is that then I am putting good bacteria into my stomach each day. In the most part, this technique seemed to work well, and I had few stomach problems in India. Alas, today was not one of those times. Thankfully, the next morning I felt a little better, and we decided to head to the Fort. We'd heard there were zip lines that you could go on, and we wanted a go. While we were a little forted out, it seemed Jodhpur had an interesting offering for us. There were six zip lines in total, going back and forth across the moat and battlements, and we had great fun with our small group whizzing through the sky. It was our last day in Jodhpur, and indeed in Rajasthan. Later that night, we would board another train for the 15-hour trip to Delhi. After our first rail journey here in India, I was surprised John agreed to such a long ride again, but thankfully, all went well this time as we were able to secure seats in a different class.

While as far as I was concerned, Delhi was good only for shopping prior to heading home - something we were not about to do just yet - this was John's first trip to India, and so he was keen to see one of its biggest cities. We didn't plan to cycle much here, but we would head out and see the few attractions it offers and take the opportunity to drink good, strong coffee and eat cake.

I'd pre-booked a hotel for our arrival, and while it's good to have somewhere to head for on arrival, the challenge, of course, is then that you must find it! The roads in Delhi were the busiest we had seen as cars, rickshaws, bicycles, animals, and pedestrians were all rushing, beeping, and constantly swerving between each other in a bid to reach their destination as fast as possible. Fortunately, I'd had a brain wave. We hired a cycle rickshaw. It took some time to explain, via an interpreter, that we didn't want a ride as such - we just needed him to take us to the hotel as we followed on our own bikes behind. After about a ten-minute debate, we were off. I don't think the rickshaw rider could believe his luck - if only all his rides were from passengers who weighed nothing and carried their own luggage.

Having settled in and completed our normal ritual of showering, laundry, email, and Facebook, we had a few jobs to complete before we were once again out seeing the sights. Visa applications completed and a 70th birthday present purchased and posted for my father we were off. First to the mosque, and then to the Red Fort.

This great mosque of Old Delhi is the largest in India, with a courtyard capable of holding 25,000 devotees. As is customary with visiting such places, I would need to hire a robe. Even though I was wearing long trousers and a 3/4 length blouse, apparently there was still too much of me on show. While the Delhi tourism guide notes that "this may be the only time you get to dress like a local without feeling like an outsider", I certainly felt conspicuous as I walked around in a bright blue 70s pattern robe-style tent. Flattering it was not, and it certainly did its job of removing any sense of sexuality. I wasn't sad to return this garment before making my way to the fort. The fort was still heavily guarded (tanks and armed soldiers are camouflaged at the entrance) as we made our way in. It was all interesting to see, but we were ready to leave Delhi.

We were heading South, and with another train station to find, another cycle rickshaw was hired. Alas, this one did not know the way. We would spend two nights on the train down to Bangalore, a 36-hour journey in total. We shared our four-berth cabin with two guys, Sham, and Arif, from Blackburn, Northern England. The level of service on the train was incredible. Hot, tasty food came at regular intervals, chai was plentiful, and the cabins were very clean. Mosquito repellent was sprayed at the critical time, and the journey passed quickly. It took a while for me to locate our bikes, but around an hour after our initial arrival, we left the station. We were cheating again, but this time it would be the bus. Known more recently as the up-and-coming high-tech centre of India, Bangalore is the capital of India's southern Karnataka state and home to over four million inhabitants. Despite having a few sights to see, including one palace apparently modelled on England's Windsor castle, we had decided we would start our ride in Southern India, in Mysore, approximately 90 miles away.

We arrived in Mysore three hours later and checked in to the hotel. While the room was nothing special and we had stayed in much grubbier surroundings than this, it was the lack of friendliness and particularly unhelpful staff that made this one of our least favourite stays. I'll take dirt with a smile any day. Despite it being many days now since we had last cycled, we were intent to be tourists for a few more days yet. The palace here is an incredible building completed in 1912 by

English architect Henry Irwin. Yet again we'd hired a local tuk-tuk driver for the day, and as well as taking us to his local cafe, he could take good photos and let us pose in his tuk-tuk - an Indian highlight for me.

Tourist trip over, we decided we would need an early start for our ride the next morning. While we were planning a two-day ride to our destination, we knew the last 12 miles of the journey was a very steep climb. Even the bus journey took four hours. We left Mysore at 7am. The road was good, the scenery okay, and the first stop came about 18 miles in. Refreshed and full of cake, we set off again. The scenery improved, but what we didn't know about the road was that it passed through a tiger reserve. We stopped at the gate marking the start of the sanctuary. We weren't sure what to do. Signs warned drivers not to stop, and it's fair to say we felt a little vulnerable. At least we'd just had a good rest, and if we wanted to get to Ooty, this was the only road. We didn't stop, ensuring our ride through the reserve was complete before the sun started to set. We crossed the border from Karnataka state to Tamil Nadu, entering a second tiger reserve, another one we'd not banked on, before checking into a hotel in Masinagudi. The owner also organised local safaris, and so after a quick shower and lunch, we made our way to join the safari tour. This time, of course, we would have been chuffed to see a tiger, but alas, the safari highlight seemed to be the frequently sighted jungle hen, AKA a chicken! Oh well, perhaps our bike trip through the reserves was not so risky after all!

We were not too far from Ooty now, and since we left again after an early breakfast, we were confident we would arrive for lunch. We knew we had some climbing, and while the first 10km were a steady and easy-going climb, nothing quite prepared us for the ride we had left to do. It was hot and clammy, our bikes weighed around 40kg, and we had 36 hairpin bends to navigate. The scenery was spectacular, but we both struggled and stopped frequently to "take photos". Our favourite picture of the day still being the sign at the fifteenth hairpin advertising the number to call should the mortuary van be required. We certainly hoped not!

When we finally reached Ooty, we were very cold, tired, and hungry. The sun dropped and as the altitude increased, the temperature was reducing. We looked around for a hotel, and given we were cold, decided to go for one that looked smart. It was a mistake. The room was freezing, and we were told we would have to pay more for a heater. The shower ran out of hot water as I tried to get warm, and so, rather than shower and explore, we both hibernated under the duvet trying to warm up, eventually, hunger set in forcing us to leave the hotel and cross the street, where we rapidly consumed absolutely delicious home-made chicken soup, chicken kebabs, and copious amounts of hot, sweet coffee.

Ooty itself wasn't what we'd expected - it was very dirty, busy, tourist-oriented, over-crowded and expensive - though the surroundings were quite beautiful, and we still talk very fondly of the food we ate here. The next morning, our day would begin with a newfound phenomenon – deep--fried cake. Crisp on the outside and soft sponge on the inside, it paired perfectly with our morning chai, and soon we were on the road again. We were heading for another Hill Station called Kotagiri. The ride was fabulous, with the climbing done, we were already on top of the hill as the road just meandered around the valleys, throwing up gorgeous views and brightly painted houses around every corner. Amazing. We made good time to Kotagiri, but again found the actual town disappointing so, after a quick cup of tea, we continued to Coonoor.

Riding in the hills was a great break from the intense heat, and it makes it clear why hill stations were popular with the British Raj. Terraces of the tea plantations all around, dotted with blasts of colour from women out in the fields. The one great advantage of climbing is you're going slow enough to appreciate all that is around you. The other great advantage, of course, is the descent, and as we set off for Pollachi the next day, our ride would start with 20-miles downhill. It was stunning, and we stopped so frequently for photos that we still barely made 10 miles an hour - it was a lot easier on the legs, though.

However, we were in the hill stations for a few days yet, and so, a big consequence of such a long downhill was that we would once again have a tough day ahead. The road to our next stop, Munnar, was flat and mainly agricultural. We were making great progress and even came across "Only Coffee" - a growing Indian franchise that specialized in something other than tea, despite being amongst all the plantations. They made delicious snacks, provided great chat, and wished us well as we continued. Progress was good, and so as we passed through a large town where we were originally going to stop, we decided to keep going. It seemed like a good idea at the time, but we were soon proved wrong. The road had started to climb again, it was sweltering, we were running out of water, and once again we found ourselves at a barrier situated to the entrance of another tiger reserve. We still had 28 miles to cycle before we would hit Munnar, and the guard at the entrance informed us that there were no other towns enroute. There was no way we would reach Munnar, and even had water been available, I did not fancy cycling at dusk if there were tigers around. Only as I stopped did I realise why I was so popular even with the monkeys...for some reason, I had wrapped up some spare chicken tikka which was now strapped to my rear rack, and they could smell it! I wasn't sure if tigers had the same taste buds, but this was no time to take chances.

Buses were stopping at the gate, given it was on the Keralan border and we knew all we could do was wait until one of the drivers was willing to take us and our bikes. Several buses went by, and by now three drivers did not want us to board. Eventually, perhaps realising time was getting on, a driver finally agreed. He was obviously a risk-taker – based on his driving not because he picked us up though!

Bikes loaded or at least lifted on to the roof rack, we took our seats. It was like being on a roller-coaster. I'm not sure if this was how he normally drove or if he was trying to make up time, having waited for us to load, but as the bus careered round sharp bends at ever-increasing speeds, we were both holding on tight to the bar on the seat in front, checking behind us after each bump that our bikes were still on board. It was reminiscent of the bus ride in Nepal, and we were relieved to pull up in the bus station.

Munnar was a lovely town, much cleaner, friendlier and less crowded than the other hill stations. We waved goodbye to the bus conductor and walked up the road a short way to find a local hotel. It was only as we checked in that we realised we'd left our bike pump on the bus. Thankfully, the conductor was as helpful as he was friendly, and while our bus had now continued its way, he told us it would be back if we wanted to collect our pump the following morning.

Pump collected, we had around 75 miles to Fort Kochin, down on the coast. The first third would all be downhill on well-paved roads. I had such a big smile on my face and can still remember the amazing aroma as we rode past a spices factory. A few miles on, I ordered a biryani for lunch. It had never really been a dish I'd tried, but I've certainly eaten many since. The flavours just seem to get locked in, and the smell remains evocative each time I put my fork in to pull apart the rice. Yumm again!

We were on flat roads and making good time. Soon, the outskirts of Kochi and Ernakulam came into view. Kerala is an area famous for the "backwaters", and the bridges, fishing boats, and nets add to the colourful scene. We found a great little hotel in the tourist area and quickly settled in. Laundry, bike maintenance, and showers all completed, we once again set of to do the tourist thing. Cafés were plentiful, and while I perused the shops, there is, of course, little one can buy with panniers already full of necessities. We had two good nights staying here before we opted to dip our toes in the ocean. We were heading to Alleppey. It was a short ride with flat roads, and just as we were approaching, a young chap pulled along-side us to ask if we were looking for a room. It was right on the beach, and we decided we had nothing to lose in looking. Undeterred by the Disney print bedding, my bags were soon unloaded, and I lay in the hammock with a nice cold beer. Bliss. The sand was soft, the sea was warm, and the beach ruined only by watching the next-door neighbour bury her waste on the beach. I guess you can't have everything.

We watched the sunset and played cards with other guests before going into town again the next morning to organise our backwater boat trip - a popular tourist activity. It was luxury. The six-berth boat was just for us, and our crew of three looked after us like we were royalty. It was here that I first tried beetroot raita. Keralan cooking seems to have real delicacy, and we enjoyed two days of just kicking back, drinking beer, eating great food, reading, and appreciating the beautiful scenery.

It was also noticeable to us to see how different Kerala was to other Indian states. Beach-based landfill aside, it was clean and just appeared much more prosperous, border changes often even more noticeable when travelling by bike. We were now on the last couple of weeks of our Indian adventure as we headed in a northerly direction towards Goa - we had decided to finish our trip by the beach before having our final days in Mumbai. We were making good progress, unaware of the eventful days that we would soon encounter. As we left Calicut, we were completely unaware of the attention we were about to receive.

My research had informed me that there were hotels on the beach at our next stop, and we asked after rooms in the Blue Nile hotel. It was beyond our budget, and we carried on. An hour later, we were at a dead end. There were no hotels and all we could do was head back to the Blue Nile. The price, of course, had remained the same - all that had diminished was the amount of time we would spend in the slightly more upmarket hotel. Oh well, sometimes that's just the way it goes. Despite our room and bathroom being a little nicer, it didn't take long before it was adorned with laundry just like everywhere else we stayed. We moved down to the hotel lobby to use the Wi-Fi. Little did we know we were about to become famous.

We were merrily minding our own business when the Indian gent, Hassam, who sat next to us, struck up a conversation. He was keen to know where we from, and after a few more follow-up questions regarding our bike tour, we assumed this was just the usual inquisitiveness we had encountered both before and during our journey so far. However, Mr Hassam had other ideas - this businessman saw opportunity in our positive reply to the question "Would you like to be in the papers", and it would lead to a few interesting days. Ten minutes after saying yes, the local press arrived. Interview complete, we posed for a few pictures - the story would be in the newspaper the next day. The local hotel owner also saw a chance to get some publicity soon, and we were also being introduced to a multi-millionaire jewellery shop owner, Bobby. I've never really been a massive jewellery wearer, and I'm not sure the gold and diamonds really went with my purple merino T-shirt, but I smiled for the camera nonetheless. To be fair it wasn't the jewels that interested me - we were also asked if we wanted to visit a house he had established for homeless men, struggling with mental health problems. His aim was to establish a home in each town he had a shop. It was good to connect with projects like this on our trip, though my favourite visit was yet to come.

We'd stayed the night at Bobby's beach house - a simple place, far from grand, but with great company and food. I liked that it lacked richness. There was no showing off here - perhaps just a break from a grander life elsewhere. The next morning, we would head back towards the start of our detour, but first we were to visit a small primary school. The school was set up by Hisham's family in the village he had grown up in. It was such an honour. The children, smartly dressed in their beige uniforms, lined the pathway to the school, singing and clapping at our arrival. We were the guests of honour, and once again the press were there. The children were so excited as we signed their exercise books - it was the first (and last) time I have ever been asked for my autograph! It was hard to leave, but we knew we needed to continue with our journey. One of the real advantages of independent cycle touring is the ability to deviate from initial plans, but we still had more we wanted to see on loose schedule too. Hisham would drop us off just north of Kunnar, from where we would ride to Kasaragod before catching another train to Margao, where we would spend time in Goa, chilling and relaxing before the final few days in Mumbai.

The route was mainly flat road, and so we made good progress, and occasionally we were cheered at and photographed by passing kids in minibuses. Roads were dotted with stalls of beautiful fresh fruit, the colours coming to life in the bright sunshine; traders shouting hello, kids chasing you down the road, and the constant car, truck, and lorry horns. We would soon be at the beach, and after a night in Udipi, where I took time to visit the temple, we rolled in to Murudeshwar. Despite being a sizable beach spot, it was not listed in our tourist guide - more of an Indian resort for either sun-seeking Westerners or the Goan hippy. Given we had read nothing about it, we were very pleasantly surprised.

Despite its lack of inclusion in the guidebook, Murudeshwar - another name for the Hindu god Shiva - boasts the second highest statue of Lord Shiva in the world. While some visitors note it is busy, dirty, and lacking in good restaurants, we loved it, and it is still fondly remembered for fresh onion bhaji. Dished up in wrapped-up newspaper, it was like an Indian-style fish and chips at the seaside. Just brilliant. Maybe we'd just got too used to mess and dirt to notice? For us, we still talk of Murudeshwar as an unexpected treasure.

The next morning, we were still smiling, feeling good, and headed for Gokarna. As was becoming our normal practice, we stopped at the first chai stall and drank sweet, spicy tea We were never alone for long when we stopped and were soon surrounded by curious people asking where we'd come from and where we were going. I really enjoyed the curiosity and enjoyed sharing laughter - sometimes at our own expense - with the locals. We were beaming, and, as John noted in his blog, he didn't "know whether it was just because we were on a high from Murudeshwar or whether India just threw all the good stuff at us in one day, but the journey seemed even prettier than normal" ... We were five months into our tour, and it was brilliant. It was a new routine, yet one so different from the lives we had left behind, and even despite occasional setbacks and disappointments, we loved it.

It's funny how great surprises can be very quickly followed by small disappointments, but we were about to have one of those said setbacks. I was always the one who planned routes and activities. John always said if he read the guidebooks, he would just want to see everything, and so he left the sifting to me. Luckily for me, I really enjoy planning the logistics, and today I had decided we would head to Om beach, just outside Gokarna.

Despite having gone almost through Gokarna, the guide-book notes had convinced me that even despite the searing heat, it was worth doing the extra few miles to Om. It wasn't far, but the climb was tough and there was no shelter from the burning sun. It took much longer than we expected, but the beach looked incredible as we looked down. Sadly, however, it was all we could do. Steep steps led down the cliffs, and the best accommodation was all at the other end of the beach. There was just no way. We were disappointed not to reach a beach shack, but there was a hotel at the top of the road, and we conceded that we could make inquiries and walk down to dip our toes in the ocean later. They only had double rooms, and they were top budget for us. Further, the double bed was 3/4th size. It was definitely made for couples, and even then, probably couples who were both small, not in the early stages of a relationship (!) and at a different time of year.

It was also way too hot to ride back under the sun's glare. Soon, with my inventiveness and the Indian mentality to help and make money, we had an answer. We both loaded our bikes onto the roof of a tuk-tuk and headed back to find a room in Gokarna. We found a room by the beach and set off for a wander. A pleasant stroll, despite being attacked by a grumpy cow through the beach, was not a patch on our following night. We only had a short ride the next day before booking into a bamboo shack opening out directly on to a stunning beach with bars and restaurants. Still too built up for some, perhaps, but I enjoyed Palolem with beers and sunset gazing, and as it turned out, the fact that it was easy for me to just wander around on my own would be a distinct advantage. John was ill, unable to eat or move far from the room. We did little but read books for a couple of days, though I guess this had always been part of the plan once we reached the coast.

We'd finally made it to Goa. The sand was soft, the water warm, the sky blue. This perfection could only be improved by a cold beer and, for John - less trips to the toilet! Thankfully those days were coming and once John felt better, we were back on our bikes and heading to Benaulim and another bamboo shack right on the beach. Tough life, this cycle touring!

Our beach tour continued as we took in Anjuna and Mandrem in Northern Goa, again staying in simple accommodation before we had decided to treat ourselves to a slightly more upmarket hotel for a couple of nights In Varca. The beach here was phenomenal - substantial in size yet empty - with just one restaurant on the sand we would head to for drinks and dinner. Sadly, for local entrepreneurs, the local restaurants don't seem to fare too well with guests of bigger resorts. Nervous, perhaps of cleanliness, they stayed away, but it wasn't an issue for us.

After three nights though, we'd had enough and decided that for our last night in Goa, we wanted to return to Benaulim. We were pleased to arrive, and the shack owners were certainly pleased to see us. Having both assumed the other person had paid the bill on our last stay, sadly, we had left owing money. Problem rectified; we were soon made welcome again. Oops. It was the first and last time we would do this on our whole trip. It was a perfect end to our time in Goa. We were going to catch the train from Margao to Mumbai, and having booked in our luggage, we went out for a final and delicious biryani before the nine-hour overnighter. Before leaving the restaurant, John threw away the cycle gear he was wearing. We were coming to the end of our first five-month trip, the fabric had worn thin, but our smiles had just got wider and wider. Relieved we were getting on well; we boarded the train with mixed emotions. I think we both felt a little sad at this point as we knew our time away was running out, nearly five months to the day since we started, and we only had a few days in Mumbai left.

While the food in Goa had been somewhat disappointing compared to our general experience, we were heading to the street food capital of the world. Our stomachs were generally pretty hardy, and we were ready. First, we just had to find our bikes. They were not there.

Usually, each time we used the train, John would wait with our luggage while I went off in search of our bikes. On each occasion, thus far, I would return slowly wheeling two bicycles along the platform. We'd load up and head off in search of our next accommodation. Our experience in Mumbai, however, was much more anxious. Almost an hour after leaving John, I returned - alone. Following numerous conversations with the porters, luggage office and train guards, it turned out that our bikes were not on the same train as us. The route into Mumbai was much busier than any other we had used - trains were more frequent (hourly rather than daily or twice weekly) and I was told our bikes would be on a later train. There was little we could do but trust what we were told. We placed our bags into the luggage store and went off in search of breakfast. Strong tea and curry later, we returned. It was not good news. Our bikes still hadn't arrived, and we began to talk of contacting the police, putting in a formal complaint, and notifying our insurance company. We would need new bikes for our Africa trip and had started to panic. Thankfully, we were saved by Indian nosiness. Just as we were trying to decide what to do, a porter who'd heard our conversation told us that there were bikes on platform 17. We legged it, running the whole length of the platform, and there they were, the Captain and Kylie just waiting for us as if there had never been a problem. What a relief!

*

Finally reunited and reloaded, we set off through Mumbai in search of our hotel. Given it can be much more expensive in Mumbai, I'd pre booked a room. We were staying in the Sea Green Hotel on Marine Drive. The hotel had been selected for its hopeful ease to find (just head for the coast) and sea views. It was wonderful. Nothing posh but brilliant staff, in a nice part of Mumbai, and at a reasonable price.

I'm not sure they had many cycle tourists stay there, but soon they were helping us with their local knowledge of bike stores (we needed boxes to pack the bikes for our flights home), taxis, barbers, ATM machines, and last but not least the office for the courier company that were looking after the rest of our kit. It had been six weeks since we left it with them in Jaipur, and we were nervous about its return - especially after our recent bike fright. We had nothing to worry about and were ready to pack up for our journey home, though not before we took the time to complete our culinary journey.

A friend of mine was in Mumbai for work, and as she joined local friends for dinner, John and I were also invited. It's fair to say the restaurant was much higher end than much of the food we had sampled so far, and it really was delicious. However, as their chauffeur dropped us back at our hotel, it was also a final stark reminder of the vast divisions between rich and poor in this truly incredible country.

The Stats; A Tour of India
1,850.1 Miles

Destination	Total Distance	Average Speed	Metres Up	Metres Down
Gorakpur	59.4	-	78	153
Agra	(Train)	-	-	-
Fatepur Sikri	26.8	-	40	27
Bilaji	63.1	-	173	111
Jaipur	64.4	-	270	99
Tonk	49.3	-	119	227
Devli	40.7	-	87	28
Bundi	29	-	87	131
Bijapur	54	-	517	357
Chittor	23.8	-	295	354
Udaipur	81.3	12	425	207
Kumbhulgarhh	51.5	7.2	1067	682
Deogarth	52.2	10.5	564	833
Ajmer	82.9	11.5	398	526
Pushkar	10.8	7.2	180	130
Jodhpur	38.6	11.3	141	355
Bangalore	(Train)	-	-	-
Mysore	-	-	-	-
Masinagudi	61	8.3	885	717
Ooty	19	3.3	1543	290
Kotagiri, Coonor	30	6.8	681	984
Pollachi	68.7	10	500	1872
Munnar	37.2	10.4	374	237
Fort Cochin	83.4	10.7	503	1900

Destination	Total Distance	Average Speed	Metres Up	Metres Down
Allepey	37.4	9.8	26	25
Kumakaron	27.3	8.7	43	30
Purvur	58.7	8.5	128	110
Calicut	82	10.1	154	183
Kannur	74	9	441	435
Kasagurud	21.9	7.5	217	198
Udupi	72.7	8.9	519	528
Murudeshwar	68	9	347	395
Gokhara	79	-	-	-
Palaulem	98	-	-	-
Benaulim	38	-	-	-
Anjuna	86	-	-	-
Mandrem	13	-	-	-
Colva	58	-	-	-
Palm Beach Resort	9.1	-	-	-
Benaulim	-	-	-	-
Margao	-	-	-	-

Notes

• Data shows a mix of distances and terrain as well as train use – something we chose to do to enable us to choose our cycle areas and make the most of travel in this amazing country.

• We cycled a total of 1,850.1 miles through India (based on data above) alongside trucks, animals, rickshaws, cycles, and private cars.

Based on averages of speeds listed above in India we cycled at an average of 9 mph.

1.

SOLITUDE

"Loneliness expresses the pain of being alone and solitude expresses the glory of being alone."

Paul Tillich

One thing I've always loved about cycling was the massive sense of freedom. Being on the bike offers an overwhelming sense of empowerment - ownership of one's destiny. Even when riding with a few friends, I enjoyed the solitude of being in my own space - alone with my thoughts. I'll often miss signs, animals, landscapes, and other landmarks as I retreat into my own thoughts and new ideas. I'd never really experienced loneliness, and it was ironic that as we joined a group ride for the next part of our journey the feeling, I was on my own would be overwhelming.

I'm not sure how we came to do the ride from Cairo to Capetown. I think it was just another of those back-up plans in case John, and I found we didn't get on. My mate Steve, who I'd met on a bike tour through Sri Lanka, had told me about it. The tour was organised by a company then known as Tour D'Afrique (TDA) - established by Henry Gold back in the late 1980s. The company took great pride in running the longest and toughest cycle tours and the first TDA Africa trip had taken place in 2003. It was a mix of road and off-road riding over 7,325 miles (11,793km) and averaging 75 miles (121km) per day. For John and me it was the second of our routes listed in the world's top ten endurance bike rides - something we hadn't quite realised until we'd signed up! Till date, 430 riders from over 30 different countries had taken part in the full tour.

We flew out just after Christmas, and I was so excited to arrive. Happy to be back on my bike and looking forward to the group tour. I'm a people lover and have always been very sociable. It was John who was more nervous of riding with others. John and I had got on great in our last tour, and while now confident we didn't have to be surrounded by others, I am essentially nosy, chatty and love a good chin wag. I was in no

Naomi Johnson

way prepared for how the first few ride days would make me feel. I hated it.

After a very hot flight from London, we were slightly flustered at Cairo. We'd met two other TDA riders on the flight, Liz, and Ali, both from London. It was well past midnight local time when we arrived at our hotel, but it didn't stop us from ordering beer and food, and while we waited for it to arrive, we took the opportunity to sort through our kit. Food devoured, the optimistic beer sadly put away in the fridge and kit sorted, we retired to bed. It was 3am and unsurprisingly we slept in way past the hotel breakfast.

Having arrived with a few days to spare before the ride would begin, and the initial plan had been that we would relax on sun loungers round the pool, enjoying the sunshine. No chance - it was so cold, and despite being layered up we still ended up turning the air conditioning in our room to its full temperature in a bid to keep warm. With few tourists at this time of year, the hotel didn't really cater for much other than sunny holidays. The initial plan aborted, we instead took the time to meet other members of the group as well as go and see the traditional sights of Egypt. Overwhelmed by the architecture and history, we were also trying our best to learn everyone's names.

There were over 50 riders setting out from Cairo, and given Fridays were less busy on the roads, that was the day that had been selected for our departure. Up early, luggage loaded onto trucks (quite a novelty for us), we were set to go. It was 5am - still dark and with the sun not even up yet it was absolutely freezing. We all just wanted to get going and while we had a short journey from the hotel the official start line was at the Pyramids. And with 50 or so riders all lined up to begin, it was quite a spectacle for the locals. We would leave the city in convoy.

Riding in convoy required a lot of concentration, and as was the norm with tourist groups in Egypt, we were under armed guard until we hit quieter roads. The escort would take us to a petrol station area about 38km out of the city, and from there we would follow the route map provided until arriving in camp. More often than not, directions were simply turn right and keep going. Africa just doesn't have a large choice of routes and roads. Today was no exception, and we would continue the same road until we reached camp 60 miles later.

No longer needing the escort meant everyone was free to ride at their own pace, and at this stage in the trip I came in at the halfway point. Despite riding with me through America, Japan, Nepal and India, John was naturally a much faster ride than me, and before long, he was well ahead. I had the odd companion enroute but spent just over 40 miles riding on my own. As I arrived tearful into camp, John was beaming. He'd had company, had been able to ride at his natural pace and had loved every minute. I had never felt so lonely. While I usually enjoyed the solitude on my bike, when surrounded by many other people, yet riding alone, I just felt isolated. I cried myself to sleep, nervous as to how the next day would transpire.

There is no way of being eased in gently to a trip like this, and besides, this approach just wasn't the TDA way of doing things. It was day two and we were about to ride our first 100 miler. I had never ridden this far in a day before and set off with great trepidation, especially given day one. We had a 5:30am start, and John had said he would ride with me. However, I could tell he found my speed a little frustrating now as he saw others race off into the distance. Helped along by strong tailwinds, we were at lunch by 10:30 with 44 miles done and 60 to go, finally arriving at camp about 3:30. I still felt rubbish. In all the five months of our first tour, I had never felt like John didn't want to ride with me - in fact - quite the opposite. It all seemed very different now. I was really struggling to adapt, and my confidence was getting low.

The tailwinds followed on day three, and John rode the first section with me, but I knew he didn't want to. Each time we were overtaken, he just seemed cheesed off. At lunch, I said I would just wait for other riders. By now, I was starting to feel frustrated with myself - I wished I were fitter. I guess I just didn't feel needed, had lost my best buddy, and hadn't yet settled in with a new bunch. For the first time ever, I was understanding what it was to feel lonely in a crowd. I just wanted to go home, but I'm stubborn and hate wasting money. There would be no refund. I just had to persevere.

We continued to 'turn right from camp and keep going, keeping the desert in view all around us. The wind was still strong as I pulled into camp, and I was soon to find out it had led to calamity. A sudden gust had taken John's tent, and it was now in the bin. Lucky, I had a three-man! Looks like I'd see a bit more of my mate again.

As with the previous day, we rode together in the morning and, as was now becoming my routine, I would ride with Irin and Sybil in the afternoon. That day we would end the ride in Safaga - a small beach town and a perfect spot for a barbecue dinner and beers on the beach. It also had a hotel, and, as would also become a regular habit, John and I would try to get a room where we could. No tent sharing tonight! John had been hoping the crew may find a new tent here, but alas, we would be sharing canvas for a bit longer yet. Selfishly, given how the trip had started for, I was quite pleased and think this really helped me adjust to this new situation.

So far, in Egypt, we had been blessed with flat roads and tailwinds but as we took a right turn out of Safaga, our climb would begin. I was looking forward to a change of terrain, and I'd also persuaded John to hang back and ride with what was becoming my new riding posse. At least, that was the plan until I got a puncture. To date John had generally fixed all punctures - not because I couldn't, but just because he was quicker, and on busy roads, among crowds of onlookers or long days, it just made sense. However, as we were now not always riding together, I wanted to fix this one. I'd obviously fixed punctures many times before, but the hub gearing on 'The Captain' did make the job a little different to normal.

*

Back on the road, we set off up the 27-mile hill. I was on the front, setting a good pace, and we were soon catching and over-taking people. My confidence was coming back, no longer feeling like the worst rider in the group. Group riding seemed to induce a sense of competition - not helped, perhaps, by the ride's very nature. TDA also ran this trip as a race, and most of us had opted to see how we went on the timing chips.

Feeling more settled and able, I was starting to see that while a group tour was very different, it was not all bad. I just had to change my perception and expectations. At least I no longer felt I had to go home. I was slowly settling in and feeling more comfortable, having decided I just needed to change my mindset. I guess I just hadn't ever thought I'd need to do this.

Day six would end in Luxor, where yet again, we had the option of a room. It was also our first day off. With today's ride being just 68 miles, we were by now starting to think of these as short days – oh, how things can change! At about 22 miles, we navigated our way through Qena, a large town, and one where we would need to follow the flagging tape. We'd been warned to expect a few children throwing sticks and stones, and they didn't let us down. I guess it was good practice for latter stages in our trip where missile throwing would become prevalent.

The road out of Qena followed a water course, and as with the rest of our ride that day, it was pretty flat with only the speed bumps causing a few issues - they were everywhere. It was late morning as we checked in, and once laundry was sorted, we were showered and beer had been quaffed, we headed out with Irin. We soon found ourselves on a horse-drawn carriage doing the tourist thing round Luxor, visiting markets, papyrus galleries, spice shops, and even stopped for lunch while the driver waited outside. Finally, we visited Karnak Temple, which was lit up and looked great, and with photos taken, we headed back to the hotel for beer, a chat, and to use the Wi-Fi before bed.

*

The morning saw about 30 of our group heading out on a tour bus to visit The Valley of the Kings, The Valley of the Queens, and Al-Deir Al-Bahari Temple. Egypt really does feel like stepping back in time.

Fully rested, John, Gus, Irin, and I rolled out of camp at about 7:15. Today, we had also been joined by Caroline. I was setting a fair pace at the front and very soon, we'd caught another 4-person group. I was about to have my first experience of peloton riding as Bridget, an experienced cyclist from South Africa, organised our little group, taking short turns on the front. We were able to maintain a speed of around 28km per hour. The kilometres ticked by quickly, and with decent roads, we soon arrived at lunch, a great spot on the banks of the Nile.

*

After lunch, we were back to our little group of five, following the river through small villages and towns, the scenery ever-changing. The sun was getting warm by now, and drinking fluids was important, and we quickly rattled through the miles. With about 17 miles to go, John started to lose the group. It was most unlike him, and we pulled in to wait. Gus offered to go back and check he was okay, though I thought he'd just stopped to take photos. He came in puffing and exhausted, though not really understanding why. We waited while he drank plenty of fluids, ate an energy bar, and had a good stretch and then checked over the bike. His brake was locked on, and he'd been riding like that for the last 12 miles. It must have got knocked on at lunch. No wonder he was tired. Brake fixed and breathing resumed to normal, we pushed on. The camp at Idfu was in a football stadium, and I was pleased to hear there was a toilet and shower. As it turned out, we were surrounded by four competing mosques, and the 'ensuite facilities' were so filthy. It was not the bathroom to get locked in – I think they could have filmed the famous toilet scene from the Trainspotting movie here.

We watched the local match, dust flying everywhere, and thankfully got an early night before the four muezzins got started with the calls to prayer at dawn. We all joked that volume, rather than tunefulness, must have been the key criteria for this job. We were just over a week in, and soon we would be completing the official forms to leave Egypt. Our last day was in Aswan, and it was another day of rest. While we had various official forms to complete to leave Egypt, as well as the usual laundry, we headed out with our small group for a boat trip on the Nile. It was a beautiful day and we set sail, the intention being to visit a few different places on route, including a Nubian village, botanical garden, and monastery. The truth is we were all so relaxed on the boat that we didn't really want to get off, so after a quick photo jaunt at the first stop point and short walk in the gardens, we just lay around, snoozing with the gentle waves. Some might say we wasted our time, but we were so happy and relaxed. We would not have the same space on our next boat trip.

Despite there being a road between Egypt and Sudan, it was not one we could ride, given there was no passport control - something I understand has now changed. Our journey to Sudan would be on an overnight boat, and after a short ride to the "port", we would load our gear and settle in. It would be quite an experience. The boat was rammed, and while there were three TDA riders in each two-man cabin, we had the luxury experience. Luggage, freight, and people were crammed into every available space as money changers and "street" sellers got to work. Absolute chaos and a disaster waiting to happen.

Thankfully, all went well, and it was late afternoon the next day when we finally arrived in Wadi Halfa. The boat soon emptied as we all waited to disembark. Two and a half hours later, with all passport control forms completed, bags, bikes and tyres searched, we were able to load our gear onto the new TDA trucks and ride to camp. We would also meet new crew members who would now ride with us until the end of the trip. At camp that night, they gave us a rundown on the next section of the tour. The temperature would rise, any luxuries would disappear. The off-road sections we would encounter would start to really show us why this is classed as one of the toughest endurance rides going. It seems our 100-mile days were just the warmup!

93 miles lay in front of us on the first proper Sudanese ride day, and the scenery looked like something from a sci-fi movie set. It was baking hot, and very soon we would get used to drinking litres and litres of water. It was here in Sudan when you could really see the benefits of an organised tour - water was purified for us, food had been cooked, and medics and crew were on hand if needed.

Camp was basic - there was no beer at the end of the day (Sudan is alcohol-free), no Western treats were available, and even shelter from the sun was often scarce or completely lacking. The tent was hot at night, showers were also now classed as a luxury, and wet wipes and shovels (the toilet facilities) would all become part of our somewhat reduced expectations. It may sound grim to many, but the fact that we were now all equal, both with other riders and to some degree the locals, was an amazing leveller. An experience we so rarely understand now as man has become more and more divided and materialistic. However, it was clear that someone had spotted an economic opportunity here in Sudan. The road through the desert was amazing.

Laid by the Chinese, as a transport route for minerals, the ribbon of smooth black tarmac that transgressed the length of Sudan would, in the most part, be an absolute delight. Smooth roads and tailwinds made for relatively easy riding, and as the racers set off each day, they would often arrive at the final day's camp before the trucks and luggage. I saw this as a reason not to rush.

Our small group was quickly joined by Alex, and that made us a six-strong crew. The road was brand new, and for the most part, flat. By the time we got to lunch, we were all thirsty and hungry. We were only halfway to camp but as we were okay for time, we planned to stop for Coke with about 18 miles to go. The riding in Sudan was so hot, and the extra break and sugar were a welcome relief from the searing heat. That evening, we were also blessed with a dip in the Nile - a very welcome cool down before dinner.

The next day, we had a 90-mile ride. The temperature was over 40 degrees and stopping to rest was not a pleasant relief. We were being followed by flies. Thousands and thousands of them, much like the Scottish midges. Attracted by the sweat, they were soon in eyes, ears, noses, and mouths within seconds of coming to a halt. Apparently, they follow the flowering of the palm trees, and while they are only around for a few weeks, we would be long out of Sudan by then.

We had another Nile camp spot that night before riding into Dongala the next day. That ride was set up as a "team time trial" and we were put in groups based on country of origin. I was now enjoying making friends all over the world. There were 12 teams riding the 15-mile time trial and, after a 5-mile warm-up, we would start taking turns on the front of the peloton. The UK team came fifth in the end, which frankly I think is pretty darn good. With more sitting around on a rest day in Dongala, I was very pleased to be able to purchase a fly net - it would make the next few days a little more bearable.

Our route from here would continue through the desert, and even though this day's ride was aptly named 'Dongala to dead camel camp', I was still surprised to see quite so many of our humped friends laid to rest in the sand. I'll always remember the desert in Sudan for very different reasons. Firstly, the most amazing skies. Through much of Africa, the lack of light pollution and our campsite in the desert rewarded us with the most incredible stars at night. It was just like the picture of the Milky Way I remembered from books at school. While lack of light was good for stargazing, there were some torch lights I was happy to see. With no trees or rocks to hide behind, it often felt like one was going to the toilet in public. The light from our head torches were the only thing that kept others from trespassing on these private moments. One evening, during a sandstorm, proved a particular toilet challenge. I was pleased the wind was blowing away from camp when losing hold of my toilet roll, and I'm even surer that my fellow travellers were relieved about this too.

My fitness had certainly improved since the ride started, and as John and I averaged 19 mph (there was a strong tailwind), I came third on the women's race that day and felt great. It made me start to contemplate going for a win.

Our journey would take a rest day in the capital Khartoum before eventually embarking on off-road sections of riding that would test even the strongest in the group. As usual, when we could we had a hotel stay - in this case, an apartment - with other riders and we all set to laundry and showers-doing our best to remove the orange glow and grains of sand from skin and clothing. The lounge area was littered with Lycra.

100-mile rides now seemed commonplace, and while we weren't carrying luggage, they were certainly the hottest conditions I'd ever encountered. Only Japan had been worse when high levels of humidity made the day even more uncomfortable. We would approach what John called the day of thorns. The temperature was rising, and as we set off with extra patches and tubes for the thorns we had been warned about, John also had his nose covered in zinc paste - it had become so badly sunburned and skinless. While John had a sunburnt nose, I had badly sunburned lips. It was painful to eat, but even worse, each smile seemed to lead to bleeding and cracking. One morning I woke only to look like the victim of a collagen implant gone wrong. In addition to sore lips, the road conditions also meant my hands and bottom was sore. My bike had turned itself into a real boneshaker.

The ride today was only 50 ish miles, but with only three miles paved, the rest was a mix of dry rutted mud, loose sand, and compacted earth. Our route followed an old, abandoned railway, passing numerous mud hot villages. The inhabitants smiled and looked bemused as we passed. One rider got 11 punctures that day, and while I had avoided the dreaded thorns, I was still relieved to reach camp. It was short-lived. The next day was 61 miles, the road was corrugated, and it was 44° out on the road. This trip was not for the faint-hearted. The day finished with a short rocky climb, and as I cycled into camp with Irin, it became clear that many riders had paid the price of going too fast. Camp was much like a hospital site. John was on painkillers, having fallen over the handlebars when hitting a patch of sand, and many riders were suffering from exhaustion and dehydration. The medics were busy that night.

The next day, we would arrive in Ethiopia. The ride was another 61 miles on predominantly flat roads, and because my bike was geared well for this and many riders were still recovering, I pushed on hard. The race would finish at lunch, and despite being unsuccessful in my attempt to win a stage (I came second), I didn't delay in swigging a beer at the border. Given Sudan was a dry country, the road just over the border was littered with bars and brothels. I'd known little about Sudan, but come the end of the African trip, it would be one of my favourite countries to right through despite the conditions.

The people were friendly, though reticent, and unassuming. I don't know whether it's because I've often lived in big towns and cities, but I loved the sense of space. It was while riding in such quiet, desolate spaces that I would really experience that sense of solitude. I felt safe, and even with a few people around, alone yet content. It was a country I was sad to leave behind.

By way of contrast, this was not the case in Ethiopia - the country we would ride through next. With a population of 85 million, there were people everywhere. Every time we stopped for lunch, we would gather a crowd, kept back from our group by the red tape that surrounded the camp. It seemed odd to create such a barrier, after all, we were there to experience close hand what these countries had to offer, yet without it, I think the constant attention would have been overwhelming. Loneliness was no option here, though neither was solitude. The only place where we didn't have an audience possible was using the toilet tent. It was not a place to linger.

As we hit Ethiopia, the climbing began. Yet again, we found ourselves riding through another country I didn't realise was quite so hilly. Unfortunately, John didn't ride the first day here. He felt unwell and decided to ride the bus. It was another of those things that differed to being on an independent tour. Had it been just the two of us, we would have taken a rest day, but in a group scenario the travelling circus simply had to continue.

Frustrated with having to get a lift in the company truck, John was determined to ride the next day. Retrospectively, this was a bad idea. We had 2,500 m of climbing to ride towards Gonder, with the first significant and steep hill coming just 13 miles into the ride. I'm not a natural climber, so John had gone on ahead. I was riding further back with Irin. At this point, I'd not taken the truck, and still had the EFI badge – 'every fucking inch'. I was so proud not to lose it on what would be a very hot and tough riding day. The smile on my face as I arrived was huge - what an achievement! Sadly, it was soon replaced. I was met by Nix, the tour medic. Apparently, John had been spotted on the road, weaving slowly from side to side. He been picked up by the tour 'ambulance' and placed on a drip. This really was no ordinary challenge.

Gonder was a larger town in Ethiopia, and thankfully one where we could get a hotel room and a rest. What a relief. Later that evening, we headed out with a few other members of the group for food. We decided on a typical Ethiopian restaurant, with its injera (a type of pancake) and kai wat (spicy stew). As we arrived, it was clear the place was full; a wedding was taking place. They were happy to indulge us travellers, and we were invited to join the dancing after dinner. It was a fun evening, and we will always remember it more for the experience than the food.

After a lazy start the following morning, we took a trip around the castle. While John was not perfect, he was determined to leave the hotel on his bike the next day. Alas, stone-throwing seemed to be getting worse, and we were advised to ride together. I can't be sure of the intention, but as riders reported being chased with machetes, my friend Erin needing stitches, and others being whipped by donkey ropes, not all our memories of Ethiopian were pleasant. It was the country that many people of the group were happy to leave. I was lucky and took the approach of smiling and waving at everyone. Having again decided my enjoyment was all about my mindset, I'd rather remember the beautiful country for all its calls of 'where you go' from the children of the surrounding villages.

Having climbed 2,502 metres into Gonder, we were now blessed with a day that had more downhill than up. Following a night at 'farm camp,' we would reach Bahir Dar, which the Ethiopians like to describe as their Riviera wide streets, palm trees and lakeside restaurants. We also took the opportunity to visit the Blue Nile falls from here before continuing our journey. The scenery was fantastic as we roller-coastered up and down the hills. The climbing continued, and as we would soon find out, these hills were merely a training ride for the Blue Nile Gorge individual time trial, two days later.

The 12-mile time trial would begin at the bottom of the gorge and climb 1,362 m to the top. By this point, we had already ridden 30 miles. It was roasting, and while one could enjoy the magnificent descent to the start line, it also made us much more aware of the trial we were about to endure. Riders generally set off at intervals, based on their current standings in the overall race. Before I'd even started, a few of the fitter riders had already pulled out. Irin and I decided to ride together. The route twisted and turned, hairpin after hairpin, and simply completing it would be enough for me. While perhaps serious time triallers didn't stop for Coke and sugar boosts, for us it was a necessity.

The results of the time trial would be announced after dinner. Pal (a rider from Norway) was the winner, completing the ride in just one hour 29 minutes. I was a little behind, though speak cheerfully of my four-hour plus adventure. I guess I was never going to win the stage, and while I was last in the race, I was first to bed.

As we continued our journey, so too did the climbing, hilly stage after hilly stage. The day after an epic time trial, we would reach the highest point of our African tour at 3,104 metres. No wonder I was feeling breathless. The downhills were fantastic, building up speed to get through the start of the next climb. The roads were of good quality, the views spectacular, and every day was like a rollercoaster. I was glad we didn't have to carry out panniers and camping gear here - doing the route on touring bikes was hard enough. We would be so grateful of our rest day in Addis Abba, drinking juice, eating ice cream, and generally doing very little, resting our legs before we needed to get them working again.

At some stage through this section of the tour, it seemed everyone had a stomach bug of sorts. It was also now my time to get the lurgy. I think most of us had a stomach bug at some stage of the Ethiopian route. It was just my luck to coincide the squits with a meal dominated by beetroot. I avoided the red stuff much after this. I took the bus into Arba Minch and was at least grateful that while camping, we had hotel facilities. I was not restricted just to the toilet tent. The next day we would ride to riverbed camp. The road was gravelly, and while yet again we did more descending than climbing, it required full concentration. The paths had quietened, and while grateful for a little peace, it also meant the crew struggled to find much food, and dinner at camp that night was somewhat rationed.

Having lost my EFI status, I also now decided to ride just half of the following day as we headed to Yabello. Noted as a particularly tough off-road day, I didn't want to arrive too late. Yabello would be where I celebrated my birthday, and I wanted a hotel room. Rooms were allocated on a purely first-come, first-served basis, and without taking the truck, I would have spent my birthday in a very, very hot tent.

As it happened, our room was dreadful. The bed and floor were covered in sand, the shower tray was merely a fly collector, and the water ran out during our rest day. Not being able to flush the toilet when dealing with an upset stomach was almost as bad as the toilet tent. It seemed there were few luxuries for my birthday stay and I made do with a birthday cake comprised of a tub of Nutella topped with candles. Travel really does open your eyes as to how fortunate we were, and I was more than happy and grateful to be spending my birthday here.

We were now around 40 days into our African tour, and I was so pleased that following my initial reaction to the group trip, I was now developing the most amazing friendships. I had settled into the new regime and was no longer lonely. Travelling in a group, while challenging in many ways, did also come with great rewards. In Sudan, I'd started enjoying being on my bike again, and having started with an overwhelming sense of being alone in Egypt, I was certainly not on my own here in Ethiopia.

Notes

• I haven't included a full trip breakdown for the Cairo to Capetown route given we completed the tour through a commercial company.

• The total mileage of the Cairo to Capetown tour in the end would be 6,818 miles over a mix of tarmac and off-road routes.

Sadly, I also failed to record speed and so I am unable to provide data on my world at '15' mph analysis for this section of the tour.

8.

ACHIEVEMENT

"Winning is great, sure, but if you are really going to do something in life, the secret is learning how to lose."

Wilma Rudolph

No doubt, as you read of these adventures, you have a picture of a svelte, athletic, sporty type of woman? Think again. Picture instead a curvaceous size 14 (ish) who probably shouldn't wear cycle shorts, and imagine the noise of the huffing and puffing, particularly on the uphill's. I hated sport at school and spent most of the time set aside for physical education sat in the sports pavilion, drinking tea and eating chocolate biscuits. Yet, as I now stop and reflect on the fact that more people have climbed Everest than have cycled from Cairo to Capetown, I feel so proud.

I was aware TDA was a race, though in booking my place, I had signed up just as an expedition rider. However, with timing chips available for us all, it seemed silly not to record the daily achievements. I'd never thought of racing until I came second back in Sudan, but now the opportunity to get an additional reward was just too tempting. While the male race was being taken seriously - the eventual winner for the overall tour having averaged a speed of just under 20 mph - the women had a slightly more relaxed approach. Yes, some were riding for the overall medal, but there was still a chance for those of us who may want to go for the odd stage.

It had taken me a while to settle into this tour, so much so I hadn't really considered what to expect when we set off. I was so grateful I hadn't caught the plane home. I'd not set out thinking I'd be able to attempt this, but as we journeyed down from Kenya to South Africa, the lure of the win proved insatiable. We crossed the border from Ethiopia just before Moyale. The border into Kenya was closed as we arrived, and there was little we could do but take a rest. Two hours later, we were able to proceed.

We were in Kenya when the Africa I'd imagined just appeared. While in Swahili, the word 'safari' translates simply as a journey, to us, it also brings with it connotations of wild animals - the so-called big five. While I'm grateful we never saw tigers in the reserves of India or while out on the road in Africa, riding by zebras, giraffes, hyenas, and elephants was certainly exhilarating.

Our first day in Kenya would involve a 52-mile ride. I was riding with Irin and Tracey and, just after passing an old, abandoned fairground, something we hadn't expected to see, we were amazed to spot a large group of zebra grazing at the side of the road. I've never really envisaged been so close to what we consider wild animals. Camp that night was also at a wildlife reserve. Unfortunately, the trucks were running low on water and all we had was to be kept for drinking only. We were unable to shower before heading off to visit what sounded like an interesting local bar. It was in the nearby prison. Kenya, it seemed, was full of surprises. Alas, John was still suffering from his rash, he was frustrated, grumpy, and in pain. It was horrid, but there was little he could do except rest. He couldn't even be persuaded to head out for a beer.

We'd been warned that the section through Kenya was particularly tough off-road riding, and we were nervous as to what lay ahead. Fortunately, or unfortunately, we would never find out. Kenya was about to go to the polls. While the worst case-scenario, that we would all have to fly over Kenya, was avoided, our cycling here would still be severely curtailed. Tomorrow, we would ride 31 miles before boarding an armed bus to Nanyuki - close enough to be near an army base if all hell broke loose.

We passed groups of campaigners and were told to take care what we photographed. Last time the elections been held in Kenyan, in 2008, it had been a political, economic and humanitarian crisis. Police shot hundreds of demonstrators, women and children were burnt alive, and the slums of Nairobi also saw unprecedented levels of violence. Everyone was praying that this would not be the case this time round. We all hoped our army escort was just precautionary.

Preparing for the drive was a big job for the crew, taking responsibility both for the riders and our gear. While the trucks were designed to carry an occasional bike and rider when they were unwell, they had not been built with the transfer like this in mind. Extra coaches were arranged, and we were escorted by the army, and as the bus ploughed past lava rock it created huge plumes of dust. Even by looking out of the window, we could see just how tough this section of the route would have been. Even by road, the journey was exhausting. The coach was hot, and windows needed to remain shut due to the dust created as we bounced and bumped around. The motto painted on the back of the vehicles read 'Still going Strong' – most appropriate!

Given we had an unexpected number of days' rest, the crew decided to host a fancy-dress party. I had a lovely silk dress in my panniers and opted simply to put flowers in my hair. Getting out of camp gear was 'fancy' in my mind. It's fair to say I got a little carried away at the party and was in bed until midday the next morning. It was quite different to our 6am starts, though this time my illness was self-inflicted. We booked into manicure and massages at our Nanyuki hotel, but I think many of us were finding it hard to stay still for too long. Not able to just sit around a pool, we took the opportunity to do a long hike up Mount Kenya. I guess none of us had signed up for a trip full of rest days and it was really enjoyable taking on a different form of exercise for the day.

We would be back on our bikes briefly the next day as we crossed the equator. It was only our second ride day in this country, and soon we would be crossing the border. Again, however, the ride was short-lived, and soon we were back on buses heading to Nairobi. The army just didn't want us to ride, and we had no choice but to concede. It was voting day, and the streets were lined with crowds. We were warned not to go too far from camp, and while I may be adventurous, this seemed to be quite high risk. I preferred adventure to misfortune The next day, we would prepare to leave.

Voting now over, we were able to ride again before the election results would be announced. We were disappointed to have missed so much riding in Kenya, however difficult the heat and terrain may have been, yet as we arrived in Arusha, Tanzania, water hung in the air. It felt dramatic as we watched the weather roll in while riding past Mount Meru on our way to camp.

John was still not a hundred percent well, and so had needed to ride the truck again. On the plus side, it meant we had a hotel room. I was so grateful not to be putting my tent up as the rain started to pour. The heavens had just opened. It felt like we had not ridden for days, and Arusha was another place where a longer rest had been planned, given it was a key location from which we could take a traditional safari tour. Having arrived early, John had already booked a trip for us with Gus, Irin, and new rider Rob. We were going out to Ngorongoro Crater, stopping in at Tangire National Park too.

I'd been on safaris before, but nothing had quite prepared me for the African experience. While previous safari trips, including the one and I the one John and I undertook in India, had always been quite disappointing, this most certainly was not. We left Arusha early, and after a 2 ½ hour drive, we were soon observing the animals in Tarangire National Park, often used as a stop-off enroute to either the Ngorongoro crater or Serengeti. That night, we would stay at the Bougainvillia Safari Lodge, near Karatu. It was much cheaper than staying directly inside the national park. Alarms set; we would leave at dawn; the gates into the crater opened at 7am. It was misty as we left the hotel, which seemed only to add to the sense of wonder as we dropped down into the crater.

It was another world. At almost 13 miles wide, it's one of the largest craters in the world and it was rammed with a huge variety and number of animals from hyenas to rhinos, a lake full of flamingos, wildebeasts and lions. We were even lucky enough to watch a lion chase down its dinner. This was the Africa I'd always pictured with its wildlife, vast open spaces, and Masai tribesman. It was an experience I'll never forget.

Safari over, it was time to ride on. We would have eight days riding in Tanzania once we left Arusha, mostly off-road. Unfortunately, John was still struggling with his rash and simply couldn't ride. I sense he was also now feeling that sense of isolation I had felt at the start of the trip, and so at times I rode with him in the truck. I was certainly glad about my lift on the day of the mud. With vehicles sliding off the road, our driver had stopped in advance to check out the situation. John and I watched from the truck window as the cyclists approached. They were carrying their bikes through the thick, claggie mud. It reminded me of the landslides we'd encountered in Nepal, and I was certainly glad not to be carrying my touring bike over this again. With my bike weighing in at 17kg this wasn't quite so easy. Everyone was filthy as they pulled into camp, and there were no showers that night. I was pleased not to be completely depleting my wet wipe collection.

The following day, John opted for a half day ride, but his return to the bike would be short-lived. Deep sand once again sent him over the handlebars - he would end the day wearing a sling. The emotional toil of the trip was just as hard sometimes as the cycling and watching on was not an easy place. I too had been through some tough days. Mum had an important hospital check-up. We were about to find out if she would need chemo. I was miles from home, not always able to communicate, and so, so worried. Following a lot of tears and a sleepless night, I eventually heard the good news that she would not need to undergo such brutal treatment. But talking of brutal...

It was less good news for John. He had been taken in the truck by the medical team for an X-ray in Mbeya only to be told he'd separated his shoulder joint. I would find out the news as I arrived late at camp. That day, the ride had been a 69-mile route road, climbing 2,000m over the highest trunk road in the country. My race timer that day recorded an 11-hour 58 minutes ride from camp to camp, and with the time penalty used by TDA for not riding being only 12 hours, it seemed I gained just two minutes on the non-riders for all my effort. Oh well, I was still so proud I completed this day and celebrated with a large block of chocolate John had sourced. Needless to say, the snack did only last two minutes.

Mbeya, a busy town, was our last stop-over in Tanzania, and despite a climb out from the hotel, we would also be rewarded with a 2,700 m descent as we passed into Malawi. Down from the hills, we were surrounded by paddy fields, and the change in landscape from the border was stark, though my overriding memory is still of the poster on the side of the road. It was highlighting free HIV testing for all new babies.

Just over the border, my riding companion, Inga, had a puncture. We soon amassed a crowd, and the searing heat was making the patch difficult to repair. In the end, we loaded bikes into the company truck to get into camp. We camped at Chitimba beach, next to Lake Malawi, and on the day, we came to leave, it was once again pouring with rain. I woke up so grumpy. It was rare when it happened, but I just couldn't shake it. The day was set to start with a big climb and knowing my speed would be slow I knew I would also get drenched. I decided to join the ride after lunch. I hadn't skipped all the hill riding though. The next day, we would climb nearly 2,000 m on what was the second most uphill day of the tour.

With long days and lots of climbing, this trip often felt like a checklist of personal achievements. I spotted a day in the schedule with under 500 m of climbing and decided I would give racing another go. I pushed hard, something that didn't go unnoticed by another rider who decided to help me in my quest. Baz worked with me through to the lunch stop but while he pulled in, to grab some sandwiches, I decided to continue. I could see another female rider up ahead, it was Suzannah. I knew she was the only other rider I was really competing with that day. I tried and tried but just couldn't catch up to her, however, I could not remember whether she left camp before or after me. I could still be ahead in terms of time and so may still be in with a chance of coming in first on today's ride.

With just 16 miles left to go, Darragh and Stephan helped me sustain a final push to the line. I arrived at camp just after Suzannah and needed to find the race director. I'd not worn my timing chip that day, and it was important to register my arrival as soon as possible. My start time was referred against another rider who set off at the same time as me earlier that morning.

It felt like a long wait until dinner when the race results were announced. We all knew it was close. Sadly, it didn't go in my favour - I came second, missing out by just 24 seconds. I was gutted. Despite not winning the race, I was fired up. While it wasn't the be-all and end-all for me, there was still a part of me that now wanted to win a stage. I'm not one to give up easily, though I knew I would have to pick my day carefully, as off-road sections and big climbs would leave me with little chance. My forte was on the flat, partly my fitness and partly the bike gearing and weight.

The next day, my legs were tired, and I took it easy as we arrived in Lilongwe. We would again have a rest day, though if I'm honest, I struggled to find much to go and see, something the guidebook seemed to agree with. Sadly, my impressions here were further ruined - one of the riders was mugged walking back from dinner one night. It was a town I was happy to leave behind. Such a shame to leave a place with a negative impression but with the tour pushing forward there was no real chance to form a different opinion.

The TDA trip was divided into sections, and we were usually shown a weekly schedule outlining distances, climbs and camp locations. As we left Lilongwe, we had been given the outline for the next part of the trip – 94, 109, 106, 77 and 65 miles. All these days were on paved roads and had climbs over 1,000 m except for the fifth day. It was clear from the data that if I was to try at all for a stage win this week, then the last day riding into Lusaka would be my only chance.

I decided to store up my energy over the next few days. Hopefully, my competitors would tire themselves out, despite all riders being forced to slow down on the second day. Having set off from Chipata, there was nothing to indicate to us quite how the ride would pan out. Having completed the traditional 'turn right from camp and keep going' directive, we were set to arrive for lunch at 50 miles. However, as I neared into the designated eating area, it was clear that this was not an ordinary day. The racers were still there, leisurely eating sandwiches and picking at fruit. Everyone had been held at the lunch stop. There were riots in Katete, the next town on, following a murder. The TDA crew were busy working out how we would all get safe passage, and eventually we were escorted through in a single group. We followed the army who shot guns into the air as we rode in convoy behind. One guy, in a bid to avoid arrest, ran straight through the bikes. Not being one for confrontation, I was relieved when this was over. Despite struggling with a group tour at the start, this was certainly one of those days when I was glad we weren't here as independent travellers.

The next morning, we all woke wondering what lay ahead next. The day was marked as a mandatory ride, meaning that those riders who were seriously racing across had to ride to stay in contention. They were never easy days, and this one was no exception at 106 miles. The hard graft did, however, come with some reward. Our camp that night was next to the river, on the border with Mozambique. We were given the option to join a short boat trip - beer and wine included. While John declined, I was certainly not going to turn down the entertainment, despite it being the evening before another of my stage win attempts.

While perhaps the best preparation for a true race attempt, the next day would have been an early night and no alcohol, I did at least do some advance planning - I had two Nutella rolls in the pocket of my cycle jersey. This was a serious affair! I thought hard, and, as two of the other strong riders opted to support me, rather than compete, I may have stood a chance. Alas, once again I was thwarted, overtaken by another female rider. My companions became frustrated, they had also wanted me to collect a stage badge. The atmosphere on the road seem to turn a little awkward, and I knew this was not the day I wanted to claim for my win. Perhaps I just had to accept that this racing game was just not me. We all arrived at the hotel camp in Lusaka later that afternoon, and I was relieved that I'd actually prearranged to stay with some friends. They say it's not the winning but the taking part, but even joining in had not been fun today.

I met Jill, while on the MBA course at Cranfield, and she now lived in Lusaka with husband, Duncan. We were invited to stay the night and join them for dinner. It was a nice break from the group, and also made it clear to us just how many calories we were now consuming. Spaghetti Bolognese had been prepared, and by normal standards it was a generous portion and seconds were available. It was a brilliant night. However, given the miles we were now averaging, it was not quite enough to fill me or John. The following day we found a 'chippy' where we probably both ordered a family meal and dessert, much to the amusement of all the staff. We were certainly not hungry now.

The cycle days into Lusaka had been lengthy, with three days over 90 miles. It was a trend that would continue as we made our way into Zambia, towards Victoria Falls. While we weren't carrying panniers, these were some of the longest rides I'd ever completed. Once again, they were not race days for me, and opportunities for me to get a stage win were reducing.

At Victoria Falls, we would once again have the opportunity for a couple of days' rest. While relaxing was certainly an option, Victoria Falls also offered a menu of high-octane adventure. As we arrived at the hotel, we were made aware of the various activities we could choose to take part in, from bungee jumps to gorge swings or white-water rafting. A microlight flight was also available. Everyone, it seemed, was doing something, though given my fear of heights, I was a little apprehensive. In the end I decided to do the microlight flight. Providing fabulous views over the falls, I rationalised this option, since it had a steady rise and fall through the air rather than a sudden drop. It was not the easy option. Flying through the air on a lawn mower with wings was for me, a petrifying experience. I was the last in my group to fly, and I begged the pilot to take me - increasing winds had already halted other flights. What a mistake. I can smile now as I compare the free-flying bird image on John's commemorative photograph with mine. My eyes were closed, hands and feet clenched, and all colour had drained from my face. By the time we arrived back at the hotel, my fear had turned into a full-on panic attack. I was struggling to breathe. Never again will I try and conquer this particular fear. The following day, I persuaded John that afternoon tea at the five-star hotel nearby was my choice of activity. It was amazing.

From Victoria Falls, we had a 44-mile ride to our next border, Botswana, where we would use the Kazungula ferry to reach camp once border paperwork had been completed. We would stay that night at Kasane, where we had another opportunity to join a sunset boat cruise. The next evening, we would stay at 'road camp'. Aptly named, it was not so inspiring.

I'm sad to say, for me, given the monotonous tarmac and unchanging scenery, I often refer to this section of the ride as

Boring Botswana. Despite not being a natural hill climber, I do still enjoy the satisfaction of a good workout. These flat roads did nothing for me, and the only thing to really look out for were the wild elephants. While great to see on safari, they are not necessarily animals one wants to encounter on a bicycle, and so we had also been joined on this section of the ride by a wildlife expert... And his rifle. I'm pleased to say it was not needed.

Given the flat roads and tarmac, one may be forgiven for thinking I could have an opportunity to race here. However, other than the first day after Victoria Falls, when everyone had been resting, the next days that followed ranged in length from 83 to 115 miles, and my only chance to race here would come as we headed towards Maun. On this day, the race finished at lunch, just 40 odd miles to ride. John said he'd help me. We pushed hard, and so too did the headwinds. It was exhausting. Despite another rest day and the opportunity to visit the Okavango Delta, I just couldn't be bothered. I took the opportunity to rest before both the longest day of the tour and my longest ever day of riding. This almost 130-mile day would take us over the border into Namibia, where boiling tarmac roads would soon be replaced by tough off-road dirt sections. While the riding was much, much harder, the scenery meant that my smile would widen.

Our first night here was spent just past the border, the camp was great, and it had been a long time since we've been able to pitch our tents on flat grass. We were back to riding in empty landscapes. Despite being only a little smaller in area than Ethiopia, Namibia had just 1/10th of the population, and just as the name 'Namibia' translates, we were riding on fast, dry plains. I had known little of what to expect in Namibia other than the famous images of sand dunes.

As we continued our way through the deep, gravel roads, we would head to Witulei. We were back to our more basic camp. Rough ground, little shade, a few stones to avoid, and an outdoor toilet. On the plus side, with no one else around, we could spread out our laundry and pitch our tents as we pleased. Given it was our last rough camp of the trip, the crew built a bonfire and decided we would have an early celebration. We bought beers from a local petrol station and sang songs before retiring to bed. We would ride into Windhoek the next day. With its German colonial heritage, Windhoek was a much more established town, and to some degree, it felt like we were leaving Africa behind. However, given this was a TDA trip, it would not be long before the smooth tarmac would once again disappear.

We had seven more ride days here in Namibia, all of which yet again highlighted my draw to quieter, desolate places. The stars were phenomenal, the heat overbearing, and the gravel lay deep. It was hard going but a real surprise, and a country I would love to return to. As our ride took us over the Sprettschuke Pass, we stopped to observe the impending downhill. It was too steep for some riders in places, and they opted to push and walk. I took my time, hands on the brakes as I gradually made my way down the block paved road. An additional refreshment stop had been set up at the bottom of the hill. My water bottles had run dry, and I was grateful for the refill. Despite being off-road, the distances we travelled were still often over 60 miles, and we were all looking forward to reaching Solitaire. Camp here was at the Moose McGregor Desert bakery, much famed as the best in Namibia. It had been established in the 1990s when a Scottish adventurer, Percival George Cross, decided to settle here, and as we headed in past the artistically placed car wrecks, we could see some of the riders had already made a visit. Here's hoping there was something left!

We weren't disappointed. Apple pie and chocolate brownie purchased, we sat down at camp to enjoy our goodies. We had found a cake oasis and, while it may have been a well-deserved calorie boost, its timing the night before the naked mile was perhaps less well-planned.

The naked mile was a long-standing TDA tradition, and while the tour leader told us all about this non-obligatory bit of fun, both the girls and guys planned to meet and take their turns in this time-honoured activity. We even heard how one year, a rider cycled the full distance, 52 miles, from camp to camp in merely his birthday suit. Having researched TDA before I left, I knew about this option, and I had come prepared. Since I left Cairo on 23 January, my luggage had also carried a special outfit, that of a flesh-coloured bra and pants set to which I had attached fake leaves. Well, I'd always loved a bit of fancy dress, and I wasn't 100% about the full naked experience.

Given I'd gone to all this effort, I decided riding with the girls for just a mile was not quite enough so, as John and I made our way to lunch, we took time to slip off the side of the road and get changed so to speak. It was great to bring a smile to the faces of the other riders as we rolled in just past the lunch truck. What a giggle! John then headed off with Gus for his naked mile stint and, following a short sandwich break, I set off with the girls as we lined up for our once-in-a-lifetime photo shoot. It was so much fun I decided to continue in my 'outfit 'with one of the other riders. Waving at the odd few passing vehicles, we finally arrived at camp with beaming smiles. It had been quite a day to remember, though one I will never repeat. A small patch of skin on my back had missed out on the sun cream. I had bad sunburn, and my back began to blister. The medics would be patching me up for the next few days.

An early night ensued as the following morning we would be up early to climb to the top of the dunes for sunrise. Wow! We watched the shadows all around as we placed our feet into the path of the previous footprints on the ledge of sand. Another experience I'll certainly never forget, even if my fear of heights kicked in again slightly. The dunes can reach as high as 325 m. Heading back down the sand, I left the group on the hill, taking time to explore the area around. The dunes were part of one of the driest ecosystems on earth, and I enjoyed taking photographs of the few trees that were surviving in this landscape.

As we left the dunes, our feelings were mixed. We were excited about reaching the end, while also desperate to get a break from the travelling circus. With five days' riding left in Namibia, the route continued to be a challenge. Distances remained long, and the scenery much the same. After three days of riding 86, 95 and 78 miles respectively, we were looking forward to a shorter day - the 58-mile ride from Seeheim to Canon Roadhouse. Based just 9 miles away from the Fish River Canyon, this was one of the largest canyons in the world and part of Namibia's newest national park. We were looking forward to an early arrival and a little bit of sightseeing. It was not to be. Lots of riders has expressed an interest in making a visit, and the crew were busy looking at how this might be possible. We had high hopes, but it was not to be. The headwind was horrendous, possibly the worst of our entire African route, and consequently the ride took much longer than anticipated. While we were disappointed, Canon Roadhouse at least was another oasis - full of vintage transport memorabilia and very good cheesecake.

For our last day here, I opted to ride the truck. Our accommodation that night was a holiday spot next to the Orange River, just 8 miles before the South African border. The setting was incredible, and well-blessed with a hotel room, given my early arrival, it was one day I did actually regret not being on the bike. Independent riding never gave us the opportunity to miss out the miles, and in retrospect, I think that's a good thing. They say you only ever regret the things you don't do, and that was certainly the case here.

The next day we would cross the border into the last country of our African adventure. I loved the ride into South Africa, and it was great to read the signpost saying Cape Town, '678 km'/421 miles. The road was surrounded by rocks as once again the scenery changed at the border crossing. As we made our way south, our first stop would be Springbok.

The ride from Springbok to Garies was 73 miles, and we had 1,021 m of climbing. I set out at a good, but usual pace. By now I didn't think a stage win was possible, and I'd even visited the toilet after clocking out. I was not thinking of the 24-second gap today. It was only as I went to pull in for lunch that I realised the racers were all still there. This was it. This was my chance.

I knew the route finished with a long, winding downhill to camp, and the worst of the climbing was already over. I wanted that win, and as I saw John up ahead, I shouted my intention. John picked up the pace and set about helping me up the inclines, yelling at me to keep pedalling even as I raced downhill. My speedo hit 45 mph, and no one had overtaken me. I flew into camp, and as the crew realised I was first in, they also seem to share my joy. It was the last day I could possibly have done this. I'd been close to a win before, and so I was waiting on tenterhooks until the announcement at dinnertime.

I'd tried several times and failed, but as they made the announcement at dinner that evening, I almost cried. I had finally come in first.

With my legs tired and another mandatory ride day the next morning, I opted to cycle just from lunch. We were heading towards the coast again where the final race point would be at Felands Bay. The night-time temperature had dropped, and we were freezing again. Early morning starts required gloves, jackets, and legwarmers, and I was grateful of hot coffee at our final lunch stop. All riders congregated on the beach, holding bikes aloft, Table Mountain clearly visible behind. Our African adventure would finish with a 19-mile convoy ride into the harbour area of Cape Town. Some of the riders had arranged for family and friends to meet them at the end of the journey, and an arrival ceremony and final night party had also been planned. Flags representing the countries of all participating riders were on show and following the race announcement we were all called up to collect our medals.

The African trip really did provide a sense of achievement on many levels. The race attempts and final stage win, the emotional ups and downs, and of course, simply getting to the end was a success.

Notes

While again full data is not available, I can share the following statistics from our Cairo to Capetown journey:

- The longest day saw us ride 128.6 miles as we crossed over the border in Namibia.

- The trip has an average daily mileage of 76.4 miles, and the journey 11 days also saw us cycle over 100 miles.

- The biggest climb day saw us ascend 2052 metres into Mybeya – riding for almost 12 hours over 69 miles. The second longest climb day taking us up 1966m over 83 miles.

Let's just say my average speed on the day I won exceeded 15mph!

On the day I lost the race by 24 seconds my average speed was around 26mph and while I don't have the stats from my winning day, I did reach speeds just over 45mph. Not bad!

9.

FREEDOM

"There is no easy walk to freedom."

Nelson Mandela

It's ironic that the land where freedom was, for many years, so curtailed, was the country that epitomized my own sense of freedom, of choice, of decision. I've never liked being told what to do and while, of course, we are all influenced by those around us, and at times have to do as others ask, I much prefer to do my own thing.

Before joining the TDA tour, I had been the route planner, accommodation booker, and sightseeing guide. John had definitely been a massive influence - he wouldn't be there simply as a follower - yet I was aware that I was still a key decision maker. I enjoyed the company of others, and even elements of the daily routine, but as I rode out from our group hotel, my grin stretched from cheek to cheek. John and I were back on our bikes, and this time we weren't following the flagging tape. We could get lost, stop where we wanted, and plan a route taking in the sights and doing the things we enjoyed. We may get lost again and not be on the best roads, but we would set the pace, distance and rest days ourselves. Whether it's about control or simply balancing a cycle tour with sightseeing, I was really looking forward to planning our schedule again.

Having completed this demanding ride from Cairo, we decided that our time in South Africa would be the holiday ride before flying home. Consequently, cycle days were much shorter, and we were joined by one of my friends. We treated ourselves to a luxury 'foodie' weekend in Franschoek where wine tasting would also be part of the course. Many of the TDA riders had already left for flights, but as the final few were still busy packing boxes, John and I headed off into central Cape Town.

I'd booked us a couple of nights in an airstream trailer, situated on the roof of the hotel downtown. The trailers were all themed and decorated very differently. It seems like a great, quirky thing to do, though in reality we were in a very pink, lacy caravan with lots of luggage and little space. It was more amusing than comfortable.

After a little repacking back into panniers, we set off in the direction of Paarl - lying east of Cape Town. The first part of the ride was on a busy three-lane highway the N1 and while it felt more like a motorway it seemed we were allowed to ride on it. It was not pleasant, and we exited as soon as possible. With 40 miles to do, not the 75-mile averages of the TDA, the route was flat, and we weren't in a rush. Our room at the other end was pre-booked and guaranteed. Paarl, the third-oldest town in South Africa, is surrounded by domes of granite, including pole rock: the second-largest granite outcrop in the world. Having left the chaos and fast traffic behind, our ride made clear that the divide between black and white was still prevalent, noted by the difference in privet hedges to townships and shacks.

We were heading to Franschoek, where we were looking forward to meeting friends and indulging in the fancy food weekend I'd booked in a world-renowned hotel and restaurant. Our first night in Paarl had already excited us regarding the quality of food and wine available, and our expectations were high. They were transcended.

Far from a tent and shovels in the desert, our room was more like an apartment - we had a huge complimentary bar and a log fire (which the staff would prepare). The room had its own lounge, bedroom, kitchen area, and magnificent bathroom. This really was the most luxurious place I had ever stayed in, and it proudly displayed a guestbook signed by many honey-mooning couples. Hmmm.

My friend, Sam had unfortunately not been able to get a room quite like ours but she had travelled from Zimbabwe to meet us for a few days. The food experience was something we could all share. The five-course tasting menu, paired with wine, was a stark contrast to the shovels and tents we had become used to through our journey from Cairo. We also been joined by another friend, Craig, a South African who I'd also met while studying. He was now living back in Franschoek, and so we had a great time catching up as we shared tales about African adventure with them both. After dinner we went back to the room and complimentary bar yet perhaps as I remembered the party night in Nanyuki and its aftereffects the extra drinks were not so appealing.

Two days later, we would ride to Stellenbosch, passing many vineyards as Sam took a taxi to meet us there. It seemed there was still more local wine to try. Budgets splashed, we down-graded our accommodation this time and booked into a cheaper hostel. It really made me chuckle that the bedside lamps were impossible to use - no plug socket anywhere near them rendered them obsolete.

The trip was really slowing down, but as we made our way from Stellenbosch to the coast, we would realise that the group tour did take some of the pressure off an African ride. We had just over 30 miles to get to Kalk Bay, but as we steadily made progress, a guy in a pickup truck kept trying to get our atten-tion. We weren't sure what to do, and initially just kept on riding. Undeterred, he eventually shouted, "It's not safe!" from his jeep window. Unusually, I was cycling behind John, and I suggested perhaps we ought to hear what he had to say, while keeping ourselves ready to ride on should we need to. How we would make a quick getaway from a jeep I wasn't quite sure though!

He wanted to let us know that we were heading towards a very large township, Khalisha, and apparently it wasn't safe. The township had been created several years ago, as black residents were moved out of District Six in the centre of Cape Town. Two tourists had been killed riding near there in recent years. We really weren't sure what to do. It was the only road to our next destination, and the driver we were talking could tell we were assessing our options. He flagged down another car. I felt very uncomfortable with the two white guys sharing their advice. I deplore racism, and I felt very uneasy. However, we didn't want to be stupid, either. The pickup driver offered us a lift for a short distance, which we eventually did opt to accept.

He dropped us off 10 miles later. From Kalk Bay, we were heading down to Cape Point. While we hadn't started at the most northern point in Africa, we were determined to reach the most southern spot. The ride down was fabulous, and we followed a small road through the national park. Even better, we were able to leave our baggage at the park entrance. Obligatory photos taken, we turned round and started heading to our next destination, Kommetjie. We were woken in the middle of the night by an incredible storm, lightning, thunder, and driving rain. Who knew what the next day would bring?

The rain had passed, and we were left with strong winds. It made the cycle much harder, but most alarming was the way the wind was trying to push us off the edge of the road as we headed down Chapman's Peak Drive. This section of coast road is a well-known route on the way back to Cape Town and the end of the Africa ride. Soon, we would begin what was becoming another routine by dismantling and packing up before heading home. We would have a few days to be tourists, and as we had not been to Robin Island, where Nelson Mandela was imprisoned for so many years, we decided to take a look. It's hard to convey just how austere the foreboding prison was or contemplate what it was like to be confined to a small cell for so many years.

I had just completed the most phenomenal ride from Cairo to Cape Town, yet I still beamed as I rode off independently. The ability to make choices, change our mind, and be where we wanted to be is a position I will never take for granted, and there was no better place to be reminded of that than here in South Africa.

The Stats; A Tour of South Africa
180.8 Miles

Destination	Total Distance
Capetown to Paarl	36.7
Franschoek	23
Stellenbosch	23
Kalk Bay	29.8
Capepoint	21.7
Kommetji	21.1
Capetown	25.5

Notes

• Of the data listed above, just under ten miles were covered in the back of the truck past Khalisha.

Sadly, I failed to record speed and so I am unable to provide data on my world at '15' mph analysis for this section of the tour.

Roads were good and I was by now at my fittest, and with reduced pannier weight so it may just have been possible that the target speed was achieved in this short section. Well, that's my story and I'm sticking to it!

10.

COMMUNITY

"Chapeaux"

All cyclists riding up
Alpe D'Huez

It's very own 'community of interest', the cycle gang are undoubtedly held together by the passion of the two-wheeler. While back home in the UK, the relationship between driver and cyclist can at times feel antagonistic, in France and Italy the sheer love of cycling as a sport offers a completely different cycle tour experience.

For those who follow the sport of cycling, particularly the road race you'll be aware of the big Grand Tours that take place each year: The Giro D'Italia, the Tour de France and the Vuelta a Espana. All set over three weeks these extensive races see riders complete for the key positions and associated jerseys of overall winner (General Classification, yellow jersey); King of the Mountains (polka dot jersey) and Top Sprinter (green jersey). Of these, the Tour de France is the oldest race and the most widely attended sporting event in the world. Each year keen followers set out to complete stages, follow in their camper vans, and tune in for daily TV coverage. Around 12 million people watch the race and as we cycled down to meet up with the biggest cycle race in the world it seemed the influence of the sport on the road was implicit in the way drivers treated us with respect. Whether riding through Paris, heading slowly over the Alps or needing to load bikes onto the train, these countries certainly seem to have got it right from a cycle perspective.

I often describe this section of our trip as the filler, it was what came before Southeast Asia. We never intended to ride so close to home given all this would be available in the future should shorter trips become the only possibilities. However, leaving at this time for Southeast Asia in July would put us right in the monsoon season and as we looked for something to do while the rain came down, John suggested we ride out to visit his father, resident in northern Italy. We would get a warm welcome and the distance and time scale seem to fit so the decision was made and while his father would now be on holiday in the south of the country we just added on a few extra miles and of course the additional sightseeing. Afterall, what were a few extra miles to us now?

I started looking at routes and in so doing we decided to invite friends to meet us in Epernay, heart of the Champagne region, 80 ish miles northeast of Paris. Having been here before the area is an easy get to from the Eurostar and Gare du Nord and with a cycle path leading from Epernay station to the municipal campsite by the river it's an easy bike getaway. This time however, rather than just a long weekend, it would mark the start of our route south over the Alps and into Italy. While perhaps we should have started from the UK, catching the train to this point meant I was still able to embark on my regular trip to Glastonbury Festival while back in the UK too.

We had a month or so at home before heading off again – just enough time to recuperate from the challenges of Africa. Date set, trip planned, and my bike booked in for a service I was looking forward to setting off again. It nearly didn't happen. I'd never really enjoyed bike maintenance in fact my friends often used to joke that I would find another bike before I would even fix a puncture. However, the bike had taken quite a pounding on African roads and while I had no specific issues, I decided a preventative service would be a good idea. The complexity of the Rohloff system meant the hub gears could only be serviced in Germany, so the wheel was promptly removed and shipped off as opposed to going to my usual Edinburgh bike store. The rest of the bike stayed here in the UK where I'd organise the remaining maintenance schedule to be completed while I was at Glastonbury Festival. I would then have two days to attach the wheel and undertake any final packing. Precision planning - what could possibly go wrong?

The wheel was waiting for me on my return and with the rest of my bike at a small, local bike store my mother drove me to the shop where the wheel and belt drive system could be reconnected. Sounds easy, however, it seemed the rear sprocket had also been updated and was now different to the belt drive system. I was due to leave the next day leaving only a few hours to fix the issue. So far, the bike and belt drive had made the trip go smoothly, we'd had little to worry about bar the brake blocks in Nepal. However, with such a specialised setup my options were now severely limited. I finally had to concede that fixing The Captain was not a 24-hour job. I would either need to delay, cancel, or find an alternative option. Stubborn and solution focused, a plan was soon formed. I was determined to complete this section of our ride.

Many years ago, while living in Bristol, another friend Cath was setting off on a ride to China. At the time I thought she was completely nuts. My longest cycle ride at that point was probably to the pub and back. Cath now lived the other side of Birmingham, around an hour's drive from my mother's. I knew she had a touring bike and with my folding bicycle also at my mums at this time I asked if she may be interested in a two-month bike swap. While she didn't want to consider my Brompton folding bike for her daily commute; she did have a spare tourer. We were roughly the same height and although it hadn't been used for some time, I knew I just need to get it to the start line I could update brake blocks, tyres and other bits as needed. Finding bike repair stores in France would not be a problem. The cycle community, or in this case, my friend Cath, had come up trumps.

The trip was back on, and I gave myself a big pat on the back for finding an effective solution. Panniers loaded; I caught the train to High Wycombe ready to meet John. Another train journey into London and then through Paris would take us into the heart of the Champagne region.

Our friends had also taken their bikes and we planned a few short rides out to champagne houses the next day. While the riding was fabulous in terms of setting-wheat and poppy fields, rolling hills clear blue skies-the bike was a nightmare. It was my first full day of riding and my shoulders and back hurt so much. I'd found a good bike to borrow but it just didn't fit me properly, and I was unsure how long I'd be able to continue. At camp that night we were back to scenario planning. While other bikes were available from friends, they too were not set up for me or indeed heavy panniers and a touring setup. We would need to make some adjustments to the bike I had. The next day we headed to the bike store. The handlebars were raised, and I hope with this an improvement to the bike geometry would give me a better riding position. Whether champagne induced or just sheer dogged determination I decided that the stem raises were doing the trick. What a relief.

Thankfully the bike was sorted before we were joined by another friend, Thijs, a Dutch rider from our African adventure. Like us, he had time to fill to before returning to work and he would head off with us through France and into much of Italy. Thijs was younger and fitter and whether it was because we were spurred on by him or simply because we were used to triple figure ride days after Tour D'Afrique we found ourselves doing 100+ kilometres the first few days. While I'd prepared a rough plan for our daily destinations, we used Thijs and his bike GPS to calculate routes. Whether all roads around here were quiet or the sat nav had deliberately sought them out I wasn't sure, though it certainly made for some great riding as we passed through Troyes, L'Isle sur Serein and Chalon sur Saône.

I was settling in to my 'new' bike and as was customary he was also given a name - Bob. As well as the bike, we'd also both been adjusting to a new routine and a new rider. I guess John and I had got used who did what at camp, how we navigate and ride and how we plan what we were doing next. It's fair to say there were a few tensions with debates over camp spots, routes, and food choices. Having demonstrated my problem-solving abilities, it was time for diplomacy.

We made great progress both in settling disputes and clocking up the kilometres, passing quaint villages vineyards and château's, rolling in at the boulangerie for pastries selecting from the vast range of cheese and ham in the supermarket. We soon got into the routine of shopping early, avoiding afternoon closures, eating picnic lunches as we sought shelter from the heat of the midday sun. While not quite as cheap as the hiker/biker states of America we found the municipal camping areas, well located and with reasonable prices. We made buying the cheapest wine available to have with dinner a bit of a contest and with only one box of wine I suspect the French wouldn't even use for cooking, the experiment was deemed a success.

Our fourth night with see us arrive in Louhans and having located the campsite and set up as normal we decided to venture into the town, taking in the sights we glimpsed on our cycle in. While renowned for its famous poultry market – which we didn't see – we did have the opportunity to explore the Grande Rue, known as the largest arcaded street in France boasting 157 arches. The town was very quiet for exploring though this did also mean we found few places to eat and drink. The next day saw us heading for Bourg en Bresse where we made up for eating and enjoyed taking photos in front of the old timber framed houses, dating back to the 16th century. The beautiful scenery continued as we pushed on following small bike paths out from the town, stopping off at a local market.

I've always enjoyed the food markets of France, stacked full of fresh local produce where the focus is always on flavour as opposed to supermarkets here that reject food that isn't the right colour, showing much less concern for what it tastes like. Interested in our ride, one of the traders – interested in our cycle tour – had given us some raspberries. We were making good progress though we were about to take an enforced rest as John become unwell. That day we would finish early, camping on a farm site just south of Montalieu-Verlieu. John slept all the next day as the lady who ran the site offered to call a doctor. Thankfully, the illness passed though it does always highlight why flexibility must always be built into tour planning. Goals and destinations are always good to have in mind, but adaptability is key to ensuring rides remain a pleasure and not a stressful race. That said, I think we were all relived – being ill in a hot tent is never great but we were also keen to make it to Alpe d'Huez in time to watch the world's greatest cycle race pass by.

Grenoble was our final stop before the climbing started and as we got closer a local rider would point us in the direction of a cycle path into the town/city. We had a hotel booked, thinking it would be a good chance to relax post being ill and before the hard work really started. The room was so hot though and we couldn't help thinking the tent would have been a better option. We were truly becoming accustomed to the migrant lifestyle!

It was heaving as we pulled into Bourg D'Osians and after a six-mile climb, we were ready to relax for a while. Recuperation before the big climb the next day. There were camper vans and tents everywhere. All hotels were booked though as one camp site was able to find space for three touring cyclists and our tiny tents, we were pleased to be travelling so light. We were soon pitched up and it was time to absorb the event build up, visit the numerous bike related stores, and get some food. With the town so busy we opted for pizza, finding a quiet spot to sit next to the water.

Alpe d'Huez is one of the most iconic climbs of the Tour. With its 21 hairpins and 1,120m gain in elevation it's a challenging 8.5-mile ride. It was no wonder I was a little apprehensive about the ride. There were people – mostly men - riding all around us. Dressed in all the latest gear and with light road bikes to match, our kit made us the juggernauts of the road. By contrast, my kit came in at 26kg in panniers with 3kg in sundries and on a 17kg bike. I felt sick as I started, not sure if it was nerves or just the fact that I had set off too soon after breakfast I encouraged Thijs and John to go on ahead. The steepest climbs came early on, averaging an 11% gradient. On these climbs you simply have to climb at your own pace and mine, it turned out, was 3.6 mph! In my lowest gear I just kept my legs turning – that is until one rider, who had pulled by for a chat (!) clipped my front wheel. I had to stop. However, the challenge now would be to get going again. Surrounded by bikes – both ascending and descending - it was hard to traverse the road and get going again. Despite nearly causing an accident as one rider came downhill so fast, I finally managed to start again much to my relief.

Having passed by the Joachim Agostino monument (a famous rider who'd won this stage in 1979) the gradient had eased a little to 8% and while Huez village was still not the final marker I was happy to know there was just over a mile left to go. I'll never forget that day and often like to think back to the sound of other riders shouting 'chapeaux' as they passed me by. One very fit bunch of guys (of course I noticed them!) even commented to his friends that he wasn't sure he could ride as I was. It kept me going and while it took three hours to go just 11 miles, I was so proud. Having posed for photos at the top of the climb we found a space to pitch the tent, grabbed a beer and planned the spot we would watch the elite riders from the following day. I say planned, there was only one spot we wanted to be in – Dutch Corner of course!

The atmosphere was electric-and despite having 5 hours to wait before the professionals passed, the time fled by – as did the riders. It was the 100th Tour de France this year and today was the 'Queen' stage– the day classed as the hardest and most demanding one to ride. While riders may not have been so pleased to see a double loop up the mountain, as a spectator we were delighted to know we would get to watch the riders once more that day. Hours to wait and minutes to watch. The professionals' top speeds to climb this great mountain are nearing 10mph. In fact, Marco Pantini, a holder of the record for the fastest climb up this inimitable mountain completed his ascent in 37 minutes and 37 seconds, just a little quicker than my three hours! Thank goodness we only did the ride once though – we still had a lot of climbing to do now as we made our way over the Alps to Italy.

Our next stop was Les Graves, then Gullestre with Larche our final rest spot in France. The days were so hard, but the views were breath-taking – it was worth going slowly and while riding a bike in this type of environment is hard going it's so nice to not be rushing through as one might in a car. The downhills were awesome too and I was finally able to ride somewhat faster hitting maximum speeds over 30mph now. It's hard to imagine how others do this on flat and undulating terrain. Still, at least the shouts of chapeaux continued. We saw many other riders bagging the 'Cols' and with Col de Vars seeing us climb to 1,155m over 12 miles and Col de Larche another 10 mile climb it was great to still hear the encouragement from others.

As we crossed over the last climb of the Alps our own 'detour de France' was over. We made our way to Peveragno for our first Italian camp. We still had a month for our 'detour de Italy' as the rainy season continued in Southeast Asia. New countries always bring in a bit of adjustment - we moved from cheese and ham to cheese and tomatoes, from vin rouge to vino rosso. What remained constant was the ongoing respect for cyclists on the road. The community and positive cycle culture continued.

Other than a brief weekend in Venice I'd not travelled through Italy before and with our ride taking in the Cinque Terra, Amalfi coast and cities like Siena, Rome, and Naples there was much to look forward to. We would drop in at beach-based campsites, with their orderly umbrellas and rows of sunbeds, see religious procession and fireworks in Levanto with our first rest day visiting the Cinque Terra. This area was our first major Italian tourist spot, and it did not disappoint. Set on the rugged coastline the 5 towns that give this area is name – Monterosso, Vernazza, Corniglia, Manarola and Riomaggiore – are all connected by a series of hiking trails and for weary cyclists, trains. While all the towns had their own character the coloured houses, harbours and fabulous eating spots were common to them all – what's not to like?

Were we not on bikes we would have taken more time to explore but with our rest day over we had a 500m climb as we made our way to Via Reggio. Another beautiful coastal town though lots of the area here by the sea was private beaches and bars making it feel somewhat inaccessible to us even if we had earnt a dip in the sea. The next day would see us head inland – Thys was pleased to head away from the coast; John had wanted to follow the sealine – I was happy doing whatever, but it did remind me again that three could be a crowd and I was always the diplomatic one... Oh well. San Gimignano was a beautiful medieval town and a great lead introduction to Sienna, our next location.

As we arrived in Sienna the rain poured, and a full-on thunderstorm was soon overhead. While home to the oldest bank in the world, it's the biannual horse race that brings the crowds here and it was easy to imagine the Palio filling the square at Piazza del Campo. Always keen to find the best vantage point in any town or city we visit the three of us had soon climbed to the top of the bell tower, looking down on this UNESCO World Heritage site, imagining animals, riders and spectators crammed in just as the paintings and photographs in all the square restaurants depicted. Again, as was standard on our trips we opted to take in the site with a large beer.

Looking back, I always feel like we were in Sienna for a few days – I'm not sure whether that's because it seemed like we did so much while we were there or because the sat nav seemed to make it a hard place to navigate out from. Steep climbs up and down seemed to get us nowhere and tempers frayed as we pushed our bikes up the hill to leave. Finally on our way again we spent a night in Monitcella Amati before calling by Porto Ecola and Tarquinia on our way to Rome. I loved riding through Tuscany with its rolling hills, great lunch stops and fabulous viewpoints. That said, for cyclists it was not without difficulty.

Having left Porto Ecola, we enjoyed a long descent where after around 28 miles we would be in Grosetto. It was all part of the plan we had mapped out, but we would soon find that it was not the best place to have ended up on our bikes. It seemed that from here there was only a 'cars only' highway heading south. While some cyclists do take their chances - given no road alternatives - we were less certain and after much debate we agreed that the train was the best option. While not what we really wanted to do it's not like John and I hadn't used the train on previous trips.

Much like France, the trains in Italy are well equipped for a bicycle. There was no pre boking for one of the few spaces available. No need to check availability before booking and then hope the tickets you were holding in an online cart were still available and of course, given we were 'boarding' with immediate effect there was no concern that a delay, cancellation, or reduced service would affect our bike reservation. Sadly, I've experienced all these scenarios in the UK. Thankfully this ride went without incident, and we were soon in Porto Ecola.

The campsite here was rammed but we soon pitched up. That said, noise or sand did lead us to a B and B booking in Tarquinia. I'd not really heard of this place but having altered our route following Grosetto we chose to stop here given it too was also UNESCO listed. While the ride through France was very much one of passing through traditional towns and villages with no real attractions to see, the route through Italy took in many great historical landmarks -Tarquinia was known for its Etruscan tombs. Having taken a short walk to take in the ancient site we tucked into food prepared by our B and B host. Not a bad diversion after all.

Next stop was Rome and with a couple of days here we had a lazy morning at camp before hitting the sites. We had opted to stay about 10km out of the city. The campsite was huge but this time we did actually want a laundrette and ever important Wi-Fi access for blog writing, skype calls and a general email and news catch up. With jobs completed, the following day we would visit Vatican City - though it did not start well. Buses went from the campsite to the local train station for us to head into the city. Normally an 18-minute ride, today it was more like one hour 18 minutes. The weather was scorching, we were surrounded by three coaches of French tourists and a very rude priest, and the scheduled train did not arrive. The next train was heaving. People were standing, including us and the sweat was ruining any attempt to look fresh in our now clean clothes. One girl fainted, the train halted while water was sought, the driver had a fag, and then we were back on our way.

We were due to meet one of my mom's former student lodgers. He was now back in Italy and having had a father who had worked on security for the Pope we were being escorted in – avoiding the long queues which by now would have kept us waiting into the midday sun. It really was an incredible place but if ever there was an attraction to note 'exit through the gift shop' – it was here. I have to say the excessive commercialism in a church setting sat uneasily with me and I was very much reminded of the New Testament story as money changer tables were overturned. We didn't have time to see all the sites of Rome, but we did find time to see the Colosseum before riding through the city the next day riding alongside the Tigris River as we continued our journey South.

A few days later we would be in Naples and what a contrast. There was a lot more glass on the road as we cycled in, and the city was full of graffiti. Once again, we'd opted to camp just outside at a campsite near to Mount Vesuvius. The bubbling crater made for an interesting spot though sadly the heat also seemed to attract wasp after wasp. Ah, the joys of camping. With our rest day here in the third most populated Italian city there was much to do and as well as the volcano we did of course make sure we fully tested Napoli pizza.

More history came as we went to Pompeii before we continued onto Sorrento. I'd really enjoyed all the UNESCO sites, but I do also have very fond memories of Sorrento. As home of limoncello it is also the stop I will always remember for hosting the best gelato (ice cream) shop I have ever seen. Still the best I have ever seen to this day.

The next evening, I got an email from an old friend, and I have to say, it threw me. The email questioned my whole trip and the way I spoke of it. Noting that I kept flying home from an extended cycle holiday while seemingly raising money for charity the message certainly poked me right at the heart. I wasn't sure where my reply would leave things. A natural conciliator I'm always one for making friends not having fall outs but sometimes you can't just keep quiet. I'd always been open and honest about the charity links (not my primary purpose but there as people often asked me) and my reason for going (a much-needed life change). I can only assume he hadn't realised why I kept coming home. I was fortunate to be able to do this and to this day remain fully aware of this, but I would not be made to feel guilty. No wonder I remember the gelato.

Speaking of friends - we were about to say goodbye to Thijs as his time for an extra ride post Italy was coming to an end. He would leave us in Bari and our last day saw us on a final discussion over food and sharing some awful cheap wine. There had of course been great moments with Thijs but as with the end of the Tour D'Afrique tour, it felt great to be just John and I again. The group of three pressure had been reduced as we continued, though I felt awful. The mosquitos on that last night had been a nightmare. I was covered in bites, but my misery was made worse having been attacked around my eyes which were now swollen. Alas, as we pitched up again, we noted that while we may have lost Thijs, we had not lost the mozzies and another itchy night followed.

Despite a bad night's sleep, it did not seem to deter our ride which would see us pedal 68 miles the next day into our final destination – San Foca. We were a day early to meet Paulo and Ivana, who despite being taken a little by surprise, made us feel very welcome. Our Italian journey had ended and while not really beach people we enjoyed a week by the sea and took the opportunity for a brief rest before a frantic turnround for the next tour.

Bob had done a good job as a stand in bike in the end. Our filler trip had turned into a great and while adjustments had been made to ride as a group of three, I was really looking forward to the next tour being just the two of us again... and of course – riding on The Captain. The cycle community and riding through France and Italy really had been wonderful. Drivers were patient and roads felt safe. There is much we can learn from the culture that exists here. I'd like to hope the growing interest in professional racing will help though in reading social media comments as roads close, sadly I fear back in the UK the anti-cyclist vitriol will always remain.

Finally, to pinch more of the Tour de France lingo, it was time to allez, allez, allez before awarding the jerseys on our own tour podium.

- Yellow jersey – John

- Polka dot jersey – Thijs

- Best diplomat and domestique - Naomi

The Stats; Epernay to San Foca
1,565.7 Miles

Destination	Total Distance	Average Speed	Metres Up	Metres Down	Time on Bike
Epernay to Troyes	100	10.9	-	-	c. 7.5 hrs
L'Isle sur Serein	60.9	9.7	-	-	6 hrs 08
	72.1	9.1	-	-	7 hrs 57
Chalon sur Saone	53.9	10	-	-	5 hrs 24
Bourg en Bresse	97	-	-	-	-
Montalieu Vercieu	51	-	315	288	-
Grenoble	59.8	10	824	1038	-
Bourg d'Oisans	31	9.2	285	15	3 hrs 22
Alpe d'Huez	11.2	3.6	1123	-	-
Les Graves	18.2	6.5	698	123	2 hrs 47
Guillestre	49.3	9.3	755	1380	5 hrs 17
Larche	29.6	5.6	1302	796	5 hrs 13
Peveragno (Italy)	49.3	10.9	446	1460	4 hrs 32
Celle Ligure	60.9	9.4	698	1425	6 hrs 26
Nervi	36.2	8.6	430	369	-
Levato	55	8.1	1110	1429	6 hrs 41
Via Reggio	55.4	8.9	767	863	6 hrs 12
San Gimignano	61.4	9.5	598	526	6 hrs 27
Siena	26.3	7.8	476	499	3 hrs 21
Monticello Amiata	48.5	7.4	1100	914	6 hrs 35

Destination	Total Distance	Average Speed	Metres Up	Metres Down	Time on Bike
Porto Ecola	34.8	11.7	152	745	2 hrs 59
Targuinia	9.3	7.2	97	25	1 hr 17
Rome	64.1	10.6	507	787	6 hrs 02
	71.3	10	168	223	7 hrs 06
San Felice Circeo	28.7	9.7	25	47	2 hrs 57
Baia Domizia	45.2	10.5	140	109	4 hrs 19
Naples	39.6	10.2	179	269	3 hrs 51
Pompeii	23.9	8.9	203	318	2 hrs 40
Sorrento	16.8	7.6	163	183	-
Nettuno	13.6	6.6	291	381	2 hrs 03
	29.1	6.4	773	737	4 hrs 32
Bari	15.7	8.8	215	362	1 hr 47
Alberobello	37.4	9.6	417	224	3 hrs 35
Specchiula (via Ostuni)	40.4	10.9	247	614	3 hrs 43
San Foca	68.8	10.8	138	219	6 hrs 21

Notes

• Estimates shown in italics as data not recorded in diary. Some place names unknown.

The world at **8.9 mph** (averaged from averages). Still much slower than the 15 mph BUT I did also note a top speed of 45.7mph.

11.

MAPS AND BORDERS

"A map is the greatest of all epic poems. Its lines and colours show the realization of great dreams." (sic.)

Gilbert Grosvenor

(first editor of National Geographic)

Maps have a long history and broad interest. While we now often think of them in relation to journeys and travel, they can act as political and historical guides, provide inspiration for travel and adventure. They can highlight things to see and things to avoid. We can obsess about the details they hold or the space they contain. They provide connection and offer escape.

I've loved maps and books ever since I was a little girl. Even before homework was a thing, I would cycle to the library in the school holidays with a project in mind to research. I would often be found illustrating and fantasising over treasure island drawings – something about the unknown and a world yet to be discovered perhaps? Even to this day, while many head to online video, books are my 'go to' if I want to find out how to do something and investigate new ideas.

For me, travel abroad was not a childhood thing – flights and holidays abroad were more expensive then and my time would be spent in the family caravan in North Wales. Consequently, maps and geography in this sense were confined to school, to books, and to the tales of others. Looking back, it seems like a very different world with foreign travel now much more accessible. As costs changed, and I grew older my interest in visiting other places often aligned with that of learning of other cultures and ways of life. Having completed a master's degree in Buddhist studies, Southeast Asia was a part of the world I was super keen to explore.

I'd read on various cycle forums that Southeast Asia was a great area to start for independent cycle touring abroad though with visa rules, border crossings and places of interest to take into account there was much to consider. I think it was these logistics that meant it was the part of the tour I enjoyed planning the most.

We would fly into Singapore. As a global flight hub, travel costs were good and landing here would position us well for three months of exploration. We planned to visit Malaysia, Thailand, Vietnam, Cambodia, and Laos too – it was a map lover's dream. Investigating border crossings and navigating routes through multiple countries without the flight in between was different to many of our other five-month trips. While border crossings were a common feature of our ride through Africa we were of course on an organised tour. I would not have to research which crossing points were suitable for international tourists or consider VISA requirements and restrictions. However, as I started looking into the next stage of our world, I knew I was going to relish the complexities - little did I know that understanding borders would remain a research item even as we made our way through this 2,000 plus miles journey.

Having landed in Singapore we opted for a rather posh hotel by our usual standards - The Concorde. While our airport transfer was included it quite an expensive way to start the trip and we would have to adapt to our more regular accommodation standards as we continued. As per normal we spent a few days sightseeing - botanic gardens, Little India and as is customary, a visit to the highest point for views.

However, as with our arrival in America, we had itchy feet. Bikes assembled, photo taken with the hotel manager for their monthly magazine, and we were off. We left the city in a torrential downpour and the wet weather continued all day. While soaking, it was still very warm. We were hoping we had missed monsoon season, and this wouldn't be a daily occurrence and while not quite daily we did get more and more used to riding in hot yet rainy conditions.

Singapore is of course a very small country – with much of it resting on reclaimed land so to say all our riding through Singapore was in the rain is not actually as bad as it sounds, and the roads were impeccably clean as we made our way towards the border. The Singapore-Malaysia border is one of the busiest in the world with 350,000 people crossing at the Woodlands Checkpoint, the route we had also taken. We passed through with ease as we made our way to our first port of call in Malaysia, Pontian.

Malaysia - if I'm honest – is another country I knew little about and while enthused about my Buddhist inspired trip, we would first be riding through a predominantly Muslim country (around 60%). That said, it wasn't strict in its approach, so I wasn't too anxious about covering up. The usual sarong was available were it required and if getting off the bike to visit sites of interest - whether religious or not – I often preferred to wear a sarong than simply be in the bike lycra.

For the first few days in Malaysia there was it seemed little really of interest. We mostly followed route five up the West coast, surrounded by rubber plantations. While scenery was perhaps underwhelming, we were made to feel so welcome. Whether to practice English or buy us a hot or cold drink, the people were as sweet as the coffee, where in Malaysia it was made with condensed milk. Rocket fuel! One old guy on his scooter had just waved at us yet paid the bill without us even knowing. Why is it the people with the least can often be the most generous?

By the fourth day we'd arrived in Melaka. Historically, this was a town that had grown rich from trading in spices and textiles and was once an affluent place. Having also been taken over by the British, Dutch, and Portuguese the buildings also reflected a real coming together of food and architecture. However, the thing I was perhaps most taken with were the heavily decorated rickshaws. They were covered in lights and fake flowers and while I never did quite get round to fitting the lights, I purchased I could really see The Captain in a new Malaysian outfit. Well, I'd attached bright pink flowers in Ethiopia and stickers and flowers and India – why not add a few LEDs?

The lights would have been handy as it happened. As we reached a 20,000 km mark (it was quicker to get to these big numbers in kilometres) we were heading into Kuala Lumpur (KL). The rain was heavy, and visibility was low. The route we were following ran parallel to a 5- lane motorway, that is, until it flooded, and we were forced onto an alternative path. While a diversion that took us on a more convoluted route may have been frustrating it would have been safer than the option we had – yep – the 5-lane motorway! Jeepers. The sky was grey, buckets of water were pouring from the sky and while the hard shoulder was wide crossing the junctions were the cars left or joined the road were somewhat treacherous. I'd pedalled hard to win my stage race on the Africa tour, but I still think the pedalling required to survive here was my top effort so far. It had to be.

We were looking forward to a day off in the capital city and had also arranged to meet Alexander and Andy. Alexander had also paid his deposit for the original World Cycle Challenge, just like John and I way back in 2011. Having kept in touch with a few of the original sign-ups it was brilliant to then meet up with one of them on our adventure. It always offers the opportunity to consider what other friends we could have made though of course as one door shuts another one opens; we were now doing our own epic adventure instead. Funny how life turns out.

There were lots of things to see in Kuala Lumpur and as well as seeking out the high point again, this time the Petronas Towers. We would take sticky walks through the Botanic Gardens, take in another China town, and wander through the shops and markets. We'd opted to book a tour here, as we did with many places we visited. With what was often just one day to see what most tourists would take a few days to cover it was always a bit of a mission. I'm aware many on cycle trips maybe don't bother whether due to cost or simply the fact that this isn't their key focus, but we definitely took the tourist part as seriously as the riding. We were visiting countries to which we may never return, and we wanted to absorb all we could. Our day off done we would be back on the road the next day, calling in at Batu Caves some eight miles from the city too. As well as being a great site to visit - batu is the Malay word for 'rock' and here were a series of caves and Hindu shrines built into the limestone hill. We will also remember it once again for incredible hospitality as we were treated to breakfast. It stood us well for the busy roads – fuel for the legs and brain.

We were still slowly making our way up through Malaysia and in the few days following Kuala Lumpur we would come across the usual cyclist wildlife challenges – dogs. One day we were chased by dogs six times though it would be the first time I would see a big snake in the middle of the road. I wasn't sure if a quick squirt from the water bottle was the right thing to do here so avoidance seemed a much better option. Sadly, it's a little harder to swerve the canines! The dogs however were not my main problem. I was on my period and with padding already present in my cycle shorts and high humidity I needed tampons – something we often take for granted. Alas, my luck was not in and there were none to be had. I was running very low and there is only so long one can make them last. I was crossing my fingers for the following day and thankfully, just as we were leaving Lumut, a reasonable size town I would finally find the tampons I now so desperately needed.

With me sorted, John was not so lucky. His saddle had snapped, rendering the bike unusable. An emergency fix was required. Thankfully, we were fortunate to be in a place where a replacement could be sort it was not quite the match to the now well settled in Brooks. The next few days were a painful ride for my companion. We needed a longer-term strategy and a quality bike store.

Lumut is known as the main gateway to Pangkor Island – our next destination. We were meant to have a rest day bit not wanting to miss out I thought a short ride round the island might be fun. It wasn't. The replacement saddle John had was just not up to the job. We only rode 20 miles or so, but it had not been pleasant. We would have another 125 miles to ride yet to see us into Penang, where online research had identified the bike store we were counting on. They sold Brooks saddles and after a few days in agony, I was hoping the new seat would make all the difference, I remember only too well from my first days in France just how tough it can be without the right kit. Penang itself was a fabulous place and somewhere I'd love to return to. Great food, places of interest and with great streets and shops to explore. One place we loved wandering round was an old antiques store. Full of antiquities including a huge ancient boat we were surrounded by solid furniture and huge sculptures. John and I listed all we would carry back for the other, each selecting the heaviest and most awkward item we could see. It was a joke that had started with the huge stone carvings in India and continues to this day.

We had just a couple more days here in Malaysia before we entered Thailand. Having planned the route, we were getting the ferry to Kuah on Langkawi Island and from there into Satun, Thailand, It sounded straight forward and indeed it was. The impact of coming into Thailand this way would affect our trip at a later date but as we were currently unaware of the issues it would cause and were heading to the hotel we'd booked, right on the beach. It sounded idyllic and indeed the back of the hotel did walk straight onto the sand, but the front was a building site. Oh well. Day off and tourist attractions once again crossed off the list (bat caves, crocodile farms and cable cars) we made our way back for the Thailand ferry. Almost into Kuah we came across a large group of cyclists, the Associated Cyclosportif Trekkers (ACT). They had all been taking part in a local race and we were all keen to hear about each other's adventures. We spent the afternoon chatting, watching their awards ceremony, and helping them eat the buffet as part of the celebrations. A great way to close our last day in this very welcoming country.

As someone who loves new things and delights in change, crossing borders is always exciting. Of course, there is a sadness for the things you may miss about a particular country but new food, different cultures and often even a changing landscape always means I wake raring to go on these days. There are more than 20 land border crossings in and out of Thailand though as I started planning routes throughout Southeast Asia it was clear that this required careful planning. Some border points were not available to UK Passport holders and others were trickier crossing points from a security perspective.

The ferry from Langkawi Island to Satun was quick and a pleasant journey, unlike immigration which seemed to take forever and was not as we had hoped. Even with my meticulous planning, and assessment of borders, I had made a critical error. Having expected a 30-day visa it seemed that by crossing into Thailand on foot, or should I say, bike, we were only eligible for a maximum of 15 days. It was a significant disappointment and meant that we would be back to the drawing board to assess routes and options moving forward. Fifteen days was not enough time to get through Thailand and into Laos on bicycles al one and I would very quickly need to formulate a new plan. Immigration offices were closed, and with our time already curtailed, we could not simply stay here for an additional night. We pushed on to Pak Bara, our first night's stay. It was time to look over maps again.

While we could have looked to extend our visa, we were also of course conscious of the trip through Southeast Asia as a whole. Having taken two weeks to travel up from Singapore, we were already under pressure in our three-month tour if we wanted to ride through Laos, Vietnam, and Cambodia too. In the end we decided to use the train a little, doing as we had in India and prioritising riding in the areas where we also wanted to visit places of interest.

Guidebooks consulted, we decided that we would continue to make our way on the bikes up towards Hua Hin and it was at that point we would ditch the cycling. Riding in towards big cities is never the easiest and having already found ourselves on the motorway into Kuala Lumpur we didn't want a repeat of that particular experience.

From Pak Bara we would stop off at Trang and Pak Meng before riding on to the more popular resort of Krabi. For all we were looking to see key attractions, we are not big beach or resort focused people. For us, one of the real joys of bicycle touring often comes from riding through the towns and villages that are not visited by so many foreigners. Here we found both the food and the people somehow more authentic. Krabi had all we liked in a place to stay. It had a choice of eateries and places to drink where we could stay as part of a town rather than simply a tourist report. It was a great place to end up, in contrast to our journey thus far, which we'd been finding a bit of a challenge.

After leaving Pak Bara we had wanted to stay in Palian, around 50 miles ahead. On the map this was a town that looked big enough to have places to stay. We'd planned to stay next to the beach and, having asked for directions, then found only one hotel. It was way past our budget. Plans changed again and we knew we would have to head inland towards the next big town – Thrang. It was roasting and we now had another 25 miles or so to go. But we had no choice. For all the pouring over routes these are some of the challenges of travelling by bike. It was tough going and having opted to stop for a cheeky beer as we were approaching Palian we had made it even harder on ourselves. It had seemed such a good idea at the time too!

From Trang we were determined to be back at the beach – we were in Thailand after all. This time we pre-booked, but we wished we hadn't. Despite still being very hot and humid, this was one of those times when we would have chosen to ride on. Having only ridden 29 miles that day we were now faced with a long, few hours in a tourist hotel – far away from the town. We would soon learn not to book a 'resort' hotel again. The food is never as good, always costs more and you're often surrounded by holiday makers who just want to get drunk. My idea of a nightmare. Thankfully we had just one night here and while we were not surrounded by exuberant cocktail drinkers, we were disappointed by the location, struggled to taste any chilli in the food, paid a lot (comparatively speaking for our beer) and found the experience of being in a tourist mecca, off-season, even more depressing. Thank goodness for an amazing sunset. You can always rely on nature though as we sat gazing at the sky, we hoped our journey through Thailand would improve. We were working hard on the bikes each day but finding the destinations very underwhelming until our time in Krabi.

With good wi-fi and plenty to do we opted to stay in Krabi for a couple of nights. We joined a rather hectic Phi Phi island boat tour and the following day enjoyed subsequent relaxation on the island of Railay – a stunning place and somewhere I would love to return. We'd been cycling through limestone hills as we travelled up from Satun, but it was here in Railay where craggy rock formations and hidden caves providing such a dramatic showcase. Despite been known as a global climbing destina-tion, we opted for lunch on the beach and took the chance to take some cheeky photos at the Princess Cave (Thram Phra Nang). Adorned with phallus shaped carvings, given as offerings from local fisherman, legend notes that the cave was inhabited by an Indian princess following storms in the 3rd century BC.

Exploring over, we caught the longboat back to Krabi. Since the wi-fi was good and we'd opted to stay a couple of days I'd now booked us on a bus and train up to Hua Hin, cycle to Phetchaburi and then head from there, still on our bikes, into Bangkok. The roads into the city were a bit of a risk but we also didn't want to constantly be loading bikes onto trains and we 'd already decided that to fit inside our 15 days we would catch the train out of Bangkok instead. The visa restriction has meant we had needed to completely rethink this section of our ride. Still, at least we would be returning to the city for our flight home at a later date.

We arrived in Hua Hin station early in the morning. There was much to see here, and we set about crossing off the things to do from our list. In the early 20th century, the four-hour train journey between here and Bangkok was seen as a transport revolution. Used then as a place to retreat from the heat of the capital, Hua Hin is now a real blend of city and seaside town. From fancy modern shopping centres with global stores, to traditional markets and our favourite, a funky new arcade with a strong art and boutique. I'll also always also remember this as the place of the roast dinner. While my usual position is always to eat local food the lure of traditional British fodder on this occasion was just too much as was the pull to visit the Hua Hin Hills vineyard. Thai wine was a surprise to us but the professional set up and excellent food pairing made for a great change from the usual attractions.

As well as returning to the traditional Thai food, our next stop, Phetchaburi, would also see us back on the cultural trail. Known for its historic temples, this town, south of Bangkok, was a brilliant stop off point. We only had the afternoon to explore here but having packed in a few caves, some temples, and a palace we raced around town with our tuk-tuk driver. Once again, my meticulous planning was foiled. Having studied the guidebook carefully based on distances and closing times I'd handed the driver a chronological list of places to visit which he promptly ignored. Oh well – we can only try.

The next morning, we were ready to make our way into Bangkok. John had planned a careful route from google maps and with around 85 miles to ride and complex navigation, we decided to cheat and found a tuk-tuk willing to take us and our gear a little way up the road. We'd booked a hotel in Bangkok near Hua Lamphong station. Our next cycle skip was a train to Nong Khai on the Laos border and having navigated this mega city once we did not want to keep testing our navigational skills. That said, we were grateful that despite some of the roads being wide and busy, there was always a safe place to cycle.

Of course, there is much to see in Bangkok, but our visas were against us and given we were coming back this way to fly home we chose to stay just one night and then head off again. Fortunately, we did find the time for John to buy a new handlebar camera. His last one had broken during the Phi Phi island bike trip – seemingly the camera was not quite as waterproof as it claimed. Throughout the trip we'd both had a good camera for day trips and pivotal shots as well as a point and shoot. John had become quite adapt at cycling one handed and getting pictures on the go – something he wanted to continue, and we knew Bangkok was our best chance at finding a replacement. Task completed we were ready for our next country and our next border.

The Thai Lao Friendship Bridge spans 1,174 metres, stretching over the Mekong river and takes you from Nong Khai to Vientiane, just 15 miles past the border control on the opposite side. We'd made it out of Thailand just in time and were excited to explore another country, one that to date sees many less visitors. Despite being the most bombed country in history (Indochina war) and Vang Vieng being known more recently as a backpacker party and drugs capital, we found Laos peaceful offering dramatic scenery in a tranquil setting. Unlike Thailand we had a 30-day visa, however, having looked at the landscape and read about the places we wanted to visit while we were here, we would once again need to lose the bikes a little to fit in all we wanted to see. Once again, I was route planning and while looking at options we would take the time to explore Vientiane and take advantage of the French influence here. We would take a particular focus on the great bakeries, prominent throughout the capital.

Once again, we had pre booked our accommodation, something we often did when arriving at a city. It gave us a location to aim for and, in the case of the accommodation we had chosen here, Villa Lao, it lay around 1 mile from the centre. Noted as 'our pick' in the guidebook, the accommodation consisted of two large traditional houses set in a compound and described as the most atmospheric budget place in Vientiane'. For once the guidebook was spot on and with the slightly out of town location and subsequent space available it proved just the right place for leaving our bikes, and much of our kit, for a few days while we ventured north.

I'm sure as you're reading this, you're wondering what has happened to the cycle tour? It seems like since entering Thailand we'd needed to use other transport much more than we'd ever intended. I guess the main lesson here is not to try and cycle Southeast Asia in just three months. We certainly wished we'd had longer.

The landscape of Laos can briefly be summarised by the mountains in the North to the lowlands in the South. With time pressures once again influencing our journey we opted for the bus in the North where climbing would take much longer and cycling in the south. For our Northern trip, we'd booked the bus to Luang Prabang, an overnight journey which it's fair to say John found far from comfortable. At 6 ft 2 the overnight sleepers are not made for the taller Westerner, and he vowed he would be avoiding this method of travel for the rest of the trip. We'll see, eh?

We arrived at Luang Prabang at 5:30am, just in time to see the monks on their daily alms trail. It was something I'd read much about but had never witnessed. Too often, many religious institutions seem to have found new ways to skip tradition and even demonstrate behaviour which seems contrary to key beliefs and teaching. I was delighted to watch the saffron clad monks make their way towards the temple. Observations over, we needed to find somewhere to stay, dump our gear and get some food.

Luang Prabang is stunning. The buildings are immaculate, it's spotlessly clean and while no one building stands out as the key attraction, the former royal capital, and now UNESCO World Heritage Site, boasts a magnificent glory. We were so glad we came even if we hadn't cycled here. We took our time visiting the palace and local temples, eating in fabulous restaurants, and walking down to the river. Luang Prabang sees both the Nam Khan and Mekong River meet, with a variety of cafes and eateries designed to take in the atmosphere. The town has a quiet and laid-back feel and we certainly felt like we were resting even if our first day here finished with a walk up Cholsey Hill, the key vantage point to take it all in. We had a second day here too and this time took a boat-trip to take in caves, waterfalls and watch local silk makers. The tour ended with a trip to a swimming lagoon, and while we didn't partake it really was incredible to take in all that was on offer here.

The next morning, we were back on the road – still on the bus, as we made our way to Vang Vieng. The guidebook noted that the journey would take six to eight hours despite being just over 100 miles away. We were in for another long, and possibly uncomfortable ride! As it turns out the bus was okay and around five hours later, we had arrived. The journey had fled by. There was so much to see, the scenery, with its limestone mountains all around was such a joy but we know would have been quite the ride on two wheels.

I already knew Vang Vieng had a reputation as a bit of a party town with hash and opiates available should you desire. It's not our thing so we opted to give that a miss - much more interested in the adventure tourism on offer. That said, caving is out for me, as is climbing. We tried a bit of tubing down the river but the part we really enjoyed was the cycle trip. Yes, we hired two bikes. While we could have walked, we simply wouldn't have covered so much ground and we only had a short time here. The mountain bikes came with a guide and the trip was expected to take much of the day. The trip was just over 20 miles as we took in a few villages, a cave, and the river, where this time we did swim while the guide prepared lunch. We got back an hour and a half earlier than planned – I think we broke the guide. While we'd had a few days off The Captain and Kylie I guess we were pretty cycle fit. Perhaps we should have warned him?

On our second day we took a trip out to more waterfalls, opting for a more relaxing day before our last bit of adventure tourism. We could have just taken the bus back to Vientiane from here, but I'd had a different idea – kayak. The trip we'd booked included four hours of kayaking before a final bus transfer back to the city. It was not what we'd hoped. Having made our way through some minor rapids we stopped for lunch, expecting more to follow. However, after 20 minutes or so we were told the trip was complete. Finito. We were not impressed and even I made my disappointment apparent.

Seeing how disappointed we were our guide got us back in the water for another 20 minutes or so but then that was it. I think their timing must also take into account the waiting – the next part of our 'adventure'. Having booked the kayak and bus transfer through a tour company our expectation was that we would be on a bus similar to the coaches we had travelled on so far through Laos. How wrong could we be. We were dumped at the local bus stop where the non-air-conditioned bus, complete with chickens, took us most of the way back to Vientiane. We were dripping with sweat and transferred to an overcrowded tuk-tuk for the final part of our journey. It's fair to say we were not happy. The bus itself is not a major issue – while we were cramped and overheating, we have used plenty of local transport on our travels. However, we had not paid the local bus rate and soon complained to the company involved. A refund was offered, and we continued with our trip. No regrets, but we were glad to be getting back on with our bike tour.

The road out was pretty flat as we stopped in at a local sculpture park and took time to eat melon from a lady selling fruit on the side of the road. It was so refreshing and a welcome break from the muddy route we found ourselves on. While it's always nice to travel through on these quieter paths, we were pleased to see the main road that day and very much enjoyed our traditional noodles and steamed veg as we settled at Thabok for the night.

We were away early the next morning, doing our best to avoid the hottest parts of the day and had decided to ride on a while before stopping for breakfast. It was nearing 9 am when we spotted what we thought was a local shop and restaurant. Out front we were met by a group of women who encouraged us to stop with their smiles, giggles, and sign language. They were already on the Beer Lao and while they were keen for us to join them in a drink it was a little early for us to be on the booze. Food was our key concern and we joined in the sign language game to enquire. Soon enough we were given rice, veg and strong, strong coffee. We also left with big grins, satisfied with our food, though we're still unsure to this day whether we had in fact eaten their packed lunches rather than a restaurant meal.

Our route followed the Mekong, and we passed by numerous stalls selling dried fish. We were enjoying the flat and relatively easy riding. It was a chance to build up energy for the climbing we knew lay ahead as we made our way towards Vietnam. We were heading to Na Hin as the gradients changed. It was pouring with rain as we made progress though the incredible Laos landscape. It was brilliant to be back on the bikes even if we were cold and drenched on our arrival. Showered and dry we set out to visit the bakery we'd read about in the guidebook. We were really enjoying this part of the journey – food, people, scenery – all the ingredients for a brilliant trip and we had one more stop at Lak Sao before crossing the border.

The Nam Phao/Cao Treo border is just over 20 miles from Lak Sao where we had opted to spend our last night in Laos. We'd chosen to cross here given that we wanted to visit Hanoi, in Vietnam and while there was a border slightly further north, we'd opted for a place that avoided unexploded bomb debris and had sufficient facilities for somewhere to stay, given other crossing zones were described as lonely and with little accommodation etc. However, it seemed this had not been a good option and the decision would put us back on to the incredibly uncomfortable overnight buses we had vowed never to use again. Passing diggers, bull dozers and excavators, the mud had fallen on the road, which they were obviously now trying to keep open, An older man on a motorbike kept waving at us as we cycled on. The gradient increased and we continued to climb before we made our way to the offices where our passports would be stamped.

Having handed our passports over the guards seemed to disappear. Always anxious of losing sight of our official documentation, we were told to wait. We waited. And waited. Eventually, after 30 minutes had passed by, I tried to find out what was going on. No-one spoke English and we were struggling to communicate. There are some situations when sign language is not so easy, and this was one of them. Fortunately, mobile phones and online translation apps were becoming more common and as our passports were returned, with a shaking head, we were shown a picture of a landslide. The border was open to pedestrians only. Ever hopeful, we gestured that we could carry our bikes, but they were having none of it. Perhaps we should have shown them photos from our Nepal adventures?

Powerless in the situation, we had no option but to return to Lak Sao where once more I would research maps and options. If we cycled to a different border, then we would not have time to go to Hanoi. The overnight bus was our only option, though first we would need to make our way to the main transport interchange at Thadket. I'm not sure if my map skills or ability to utilise public transport was becoming a new required essential, either way we had a solution.

Bike, luggage, and ourselves loaded, we were on a jeep. The small bench seats were enclosed under a low caged roof. The roads were bumpy, and John's head kept bouncing on the ceiling. It was not what we had hoped for. I enjoyed the buzz of border crossings on a bicycle – there's something about the freedom you feel to just head off at your own pace, leaving the queues and crowded buses behind. The ride down to Vinh had sounded brilliant and a great reward from the uphill, yet we would now find ourselves on a very crowded bus. We arrived weary into Hanoi. It was 5:30 am and we had been on buses now for just under 24 hours, but we were here and despite the detour we had arrived in on the day we'd originally scheduled. It was time to explore a new country.

I'd cycled through Vietnam before around 10 years earlier as part of an organised cycle holiday. It had been amazing, and I was happy to return. There is so much to explore in Hanoi, and from here we would also have the chance to do another boat trip around the world nature heritage site, Halong Bay. We took our time to visit the sites, walk and relax by the lake and meander through the shopping streets and markets as well as booking our boat trip and planning the next part of our adventure. While the cruise we were on looked nothing like the brochure – another tour company oversell - there is no denying that the scenery of the bay is still fitting of a James Bond movie. It was busier than my first visit, something that I would notice as we continued to travel through Vietnam, but certainly no less spectacular.

I'd like to say our cycle tour was then back on but once again, having ploughed over our itinerary, we were back on the overnight bus. It feels like such a cheat as I write this, but I hope will act as a useful guide for anyone else planning a cycle tour here – you need to come for longer! Its perhaps also worth noting that while we we're not pedalling, we were not travelling in luxury either. The bus was overcrowded, there was luggage everywhere, the toilet was disgusting, and we arrived four hours late. Bags were quickly dumped, and we jumped in a taxi to visit Paradise Caves. One of the largest dry caves in the world they have only been open since 2011. We had pre booked a special tour that went beyond the cave's main barrier just over a mile in and we were kitted out with army fatigues and boots. The caves went on for some 20 miles and the usual trip also includes a boat ride. However, storms in the past few weeks, the evidence of which we had seen on our way here, meant the water levels were too high. Despite this we were not disappointed. We trudged on through mud, waded through rivers, and ducked under low ceilings before sitting by a small lake for lunch. It was perhaps one of the most unusual places I have ever sat down to eat – a real unmissable experience. Well, mostly unmissable. Unfortunately, the boots John had borrowed fell apart during the trek and he had to complete much of the walk in his bare feet. It seemed whenever we swapped the bikes to become tourists, it still came with an air of adventure.

The next day we were back on the bikes, heading to Dong Ha, with another underground stop on the way. This time we were visiting the Vinh Moc, an extensive tunnel system where around 90 families hid and lived during the Vietnam war. Set over three levels we followed our guide who gave us a real insight into life in the tunnels while bombs fell overhead. Trips to countries and places like this are always offer a solemn reminder and make us realise just how fortunate we are. Sadly, war would be a common theme of our tour here. Humbled, we set off again and the next day we would be in Hue.

Hue is a beautiful city, situated on the Perfume river and a place of great historical significance. We took our time taking trips on the river and walking through the enclosed Citadel. The temperature and humidity were something else though and as we walked around, dripping with sweat, we eventually conceded to a cycle rickshaw. How someone else could pedal us around in this heat was something else and up until the point the driver tried to scam us (claiming we'd given him fake notes) we were quite sympathetic towards him.

Alas, increased tourism does sometimes bring this behaviour and while it was not something we had encountered much of on the bikes, we were more likely to experience it in larger tourist zones. In some ways one may say the real joy of cycle touring is the time spent outside of these areas, but John and I had always wanted to be tourists as much as we were cyclists. However, having just concentred predominantly on the attractions, the next days would be all about the ride.

We left Hue, heading towards the Hai Van Pass, made famous in the BBC programme, Top Gear's Vietnam special. It would be the toughest ride day of our Vietnam tour and having ridden the pass on my previous tour here, it was, at that point in my life, the toughest, hottest, and most challenging ride I'd ever undertaken. That time I had been riding up the hill in the opposite direction, I had no panniers and there were a group of other riders cheering me on at the top. I remember watching cycle tourists on the road all those years ago; I thought they were mad, yet here I was about to do the same thing. Strangely, it was much easier than my previous attempt. Older, yet much fitter, I was beaming as we pulled in to admire the views from the 496-metre peak. The views out to sea from this Truong Son mountain range were fabulous as we made our way back down the hairpins on the other side. Our journey would end that day in Hoi An.

Hoi An is perhaps one of the better-known tourist destinations of Vietnam, described as 'Vietnam's most atmospheric and delightful town' this is one of the most affluent places here and since my last visit here there were now many more bars and restaurants forming a promenade along the river. The old town boasts historic merchant houses and tailors' shops, where made to measure clothing lure in the visitor, as well as the usual temples and pagodas. The incredible thing about wondering through this area is not just that houses have survived centuries but whole streets. Quite remarkable, given both the war and the fact that the area is prone to floods. At night, the buildings are lit up by colourful lanterns, reflected in the river and providing a stunning setting for an evening stroll. It's a must do and it's great to see the ongoing conservation work that continues here.

Having spent a couple of nights here we were up early, trying to avoid the worst of the heat as we made our way on the 80 mile or so ride to Quang Ngai. The route was flat as we passed numerous paddy fields – the sun shimmering on the water in the distance as we rode on by. This would be our last full ride day in Vietnam. We had a train booked into Ho Chi Minh City (HCMC) and from there our ride would take us into Cambodia. The train was indeed much more comfortable than the overnight buses we used thus far though as our bike had to travel on a separate luggage train, it was of course a relief to be reunited with them some two hours later. The roads into the city were some of the busiest we encountered. We were surrounded by scooters and as we stopped at junctions as required it felt very much like the race was about to begin. Having just arrived by train, our initial ride into the city was quite short. I was wearing my everyday sunglasses, not the sportier cycle ones and the shot of me among all the other riders while wearing my green heart shaped eyewear is still one of my favourite photos of our trip.

For me, I prefer the charm of Hanoi to the hustle and bustle of Ho Chi Minh City. Having renamed from Saigon, back in

1975 HCMC now generates around 25% of the GDP of Vietnam, blending the old and the new. For me, the thing I would most remember would be the trip to the War Museum. It was harrowing and we were unable to complete the full tour. One may wonder whether it's necessary to present the history in such a brutal way but if we need to be reminded of the cost of war, then this is a place that certainly does that.

We were not sad to leave the big city behind. Some may think the biking was exhausting and while it certainly could be - the time we spent in big cities, trying to fit in all the sites, were tiring for very different reasons. We were also really excited to be heading into our final new country of this tour, Cambodia.

The border between Ho Chi Min City in Vietnam and Phenom Penh, in Cambodia was once again a fascinating ride. The route out towards the main crossing into Cambodia was busier than our initial trip in from the train station and we would need to stay alert as we rode through the busy streets to our next border, Moc Bai. Despite warnings that this was a crossing that could see large queues, we soon completed the obligatory forms and handed over the cash and a photograph required for our visa.

Leaving the administration offices behind we pushed on – excited to be in a new country and a little nervous as we became accustomed to this new place. It was always a time to get used to new language, money, and dietary tweaks but as we cycled up what were now much quieter and even more deserted roads these were not the only changes on our minds. The road in Bevet was lined with casinos. In fact, it seemed that all we could see were large, fancy buildings surrounded by carparks yet at this time of day, still empty. It was weirdly unsettling and as we chatted, we noted that we were very much reminded of the border out from Sudan. Where Sudan had been a dry state and all we saw as we crossed into Ethiopia were bars and brothels, the Cambodians were targeting a different prohibition – gambling. Though rules had relaxed a little in more recent years, gambling was outlawed to the Vietnamese back in 1975. It's funny what borders can tell you about a country or neighbouring country though the immediate impact on us seemed to be that given the prominence of the gambling industry here there were no wee coffee stalls or places to stop. We were glad to turn off the main highway towards Svay Rieng where, as we checked in to our accommodation for the evening, we would also meet two other cycle tourists. We enjoyed exchanging stories and went out to get dinner. While our food had a great taste, I was slightly perturbed by the rats we spotted running around as we tried to eat. We would head to Phenom Penh the next day.

It was horrid. Not the city but the journey. I had the most horrific period pains, was low on energy and was struggling to push the pedals. At just over 5 miles we had to stop and rest, I wasn't sure I'd be able to make it, but we'd already booked a hotel in the city, and I hated to lose our money. We continued on our way, taking a small ferry where we would park up next to a man transporting a dead pig on the back of his boat. Eighty miles later and relieved to arrive, we showered though I'm afraid I had to go straight to bed, leaving John to eat on his own. It would be a day or so on plain rice for me, my exhaustion it seemed was not just down to my period after all. I guess the rats had been a clue!

Feeling slightly better the next day we went to explore. We had a pleasant day, wandering round the market and even enjoying a coffee in a well-known chain though the next day would not be quite so easy. The next few paragraphs are taken directly from my blog which sought to capture the history and our feelings around it at the time.

"Just outside Phnom Penh, the capital of Cambodia is an area called Choeung Ek. Nestled in among paddy fields, we rode down a bumpy, muddy track, passing children cycling to school and the usual hustle and bustle of village life. Our driver pulled in, under some trees and arranged to meet us there in two hours' time. We had decided to visit what in essence was a scene of great brutality. Around 17, 000 people (men, women, and children) were brought to this extermination camp from a prison, known as S-21, where they had already been held and tortured.

While much of the site infrastructure (waiting rooms, tool stores etc) have long since gone, mass graves are clearly marked, and a chilling audio guide leads you around. Steadfast on a communist ideal whereby cities were destroyed, and peasant farming and manual labour were the standards being set to bring equality to all the Khmer Rouge led a war of unimaginable proportions. Teachers, foreigners, anyone who spoke more than one language, those who spoke up against them, took rice or belongings from the collective pool or it seemed anyone even with a vague association to any of the former were simply removed. While the exact figure is unknown estimates are as high as 3.5 million deaths (half the population). 8595 bodies were exhumed; at Choeung Ek in 1980 and as you wonder through what is now a quiet memorial site, clothing remnants, bones and teeth that continue to rise to the surface each year as rain disturbs the ground are displayed.

Thankfully, those arriving at the site were unaware of their fate. They didn't use bullets here but bludgeoned people to death and the audio guide played loud vitriolic songs that were blasted out alongside the noise of the generator to cover up the sounds of people screaming as they were killed. I couldn't listen to the audio. They had done too good a job of stimulating the noise of the environment. One grave housed many bodies that had been beheaded – thought to be soldiers who had raised objections - and the site marked a tree where babies heads were thrashed before being discarded. Again, the audio was turned off. It was too much for me.

In 1988 the Memorial Stupa was built on the site. In essence, a narrow tower, ten stories high displaying the skulls and bones of some eight thousand people. I had not been sure whether to visit The Killing Fields. The War Museum in Saigon had also been vivid in its portrayal of the Vietnam War, and I saw only enough there to understand. Nothing is masked here. I had been ignorant of the full extent of the torture Pol Pott had inflicted and while The Killing Fields was far from being a pleasant experience this is history; I am now much more aware of."

So that was Phenom Penh and I'm pleased to say the next day was much more jubilant as people took to the streets to celebrate independence. The streets were busy as we rode out, leaving the city behind us. One of the other consequences of the Pol Pott regime was that much of the transport infrastructure had been ripped out. There would be less options to catch up on days by using trains here. We needed to get going.

The key site we wanted to see while in Cambodia was Ankor Wat. Situated just outside Siem Reap we would have a five-day cycle before arriving stopping in at Udong, Skuon, Kampong Thom and Dom Dek. While Udong was a former capital and Skuon is better known for its spider eating delicacies there was not a vast amount to see and we were very much focused on getting to our key destination of the Cambodia tour. In many ways it was like arriving at the treasure I used to draw on maps as a child. The secret place, hidden for hundreds of years.

We passed by the usual paddy fields, looked on at buffalo grazing and, in our usual way, we stopped in at numerous eating holes for snacks, meals and coffee. Our favourite breakfast in a while would come as we pulled into the Sister Sray café in Siem Reap. We ate baked beans, sausages, bacon, and poached eggs that were perfect. It was heaven and just a few hundred metres from our accommodation.

We had been keen to organise our few days here and not just rock up. Known as one of the greatest ancient sites of the world we were keen to make the most of our visit. Ankor Wat gained UNESCO World Heritage status back in the 90s and this religious site (Buddhist and Hindu) dates to the 12th century. The complex spreads over a vast area (around 400 acres) and, is now in part overtaken by overgrown trees and other subsequent dilapidation. The site has been used as a backdrop for numerous films, most notably Tomb Raider. In reading the guidebook we'd become interested in the photography tours listed, signing up for two days with Kimleng Sang. Kimleng was a local tuk-tuk driver who'd shown a keen interest and natural flair in photography with a Canadian tourist some years prior. Having been gifted tripods and high-end cameras he now ran these incredible tours and the next morning he would collect us at 530 am ready for a full day ahead.

There was no one around as we set off – we had just bridge cameras with us, cycle touring didn't allow for multiple lenses, and this had seemed a good compromise. Thankfully, having told Kimleng we were on a bike tour with minimal equipment, he was all set to let us try out his tripod. This, along with his practical advice on shutter speeds and local knowledge of locations and sunlight mean we still think our photos from this part of our tour are the best we have. It was money well spent and certainly rates as the best guided tour I have ever paid for. Incredible.

We'd had two full days touring the old ruins and before leaving also took the time to visit a stilted village not too far away. Based on Lake Tonle Sap we observed new vegetables with interest and looked on at the way fish and other food was presented. Living like this was very different to us - I wonder whether it's something we may all need to adapt to more with climate change. Sadly, I also think about the impact increased temperatures and rising water levels will have on these people and places. Sometimes we're just too removed from these impacts to make us really think about the behaviour change we need.

We were making good progress, stopping first in Sisyphon and then on to Battambang. For much of our trip through Southeast Asia we'd been conscious of making progress, never truer than our first ride through Thailand when the 15-day visa was a constant headache. It was a situation we were facing again. If we entered Thailand too quickly our visas would run out before the flight home. We were forced to slow down.

Despite never really intending to be here for a few days we found plenty to do and alongside the usual temples we also observed millions of bats heading out in formation from a cave we'd just explore, took a tour round a rather smelly fish farm, and visited a local acrobatic circus. Our favourite part however was the trip on the bamboo train. Much of the rail infrastructure had been removed by the Khmer Rouge but on this old track locals used an old, flat bamboo cart, known as a 'nori' to transport tourists and rice the short distance that remained. Powered by a small petrol engine the fragile cart reached 20mph when, on meeting another nori travelling the opposite way, it was quickly dismantled and rebuilt before continuing on its way. Brilliant fun though I think bike travel was less perilous and with one last day here in Cambodia we left Battambang and made our way to the final border. The paddy fields reduced in number and the landscape started to change again. We'd both really enjoyed our time here in Cambodia, despite some challenging 'tourism' and knew as we entered Thailand there would be much more of a holiday feel again.

With just a few days left of this section of the trip, and just a short time at home over Christmas before we were off again, John and I had decided to end our last days here with a bit of beach time - taking in one of the beautiful islands Thailand is always so famous for. Ko Samet wasn't quite as picturesque as we'd imagined but we definitely felt like we were at the end of the tour.

Relaxed, yet on full alert, we proceeded towards Pattaya. We were on the motorway once again - something we'd encountered before on this trip. While we still had a few more days in Thailand this was our last cycle here. It was just so much easier getting bikes to an airport with the help from friends. Even with a now well-rehearsed routine every country we would fly home from was different and the opportunity for help was just too good to turn down.

We'd travelled through 6 countries, cycled over 2,000 miles and utilised taxis, coaches, trains and tuk tuks along the way. Never bored there was always something to enjoy in Southeast Asia – it was packed with history, food and culture, all visit but also to have researched prior to leaving. I'd poured over maps for general routes, but it can be hard to really know how exactly the riding will be between the destinations we were aiming for. Our trip through Southeast Asia had been the most interesting to decipher so far though I imagine our Africa tour could have been even more challenging, had we not been following a route someone else had planned.

I remember saying many years ago that maps can be deceptive. For anyone that's cycled Lands' End to John O' Groats you soon realise that the daily weather map we often see on the television hugely exaggerates the central area of the UK while making Cornwall and Scotland appear smaller. While I'm sure this is much more for practical, population and detail requirements than political motivation, it does just go to illustrate that a map is very much a subjective representation of the geography and land it sets out to describe. Travelling on a bike helps us get beyond this and as well as increasing our knowledge of the landscape we also too see the differences in culture, politics, and way of life either side of the immigration posts.

Boundaries are a strange thing really when we think about it. In our small worlds we are taught to share yet in the big wide world we draw a line around resources, countries seek power and trade -you're either in or out. Our lives so often determined in part by something we have no control over – our place of birth. It's always interesting too to see how maps and boundaries have changed over time. Indeed, even in writing this book some years after the trip our access into Europe has changed; talks continue around trade and boundaries and for the UK cycle tourist we are now limited by a 90-day restriction. I guess, if we ever want to do a pro-longed tour of Europe, we'll have to do some careful planning and learn our lesson from our first entry into Thailand.

The Stats; Southeast Asia
2,073.9 Miles

Destination	Total Distance	Average Speed	Metres Up	Metres Down
Singapore to Pontian	59.6	-	-	-
Batu Phahat	45.4	11.1	90	117
Muar	35.5	11.1	20	35
Malacca	27.5	11.2	85	103
Port Dickson	49	11.4	219	285
Banting	59.6	11.2	168	212
Kuala Lumpur	46.8	11.5	180	189
Batu Caves to Selangor	45.6	11.6	207	316
Lemut	64.2	13.1	20	39
Pankor Island Circular	26.6	9.9	208	196
Bhukit Pakr Resort	68.1	12.3	149	199
Georgetown	54.6	11.2	97	158
Langkawi	17.4	-	-	-
Island Ride	18.6	-	-	-
Pak Bara (Thailand)	45.4	-	-	-
Trang	82.1	11.7	266	356
Pak Meng	29	10.7	64	147
Krabi	69	-	-	-
Hoa Hin	(Train)	-	-	-
Bangkok	45.9	11.3	-	-
Nong Khai	(Train)	-	-	-
Vientiane (Laos)	16.1	-	-	-

Destination	Total Distance	Average Speed	Metres Up	Metres Down
Thabok	-	-	-	-
Pak Kading	61.3	11	91	114
Na Hin	57.3	8.8	495	582
Lak Sao	36.2	8.1	648	391
Lak Sao Border	40.4	-	-	-
Hanoi (Vietnam)	(Train)	-	-	-
Dong Hoi	(Train)	-	-	-
Vinh Mac Tunnel	74.6	-	-	-
Hue	42.9	12.4	19	51
Highway 1	56.2	9.8	137	180
Hoi Ann	46.1	9.3	423	451
Quang Nai	74.6	-	-	-
Ho Chi Min City	(Train)	-	-	-
Sueing Rian (Cambodia)	71	11.4	24	40
Phenon Phen	77.4	10.8	12	16
Udong	32.8	9.1	33	40
Skun	33.1	11.1	25	35
Kampong Thom	56.9	11.7	11	19
Tam Dek	71.7	12.3	13	15
Siem Reap	-	-	-	-
Sisyphon	65.5	12.6	34	43
Battambang	42.7	12	3	9
Paulin	53.6	11.4	138	134
Chantanaburi (Thailand)	54.9	12.2	305	545
Ko Samet	65.8	11.8	-	-

Destination	Total Distance	Average Speed	Metres Up	Metres Down
Pattaya	52.9	13.7	253	328
Bangkok	(Bus)	-	-	-

Notes

• Singapore (16.1 miles); Malaysia (602.4 miles); (Thailand (271.4 + 118.7 miles); Laos (211.3 miles); Vietnam (294.4 miles) and Cambodia (559.6 miles)

• We used public transport to make up time through Thailand, make the most of our trip in Laos and to get to Hanoi following border crossing challenges.

• As we cycled into Kuala Lumpur, we reached 20,000 km.

• 6 dogs were also noted as 'chased off' on the Lemut ride day – nothing a cyclist hates more!

The world at 11.2mph (based on an average of averages).

12.

LANDSCAPES

"To the complaint, 'There are no people in these photographs,' I respond, There are always two people: the photographer and the viewer."

Ansel Adams

(landscape photographer)

At the start of our journey, back on the USA leg, I talked greatly about being back in nature. Escaping the office, the computer and the daily tasks that so often take us away from time outside. We rode through amazing scenery with the Oregon coastline as a real standout. Indeed, in the places we have passed through since then we have of course ridden through a wide variety of places but if there are landscapes that really stand out it would have to be those of New Zealand.

There's something about landscapes that have always attracted artists, musicians, photographers, and poets, amongst others. The scale, majesty, and sheer beauty they offer can be overwhelming, and we felt hugely privileged to be part of the picture. I used the Ansel Adams quote to open this chapter for that reason. The scene around us was stunning and I can't even attempt to describe all that we could see. I can however say that something about the openness and the space which surrounded us seemed to instil the same internal headroom to think. The cogs of the mind turning in conjunction with the wheels on the bike. Just as nature evolves, so too does thought and I wonder if that is then perhaps one of the reasons why being *'plein air'* offers such inspiration, such freedom, and such creativity. Perhaps it sounds a little strange to some, but while riding I developed new ideas, sketched out books and stories - dreamt of wider possibilities. Consequently, I would often miss details of buildings, people and animals and I'm certainly grateful John kept a detailed blog.

We landed in Auckland on New Year's Eve. While keen to be at home for Christmas we both thought I might be fun to celebrate New Year in a completely different part of the world. The obvious spot would of course be Sydney but due to routes we wanted to take we decided instead to start this section of the tour in Auckland.

Our flight landed early afternoon and while joining New Year celebrations had sounded fun it's fair to say it was hard work after such a long journey. I had no fancy frock or heels; little make up and bags under my eyes. The celebration was not quite as I envisaged. We were tired, yawning and decidedly scruffy compared to everyone else around us. Restaurants were booked, dinner was hard to find and even bars were rammed to the gunnels. Having lived in Edinburgh for a few years, New Year, or as the Scots call it – Hogmanay was always a big night. Alas, I was far too tired for that here in Auckland. We managed a couple of beers and watched the fireworks, but I think were both utterly relieved when our heads hit the pillow.

I can't say we woke up 'fresh' the next day - we were now contending with jet lag – but we were excited to explore and meet up with the first of our Tour D'Afrique riders, Darragh. While he too had only recently moved to New Zealand, we were grateful to hear his thoughts on our route and plans for the next two months. As part of my planning for this part of the tour I'd ordered two books called 'Pedallers Paradise'. Available only through bookstores in New Zealand this two-part series provided valuable information on roads, accommodation, and gradients and as we considered this data alongside the more traditional traveller's guidebook, I'd soon worked out my usual overly ambitious schedule.

For those unfamiliar with the geography of New Zealand it comprises two main islands, handily named North and South. Auckland, the largest city, sits around one third of the way down the North Island. There are many beautiful bays further up the coast, but we did not wish to ride North first And then come back on ourselves so instead we opted for just a minor detour towards the Coromandel Peninsula.

By the time we left Auckland we'd been off the bikes for a few weeks, both in our last days in Bangkok, over the Christmas period and then for our first few days in New Zealand. We were fit by now but it's fair to say that our legs always needed time to adjust back to the regular routine of time on the saddle and our first few days here were no exception. The ride out was brutal and while we had planned to go further, we opted to camp some 20 miles earlier than originally planned. It was so hot, and the hills had felt tough going. We were back to camping on this tour and so unlike our last ride through Southeast Asia, our kit levels had also increased. We were fully loaded with tents, sleeping bags, cooking gear, clothes, and food.

The view over the rugged coastline was a joy to look at though we were beginning to wonder whether the extra tour or the peninsula was a good idea. Thankfully, this first ride day was the hardest. Our legs were soon back to speed and the pain of the first day would soon be forgotten.

While camp sites here did not follow the hiker-biker approach we'd got used to on the Pacific Coast Highway, camping in New Zealand really is a luxury. Many sites offering lounge areas and providing kitchen facilities for those of us under canvas. I suspect fear of fires from camp stoves was a key factor here. It was great to be able to hide from both poor weather and the insects, that seemed insistent on joining the dinner table. Shared facilities were also brilliant for speaking with others and while we didn't meet groups of cycle tourists there were always people interested in our tour. On occasions we were offered cakes and beer which I'm sure you know by now, will have gone down well with us both. This was particularly welcome here given our other main adjustment here was prices. While coffee stops were always in budget for us in places like Thailand and India, in New Zealand we needed to be a little more careful. It was why our next few days would be a real treat.

Having cycled to Tirau, just 160 miles so far, we were now being met by our friend Vince, another Tour D'Afrique rider. He'd arranged a hotel in Rotorua, a town famous for its swirling hot mud pools and geysers. Despite the rotten egg odour caused by the sulphur that pervades the air, this is a town famed for relaxation. It seemed like a perfect way to relax the muscles and while we took an early trip to the hot river at Kerosene Creek, Vince had other ideas brewing. Despite being a few years older than us both, Vince was invincible. In Africa he'd fallen off one day and dislocated his shoulder. For most normal people they would have rested but not Vince. Once pinned down and his shoulder popped back into position by four other riders he was back on his bike. By contrast, my approach to injuries had been to try and avoid them wherever possible though I was not sure how this would fit with all Vince had planned – mountain biking! Just what we needed!

The Whakarewarewa Forest has around 50 miles of single tracks, weaving through the redwoods, firs, and pines on a series of graded trails. Vince thought the red route was a good option and while I had ridden trails at this level back in Scotland (Glentress), I was always a bit of a wuss. Pushing round the sharp turns and carrying my bike past the jumps I eventually reached the bottom accident free. It was the slowest Vince had ever completed this track and while I'm sure he was a little frustrated with our speed, we were both delighted to have made it to the bottom. Even a minor fall could have jeopardised our New Zealand cycle tour and it was not a risk either of us were willing to take. We would be led astray by Vince on off road tracks again, nearer to his hometown of Wellington, but for now we were looking forward to being back on the tarmac. Road bikers and mountain bikers really are different breads.

After a day at the spa, Vince dropped us in the Art Deco town of Napier. Rebuilt, following an earthquake in the 1930's, the town now boasts boulevards based on old English seaside towns as well as banks, theatres and other buildings that have been preserved to celebrate the geometric styles of the past. We mooched about for a while but given it was a Sunday when we were there the town was very quiet. Back checking out the guidebook we opted for a short bike trip to Cape Kidnappers and the gannet colony there. The bikes felt so light without any gear on them, and we were beaming. Many would think a 17kg bike was still rather weighty, but I felt like I was flying. Alas, our trip the next day would be into headwind, back with our gear and under a raincloud.

We were on a main highway and while there was a small shoulder to ride on, we were finding cycling here in New Zealand pretty treacherous. People were so friendly when we stopped but behind the wheel, they were very different. Driving past at speed, hurtling abuse, and blasting their horns. Of all the miles our 'world at 15mph' trip took us on, this is the only country where we reported a driver to the police.

John and I continued our journey and while the weather remained wet and windy, we were enjoying the views and space around us. This tour seems in such contrast to the last chapter. Here in New Zealand tourism is all about the outdoors – the space, the hot springs, the birds, and there were far less 'places' of interest. We stopped at sheep shearing museums, model railways and later on our trip even looked in at the world largest knitted jumper. Of course, Maori culture comes with a long history but unlike the temple complex of Ankor

Wat or the pyramids of Egypt, there are not buildings to look at in the same way. Here, the landscapes really are the main attraction. Mauri culture has a strong affinity to nature and for me the land is everything I think of when I remember New Zealand. Well, that and the wine. We did of course stop off at a vineyard or two as well! It would have been rude not to.

It was probably a mistake to meet Vince again the day after wine tasting in Martinborough. He had joined us, along with another of our African comrades and, with an alternative, off-road route in store, we made our way towards Wellington. There were perhaps a few regrets about that extra glass the night before. Vince and Lindsay were leading us on a bike trail over the Rimutaka Incline where an old railway line climbed five or six miles over a gravel path, the total journey being around 11 miles in total. We had unloaded our gear, which Vince had taken on ahead, before then riding back to meet us. It didn't take him long and he was soon hurtling towards us even before we'd reached the peak. While we had a wee bit of pushing and lifting it was a brilliant day and after a short transfer, we were in Wellington. Drinks and barbeque followed, and it was brilliant to receive such a welcome. Thanks Vince and Lindsay.

Our short, North Island tour was over and while we know there would have been much more to see, we were really excited about the second part of our New Zealand tour. With Mount Cook, Abel Tasman National Park, and Milford Sound all ahead of us we knew we were heading to some of the world's most unspoilt national habitats.

The ferry over was choppy and 20 minutes in, the bar was closed. Glasses were sliding around, and several people were making use of the sick bags. Thankfully John and I were fine, and it was far too early for a drink from the bar anyway. We arrived in Picton, ready to make our way to Abel Tasman. The road around the coast, the fabulous Queen Charlotte Drive, climbed up over the hills where we took in the views over Pelorus Sound. This area of small bays and beaches is famous for its green lipped mussel farms and so we made sure to try the local delicacies while stopping for lunch. As we continued to make our way towards Havelock the road descended as we passed pine trees and logging tracks.

The next day we set off – our granny gears coming into play almost immediately as the road rose steeply before a brilliant descent, on good tarmac towards the ice cream shop. I would say it doesn't get better than that, but it did and soon we were chatting to Nelson locals, Kathy and Martin who offered us a bed for the night. We arrived to cold beers, another barbeque and use of the washing machine – always a much-valued machine when travelling with so little to wear.

The next morning, we continued to follow the coast, going around Rabbit Island and into Kaiteriteri where we planned to stay for a couple of nights. We'd opted for a cabin and as we lay in bed hearing the rain pelt down on the tin roof, we felt very pleased to have made that decision. We were perhaps slightly less excited now about our pre-booked kayak trip – the rain really was atrocious, and our guide soon called to let us know the trip was cancelled. We waited until the weather improved instead taking a shuttle bus then walking back round the coast. We watched seals and took numerous photos of the turquoise waters. What a place. We were sad not to have longer to explore but as is the nature of cycle touring, we needed to push on.

We would head inland again and as well as the roads marching uphill again, we also found ourselves riding off road and into headwinds. Stopping off in Tepawera and Merchison as we passed by a variety of fruit and hop farms. The ride towards Merchison, away from the tarmac saw us hit by fine drizzle, fine that was until it met the wind. We were climbing, on an unmade road, with heavy bikes and the rain hitting our faces so hard it hurt. The scenery had changed to one of desolation, dead and dying trees were all around us and we were unsure whether this was due to disease or was simply the remnants of previous logging work. Either way it was tough going - thank goodness we were heading towards hot water bathing at Maruia Springs and that we found egg and chips on our way there. Simple pleasures. Yumm.

When looking at route planning for this part of the tour two options that stood out were riding over either Arthurs Pass or the Lewis Pass. Perhaps John and I are a wee bit crazy but the reward of cycling over these roads is so worth the hard work and, as I keep coming back to, the views and vantage points are something else. Being on a bike also means we are often able to best take advantage of this – able to stop, take photos and simply absorb the scene in places were cars and buses would have to carry on. On first glance at the map, it looked like we could miss both these passes given time constraints and a desire to visit the West coast area. Having travelled this direction from Picton it would have probably made sense to stay on this side of the country. However, given John and I were not averse to using trains and always tried to balance cycling and touring in equal measure, I came up with an alternative plan. We would ride the Lewis path and use the scenic rail line back over Arthurs Pass to end up back in Greymouth. Genuis. I should have been a travel agent!

The Lewis pass would take us from Springs Junction to Hanmer Springs and on the way I had booked us into a Japanese style bathhouse. While we had of course experienced this first hand during our first five-month tour, it was still a luxury to sit out in the natural outdoor hot pools. Our route to this point, over the Maruia Saddle had noted the road was 'extremely narrow and winding with a rough surface. Four-wheel drive recommended, six stream crossings' and we can only agree with the statement. A four-wheel drive would certainly have made it much easier. Next time?!

We were due to meet another Tour D'Afrique rider, John, in Hanmer Springs but he was just as nuts as Vince and had also opted to park his truck at the bottom of the pass and cycle up to meet us. It was a great idea in theory but alas did not quite go as planned. He arrived, we hugged and then continued. However, with a snap of the chain and a broken derailleur our friend John was soon in trouble. He'd only ridden up to meet us and so was not carrying spares. While able to roll down the hills, the push upwards was taking far too long and we still a fair way to go. In the end, we carried on and had to leave our friend to try and call for help. Finally, with the aid of a local policeman, his friend Mark had been summoned for a lift. Oh, how it reminded me how grateful I was for hub gears and a belt drive.

We were pleased to be reunited and shared lunch in a local café (actually owned by the aforementioned friend, Mark) before we transferred to Rotherham and a day or so with John on his dairy farm. We were really enjoying meeting our new friends and the theme would continue on arrival in Christchurch.

Anne had been a great character in the African team, and we'd shared many a giggle during the Cairo to Capetown ride – particularly the naked ride through Namibia. While we had no such plans for this in Christchurch, it was great to share these memories once more. Once again, our cycle friend had planned a cycle ride - so much for the rest days! We continued recounting tales of our travels and African stories as more of the Kiwi African team joined us for dinner, including Vince who'd flown down from Wellington. Just brilliant. I talk about friends in the next chapter but its fair to say they were really making our New Zealand tour too. We chatted about the next part of the journey and before we knew it, we were back on our way again. It was time for the train ride over Arthurs Pass.

The Trans-Alpine Scenic Railway is listed as one of the top rail journeys in the world and I imagine on a clear day it would be. For us however, it was grey and misty. Despite this the views were still incredible, and the train was even equipped with an observation car so you could really take in everything around you. While easier on the legs though, it was not the same as being on the bike. We were no longer emersed in the scenery but simply passing through. Pleasurable yes but definitely not the same. Maybe we were more cyclists than tourists after all? The train ride took us to Greymouth where, following a quick trip to A and E for me (earache!), we would follow the West coast down through Hokitika and Hari Hari before facing the Fox and Franz Josef glaciers. Holy smoke. Now, when I talk about the landscapes of New Zealand this for us was where the drama really set in.

Set within the Westland National Park, Fox and Franz Josef glaciers stretch some 7-8 miles long, sitting between the peaks of the Southern Alps and the coast. They are the two largest and most well-known of the sixty or so glaciers that make up the protected area known also as *Te Moeka o Tuawe* and *Waiau* by the local Maori. Our first stop was at Franz and as we got closer, the white tops of the mountains were glistening, and the skies were true, sky blue. Riding the Glacier Highway really was something else and we were blessed to have such a glorious day. Having arrived early we thought briefly about doing a glacier walk but given we had this booked for Fox we opted instead to take a leisurely walk to Peter's Pool and cycle up to the foot of the glacier.

We had a few short but steep climbs the next morning but with only 15 miles to travel we left after a late breakfast. The last steeper climb took us to a spectacular viewpoint looking down over the glacier and surrounding town. We had three nights here, given we also wanted to do the glacier walk and once again had booked a cabin. Quite often the cabin was not much more than the two tent pitches and with day trips planned it was always reassuring to know our bikes and gear were safely stowed away while we were exploring. We'd chosen to do the glacier walk at Fox given the route on the ice starts from the side of the path meaning you reach the crevasses much sooner. We'd hired all the gear and as the route first set following the riverbed it was clear that our cycle shoes would have been even less suitable here than they were on the Annapurna circuit.

We were out for around seven hours in total, climbing up prepared steps the guides had carved out for us before setting off, peering down crevasses, staring at waterfalls and ice tunnels as well as settling down to eat our lunch. Sometimes on our trip we'd booked supported tours and been thoroughly disappointed but not this time. The next night we had cycled to Lake Paringa where the views were very different. There were so many sandflies at the camp than once our tents were pitched, we left them only to visit the toilet – even then every part of us was covered until there was little choice but to offer out our flesh for the wee beasties to bite on. Other than the days of the flies in Africa, I had only ever experienced this with midges in Scotland before. No wonder they often compare Scotland and New Zealand! Other visitors to this spot did offer us a nice cold beer and, while we will always be thankful to Tock and Tara, I'm afraid it's the flies we remember most.

The Haast Pass was next on our ride, which at 563 metres is the lowest road crossing of the Southern Alps. It was cold and wet when we set off on our way to Makarora. Sometimes the rain can be a relief and I think this would be one of those days. The first 35 miles or so were fairly easy going - rolling hills just enough to warm the legs up for the big climb. The rain had stopped but mist remained low, adding to the drama, and keeping the air cool for our ascent. It came fast. Passing over a small bridge and through the Gates of Haast the road suddenly become vertical. Already in low gears we pushed on, cheered, and encouraged by passing motorists. It was certainly better than the beeping horns we'd become so used to. Further up the climb there had been a rockslide at Diana Falls. The road had been reduced to single lane, traffic lights causing us to stop. Often on a climb we both preferred to just keep going but, in this case, it was a welcome relief.

Having compared New Zealand and Scotland on the basis of flies, its perhaps only fair to also say it's the geography that also plays a big part here. While we don't have active glaciers in Scotland today, they are thought to have played a significant role in shaping the landscapes we are now surrounded by. Glencoe is oft cited here and as we made our way towards Wanaka and Queenstown it was so reminiscent for me of riding over Rannoch Moor as part of the trip to John O'Groats. Long climbs up to plateaus and open land. Few people, with little infrastructure, other than the road that passed through. The road from Makarora to Wanaka went over a route called 'The Neck' and as we looked ahead, leaving Lake Wanaka behind us, Lake Hawea stretched out in front of us. What a joy to ride. New Zealand just kept getting better and better.

We continued with our route out from Wanaka taking us up our next big climb - the Crown Saddle. Wanaka itself sits around 300 metres above sea level and as our road made its way through the Cordrona Valley We would climb to 1120 metres on what is one of New Zealand's highest public roads, twisting its way over to Queenstown. Needing fuel and the toilet, we would make our daily stop at the Cordrona Hotel, remembered for the most amazing piece of chocolate cake so far on this tour. Energy tanks replenished; the road climbed steeply before finally reaching the top. From there we looked down onto Arrowtown, our next stopover, and we couldn't stop smiling as we saw the hairpin bends leading us down, It was such a thrill to ride and with an empty road we took the corners wide, enabling us to keep our speed up and make the most of this great descent.

It was here in Arrowtown that William Fox - the second premier of New Zealand and the person the Fox glacier was named after – had first discovered gold back in 1862. History goes, that after the Europeans extracted as much as they were able, the remains of the site we left to Chinese settlers to mine. John and I went off to view the old settlement where the immigrants had lived - very basic and quite a contrast to the rest of this beautiful, heritage town. It had been a brilliant day of riding and one that had really made us smile – especially as we cycled past hundreds of bras that had been tied to wire fencing for quite some distance alongside the road. It would have been fun to add one of my own but with limited gear and a difficulty, even in the UK, of buying underwear to fit it was not a risk I was willing to take. These off-road routes could be very bumpy!

We had just one last night in Frankton before we were looking forward to a few days off the bikes. Queenstown had much to offer and despite being in the place known as the adventure capital of New Zealand, we planned to do absolutely none of it. We were having our own adrenaline trip without the need for bungy jumps and white-water rafting. Instead, we were planning a trip to the shops for ice-cream and cycle shorts. Both very different items but much needed. We also used Queenstown as the base from which we would visit Milford Sound. This had been one of the must do's we had listed but with our time in New Zealand drawing to a close and the road down to this famous fiordland being listed as one of the most dangerous in new Zealand we opted for the bus. It was a good option. It wasn't just raining as we approached – it was pouring, and the single lane road was full of tourist buses which also passed through a long tunnel. It would have been pretty scary on the bikes but instead we were able to look out from the windows at the waterfalls all around us. We had a boat trip booked on arrival too and while it was stunning, I think part of the attraction had been the journey itself. It's definitely on my recommend list if you're ever out this way.

Out from Queenstown we heading to Cromwell and on our way, we got chatting to two Hungarian cyclists. They were two and a half years into their honeymoon – cycling round the world - and it was brilliant to hear their stories. Travelling a little more frugally than us they had been wild camping and so we invited them to join us on a proper campsite that night – our treat. We didn't know if they would make it but were chuffed when we saw them roll in. Delight surpassed only by that of Arpi who went on to enjoy his first hot shower in some time. Quite the honeymoon with saddle sores and cold showers!

We now had just three more cycle days left before we'd opted to hire our car for the last part of our tour. With still so much to see and a need to be back in Christchurch for our flight into Brisbane we had abandoned the idea of trying to do this on our bikes. It just hadn't been possible. There were still places we wanted to see and with New Zealand being so far away, and this quite possibly being the only time we may visit, we couldn't simply save the rest of the wish list for another time. While we didn't quite need to pack our bikes up for the next flight, we would start a part dismantle once we had the hire car. However, before that started, we had one last, phenomenal cycle treat in store - The Otago Rail Trail.

Starting in Cromwell the route follows an old railway line for just under 100 miles. We'd loved riding through New Zealand in terms of its setting but had always found the drivers a little problematic. This ride was a real opportunity to experience all the landscape had to offer without any concern at all for our four wheeled friends. We opted to take three days stopping at Omaku, Ranfurly and ended in Middlemarch. It was 33 degrees, and we would ride through tunnels and over viaducts as we made our way for the train to Dunedin. It was amazing and as the train took us down through the gorge, we couldn't think of a better way to have ended our bike journey here.

We had a week left in this beautiful country and took the time to go up to Kaikoura, stopping off at Mount Cook and Lake Tekapo. It was of course another cheat, but had we not done this we would have missed these final landscapes we wanted to make sure we had seen. There are no real sites to visit in New Zealand and the fact that nothing has been built here to come and tick off the list is exactly what makes it an attractive place to come and see. It is all about the land and not one day had passed when we had not been surrounded by the most incredible scenery.

What a start to 2014.

The Stats; New Zealand
1,276.2 Miles

Destination	Total Distance	Average Speed	Metres Up	Metres Down
Auckland to Orerepoint	56.1	8.8	830	941
Te Aroha	66.7	10.6	221	293
Tirau (Then Car to Rotorua)	39.4	12.3	39	34
Napier to Cape Kidnapper	38	9.3	50	49
Waipukapau	43.2	9.6	198	178
Dannevirke	35.4	9.1	240	376
Eketahuna	44.4	11.2	110	183
Masterton	33.5	11.7	222	297
Martinborough	31.6	10.5	289	409
Wellington	28.3	9.7	402	180
Picton Ferry and Havelock	22.5	9.3	365	420
Nelson	46.9	9.6	580	666
Kaiteriteri	40.3	9.6	159	166
Tepawera	35.9	10.9	244	227
Merchison	44.1	-	-	-
Some Cabin Somewhere	6.5	12.2	0	19
Maruia	41.4	8.1	647	600
Springs Junction Maruia Springs	21	11.5	156	32
Hanmer Springs/ Rotherham	39.1	9.5	785	1031
Hanmer Springs to Woodend	56.5	13	168	382
Christchurch	13.2	8.1	425	434

Destination	Total Distance	Average Speed	Metres Up	Metres Down
Greymouth	(Train)	-	-	-
Hokitika	24.2	10.7	19	39
Hari Hari	45.5	11.4	401	432
Franz Josef	37.8	11	323	325
Fox Glacier	15.7	8.1	555	537
Lake Paringa	44.7	12.9	213	373
Haast Township	30.3	10.5	429	489
Makarora	48.7	9.9	747	567
Wanaka	41.7	9.7	618	689
Arrowtown	34.3	8.8	672	729
Queenstown	14	9.3	155	273
Cromwell	40.2	9.8	394	540
Omakau	38.5	9.4	170	231
Ranfurly	38.6	9.4	103	187
Middlemarch	38	11.9	81	244
Dunedin	(Train)	-	-	-
Mount Cook	(Hire Car)	-	-	-
Lake Tekapo	(Hire Car)	-	-	-
Kaikoura	(Hire Car)	-	-	-
Christchurch	(Hire Car)	-	-	-

Notes

• We used trains and cars at various points in our New Zealand adventure. Towards the end of our time, it was clear there were still a number of places we wanted to see, and our only chance was car hire.

- The route from Cromwell to Middlemarch was the Otago Cycle trail – all incredible off-road riding on an old railway line.

- Lake Paringa – thousands and thousands and thousands of flies.

- Cake stats – at least as many as there were days.

The world at 10.2 mph (based on an average of averages).

13.

FRIENDS

"You can't stay in your corner of the Forest waiting for others to come to you. You have to go to them sometimes."

AA Milne, Winnie the Pooh

I missed my friends while I was travelling. Looking back the trip would change lots about friendships when I came home. Not in a negative way, simply that people just move on in your absence and of course, your own life changes too. We just lost the regularity of things we did or daily updates. I've always valued friendships highly – perhaps as an only child good friends become like a brother or sister, though I'm sure even if I'd had siblings, I'd still cherish my pals to the moon and back.

John of course was a new friend I made when setting off on this trip. We were now a year and a half in. It was longer than either of us had expected and while there were a few hiccups, the bond and experience we now shared was something it would be difficult for anyone else to match. Neither of us knew what would happen on our return home but what was certain was that we were going to be friends for life.

In looking for quotes to open this chapter, titled 'friends' there were of course many options that summarised great connections, forgiveness, a coming together of minds. Our trip had also enabled us both to meet many other people – whether through the odd bursts of kindness random strangers offered us as we travelled, or the connections we made with other riders along the way.

Despite other riders often being a challenge to the equilibrium John and I had established, both as noted in our European leg or in the early days of the Tour D'Afrique ride, looking back, we made the most amazing bunch of friends. People that shared a common interest, people that kept an eye out for each other. We'd already caught up with a number of these new friends while in New Zealand and as we carried on to Australia, I would have the opportunity to meet up with more old pals both from the Africa tour and others.

Whether for environmental factors, cost, time, or a combination of all three, travel to the Southern Hemisphere is not something anyone does often. Indeed, we may never return and the visit we were about to embark on could also be our only trip here. We certainly had no immediate plans to return and were keen to seize all we could from the next few months.

We return to places we've been to before for all sorts of reasons. Generally speaking, I enjoy seeing new places. The world is a big place and while I've travelled a lot there are still many, many more places to experience. There is of course much to see in Australia, but I think if you were to really push me regarding what would make me return, it would be to see friends. They made our tour this time and I know they would make it again should we ever get the chance.

We left Christchurch with a flight to Brisbane and with strict bio-security rules we'd ensured our tents, bikes and general gear had all been scrubbed to what looked like new. Designed to stop pest and diseases, maintain the natural environment, we were careful to remove all dirt and seeds we may be carting inadvertently. It's the first time we'd had to worry about this, and we were a little nervous as we approached the inspection area. Thankfully, while we were prepared for a full inspection, we were allowed to pass through without unpacking all our gear – all set to visit my first friend Tamara, and the reason we'd started out trip in Brisbane.

A friend from my Edinburgh days, Tamara had unexpectedly remained in Australia a few years back following a trip home to visit family. We'd never had the chance to say goodbye the long-dormant volcano on Iceland's Eyjafjallajökull glacier grounded flights and travel across Europe. The expense and uncertainty of the situation meaning that eventually my good friend decided perhaps it was now time to move back home. I'd not seen her since and was so looking forward to a long-awaited hug.

We stayed with Tamara for a couple of nights before our rider would start and really enjoyed exploring. Often not on the itinerary for most travellers, even the guidebook notes Brisbane is often under-rated, and we certainly enjoyed exploring as we visited gardens, galleries and exploring the various areas of the city. Evenings were spent sharing updates on our lives and gathering tips for our upcoming ride.

Having cycled over the river, leaving Brisbane behind us, our first day would end in Burleigh Heads. It was getting dark as we arrived, delayed by a cold beer at Surfers Paradise as we made our way down the Gold Coast. Sun, sea, and blue skies met us as we continued our route South.

Our next well-known stop-over was Byron Bay where we managed a couple of hours on the beach - I thought we'd been there most of the day such is my tolerance for sun-bathing. We enjoyed walking up the lighthouse, taking in the stunning vista of the surrounding coast. It was a busy place and while that does often offer more to see it was noisier than we preferred so we continued to push ahead.

When the sun was shining, and the riding was going well it was easy to have a great big smile on our faces. But Australia is not always so welcoming to the two-wheeler. Riding often required great concentration as cars passed by too closely and as we left Byron Bay towards our next stop at Broadwater, sadly it was remembered more for the shouts of 'fuck cyclists' coming from a passing vehicle. We would just get used to the animosity. Despite the bad driving and bouts of heckling from passing motorists and their passengers, the welcome once we were not riding was as good as we'd found in the other countries we had visited.

The next big destination was Sydney though with a total of 16 days riding between here and Brisbane we were getting to understand much more clearly the scale of this country. I'd started to get a feel of this while in Brisbane, having looked up the idea of calling in on another pal in Cairns prior to heading South. The notion quickly rejected given a 29-hour coach journey. While my Lands' End to John O'Groats trip had been a 17-day jaunt (including rest days) most people set 10-14 days aside to ride the length of the UK and the distance covered is similar to that of Brisbane to Sydney.

The Pacific Coast Highway would be our main route from Broadwater down to Yamba and we both noted it was boring. There was little to see over these few days though as we stopped off for lunch in Grafton, we would make a new friend and someone we are still in touch with despite the miles now between us. Maria was working in 'The Albion' where a cheap pub lunch had caught our eye. It was OK. Sadly, we just couldn't afford much of the delicious food on offer as we travelled through Australia. Ironically, had we realised our accommodation that night would be free we could have chosen something other than the daily special. Maria had invited us to camp at her place having heard all about our trip. It was brilliant. We had a destination to aim for and by the time we'd arrived the camp pitch had turned into a full family barbeque and a mattress inside.

The next morning, we left just as full – the barbeque being lit for breakfast again – and for the next few days we would stop in at various coastal towns and campsites before having a short rest, with a hostel stay in Port McQuarrie. The last few days had been so hot, and it was good to catch up on washing, blogs and enjoy walks. We'd had a tough ride into Port McQuarrie, pushing bikes through deep sand for several miles in searing temperatures, but we had made good progress and Sydney was in our grasp.

Our ride would remind us of the best and worst of human nature – from a conversation with a local cyclist leading to a car ride after dinner to the best viewpoint in Lauriston to picking up litter left by others as we sat down at the picnic table on Ocean Drive. Disappointingly, there was no sea view from what we felt was a rather misnamed road, though we would continue to call in a number of great beach locations as we continued on our way to One Mile Beach.

It was sweltering so rather than camp we opted for a back-packers and having had a great night we decided to do the same again in Newcastle. It was definitely a mistake. The owner was away on the second night, leaving one of the longer-term guests in charge. Frequented mostly by the younger traveller it seemed this was just the excuse for a party. I'm normally no party pooper, but the guy collapsed naked and spread eagled in the hallway and the mess of the food fight in the kitchen the next morning was quite something. We were very pleased to leave. We'd persuaded to have a few drinks ourselves when we stopped in Taree (it was rude to ignore the locals – we had to join them for a beer!) but I'm glad I never get into quite the states we witnessed in Newcastle.

The next day to Bateaux Bay was bad for a different reason. What a day it would be. I'd never cycled in rain like it. We'd just finished a lunch stop and it was clear the heavens were about to open. I suggested staying on to let the rain pass but John was keen to carry on. We continued and just minutes later buckets and buckets of water poured down. We were drenched and while normally in hot countries you stay warm, I was so wet I was starting to feel cold as we pulled up in camp. Thankfully, the site owner took pity on us. A small touring caravan was empty, and we had never been so pleased to be offered an upgrade! We showered and soon the awning was steaming – all heaters deployed to dry our gear.

The next night we would be in Manly and as we made our way into the city; we mixed riding with ferries for what would be a much nicer day. Our friend Rosie, from the Africa trip, was based in Manly and while she was away with work for the day, she'd left keys with a neighbour so we could make ourselves at home until she returned. A seasoned cyclist the instructions were clear, and she knew only too well that the washing machine was a much-needed appliance! Thanks Rosie. It was brilliant to catch up with her when she came home and get some local advice for our next few days.

Just a short ferry trip into the main harbour area, Manley is a mainly locals' area with great restaurants and bars. It was a brilliant base and we thoroughly enjoyed taking our ferry rides from there into the harbour area. As ever, we made sure we took in the sights and while the open top bus tour day was distinctly soggy, we laughed as we enjoyed the views from the top deck. We seemed to be the only tourists with full water-proofs able to take in the experience.

We had also decided that while in Australia we wanted to visit Uluru. It was a real extravagance but knowing cycling to the red centre was out of the question, we'd booked a two-night fly over. Staying with our friend Rosie meant we were able to store bikes safely for a couple of days. It was a costly diversion but so worth the expensive and we had no regrets. Our organised tour enabled us to view this iconic site as well as visit nearby Kings Canyon. The earth really was bright red and the heat overpowering but the climax with a thunderstorm and waterfalls over the rock was incredible. In addition, double rainbows offered a backdrop to our photo as we raised a glass of fizz and joked about our day which could have ended so differently. All I can say is - be very aware of shouting 'back a bit' when taking photos of others near cliff edges - sometimes the cultural refence is lost and, as we did, you end up shouting STOP much louder. Whoops. We returned to Sydney, where I met up with another old friend (Hilary) as John did the harbour bridge climb.

Holiday and rest days over we were on our way again. Yep - we had more friends to see! An old Morris Dancing friend of mine now lived in the Blue Mountains and despite the climbing this would mean as we headed inland, it was good to get a break from the coast too. We'd opted for a ferry to Parramatta to get out of the city. While we had been riding around Australia a driver had hit a group of cyclists in the Sydney area and it made us slightly nervous. It was a good option and given the climbing we would go on to do that day it was good for multiple reasons. My diary that day recorded a couple of punctures and, while this is an oft asked question, it was a relatively rare occurrence. Typical it would happen on some stonking climbs though.

Having not seen Dave for years we had booked a nearby hotel but were heading to his place for dinner. It was lovely but we were still so hungry. Much like our Zambia dinner with friends, I'm not sure ordinary folk realised quite how many calories our bike tour required. About 10 miles into our ride the next morning I was done. We kept the day short and having already resorted to pushing I was so tired it was a relief to know the next day was marked rest.

We were in Katoomba, one of the main towns in the Blue Mountains area. From here we planned to visit the Three Sisters – the key rock formations in this Sandstone plateau but I'm afraid we would see little. It had rained all night; the air was misty, and you could barely see your hands in front of you. We'd opted for the tourist bus to make the most of our one day here but as the roads turned into rivers, we were forced to change our plans. Some of the walking was just too treacherous.

While disappointed we'd not been able to really see all we had cycled here for, we needed to continue. The road continued to climb, the mist remained, and it was a bit of a slog. We still had days of riding ahead on our way to Melbourne for our next catch up with pals and if the truth be told there was little to see. Successive diary posts noting not much to see again and notes on headwind rain and thunderstorms offering a fair summary of this part of our journey. Our ride took us from the Olympic Highway to the Hume highway, an area known for backpacker murders back in the 90s. It all felt very functional, this section all being about getting to our destination. We missed history and architecture, feeling towns had little to really see. Sadly, the time also coincided with hearing a good friend of mine back in the UK now also needed a mastectomy. It was tough being so far from home and when riding through places with less to see it did sometimes make us question what we were doing. Seeing more friends in Melbourne was a very welcome distraction and as we planned to stay here for a few days there was plenty of time to catch up with home and share a cheeky wine too.

We both agreed Melbourne was a favourite Australian city and as usual we had packed our days visiting sites and taking the chance to meet yet more friends. We were about to embark on the last part of our ride here from Melbourne to Adelaide and with the Great Ocean Road ahead we were excited to get going. Our cyclist friends, Chris and Tracey had noted that Arthurs Seat was a great climb and while a detour we opted to take on the challenge. I'd lived very close to Arthurs Seat in Edinburgh and so it seemed right to make the comparison. It was fabulous and good practice for the undulating roads we were about to endure.

We would have mixed weather as we continued, as in often the case so close to the sea - one day blue skies and the next soggy and wet. However, the key thing we noticed was just how cold it was. Yet again, I was reminded of my ignorance having been taken in by the holiday brochures. I was riding with numb toes, freezing cold in the tent and it was hard not to be reminded of the wind and rain. It was time to abandon camping – waking up to ice was simply a step too far. Some readers may be disappointed - our trip is not always one of endurance. We were here to enjoy ourselves and from now on in we were using hostels.

The route on the Great Ocean Road really was stunning as we passed by the iconic Twelve Apostles we were beaming. It was so unbelievable to be riding here – something I would never have imagined in my wildest dreams. The B100 is one of the world's most famous routes and we were on it. The first sections of this road were built in 1919, constructed by hand by former WW1 soldiers, I can't imagine this was an enviable task, despite the guidebook now highlighting the experience - 'Walk it, drive it, enjoy it'. While 'bike' it was not listed as an option we could take, we were certainly trying to follow the enjoyment direction though at times it wasn't always easy.

The Twelve Apostles can be found on the section of the route that falls in Port Campbell National Park. This is the most photographed section of the road where narrower lanes and sheer cliffs follow the soft limestone, revealing a variety of arches, gorges and blow holes. Being on the bikes was brilliant and, as we've been able to do throughout our trip, we were able to pull in and get photos that are just not so easy from a moving vehicle. Kylie and The Captain were in their element!

The other great advantage of following such a popular route was that towns and facilities along the way catered well for the traveller. It did not feel like the drudge of the country between Sydney and Melbourne and made us wonder whether we should not have tried to go inland after all. But that was past. For now, we took out time to take in the scene around us, indulge in the great cafes, visiting art galleries and local shops. We took rest days in Port Fairy and Robe, enjoying our meanders around these seaside/fishing destinations, stopping off at Mount Gambier on the way where we took the opportunity to book a room in the old jail.

It's hard as I write this chapter to not feel I'm doing a disservice to Australia and particularly this stretch of road. In parts it was some of the most beautiful coastal riding I've ever done but the poor weather and long drags between places of interest did mean it's the country we least preferred riding through. We met some great people but there were less random adventures and interactions. The drivers were not always kind, and it was all much more predictable. We both felt this was a country that may be best visited with an offroad camper to truly explore. Perhaps this is the reason I highlighted 'friends' as the key factor that stands out for this section of our global tour, and we still had more folk to catch up with once we arrived in Adelaide.

When I first moved to Edinburgh in 2007, I rented a room with Cate, an Aussie who had now moved back home. She'd really helped me settle in a new city, introducing me to many of her contacts who I'm still good friends with to this day. I was so looking forward to seeing her again – though given my nights out in Edinburgh in my 30s were a little wilder than I was used to now, there was a slight nervousness too! We were waiting on the pier in Brighton, Adelaide with a cold beer when Cate arrived. We would be staying with her for a few nights, meeting up with another pal Chrissie for a wine tasting tour and going on a tour to Kangaroo Island. It was a brilliant end to our trip. Mixing nature and culture and city sightseeing with friends I knew I would not see again for a long time.

By now we'd read many guidebooks and tourist leaflets – all too often everything is worth a visit. Sadly, we learnt that's not always the case. I hope this chapter hasn't painted too negative a picture. Australia really is amazing – I just wouldn't do it on a bike. There were many highlights, from our city tours to thunderstorms at Uluru, wine tasting in the Adelaide hills and the wildlife, beaches and 'Remarkable Rocks' of Kangaroo Island. The Great Ocean Road really was a great ride, we just wish we'd had better weather and I sense, were you not on a tight budget, the food and wine could be phenomenal. We were just sick of schnitzel and chips.

I'd never had so many contacts across the globe and while riding a bike can make distances seem huge, friendships around the world can make it feel like a much smaller place. This really was the chapter about such relationships.

The Stats; Australia
2,045.3 Miles

Destination	Total Distance	Average Speed	Metres Up	Metres Down	Time on Bike
Brisbane to Burleigh Heads	65.6	8.9	527	643	7 hrs 23
Byron Bay	57.8	8.6	914	1038	6 hrs 37
Broadwater	37	10.7	228	253	3 hrs 27
Yamba	45.3	12.6	106	172	3 hrs 36
Grafton	45.6	10.3	114	102	4 hrs 26
Coffs Harbour	49	10.2	596	744	4 hrs 48
Nambucca Heads	36.7	10.1	430	498	3 hrs 36
Crescent Heads	55.8	12.2	169	271	4 hrs 35
Port McQuarrie	21.7	6.6	85	86	3 hrs 17
Laurieston	20.4	9.9	182	206	2 hrs 03
Taree	35.4	10.5	243	311	3 hrs 22
Pacific Palms	53.2	10.3	288	424	5 hrs 10
Buladelah	29.3	8.6	508	553	3 hrs 24
One Mile Beach	34.2	9.9	133	179	3 hrs 27
Newcastle	30.8	11.1	152	65	2 hrs 47
Bateaux Bay	44.5	10.1	425	539	4 hrs 25
Manley, Sydney	39.4	8.7	392	479	4 hrs 31
Uluru	(Flight)	-	-	-	-
Falcon-bridge	33.4	9.9	451	251	3 hrs 21
Katoomba	19.7	6.2	607	190	3 hrs 10

Destination	Total Distance	Average Speed	Metres Up	Metres Down	Time on Bike
Lithgow	32.1	9.6	550	727	3 hrs 20
Blarny	61	10.2	1064	1270	5 hrs 58
Coura	43	12.7	306	941	3 hrs 22
Young	46.2	10.4	217	229	4 hrs 25
Coota-mundra	31.4	11.5	210	380	2 hrs 44
Wagga Wagga	56.4	11.9	310	540	4 hrs 40
Culcairn	50.4	10.6	133	165	4 hrs 45
Albury	30.8	11.1	26	108	2 hrs 45
Whanga-ratta	52.8	10.4	120	171	5 hrs 04
Euroa	57.4	11.5	115	117	5 hrs 00
Broadford	58.6	10.7	402	485	5 hrs 27
Yarraville/Melbourne	56.2	9.4	618	895	5 hrs 57
Frankston	34.7	10.6	103	116	3 hrs 15
Queenscliff	49.4	10.6	633	701	4 hrs 38
Anglesea	38.3	9.1	288	370	4 hrs 13
Lorne	18.9	9.1	295	310	2 hrs 04
Apollo Bay	28.4	9.2	317	410	3 hrs 04
Lavers Hill	30.2	7.4	898	569	4 hrs 06
Port Campbell	34.3	9.7	492	964	3 hrs 32
Port Fairy	60.5	11.7	236	339	5 hrs 08
Portland	44.6	11.4	151	127	3 hrs 53
Nelson	43.8	11.1	321	446	3 hrs 57
Mount Gambier	24.7	10.6	191	220	2 hrs 20
Beachport	52.6	13.1	113	170	4 hrs 00

Destination	Total Distance	Average Speed	Metres Up	Metres Down	Time on Bike
Robe	34.7	11.9	10	23	2 hrs 55
Kingston	26	9.4	40	62	2 hrs 44
Salt Creek	53.8	10.5	36	41	5 hrs 06
Meningie/ Lake Albert	38.4	10.7	92	126	3 hrs 35
Wellington	29	9.4	64	87	3 hrs 04
Strathalbyn	31.3	11.4	53	35	2 hrs 44
Hahndorf	20.3	7.5	423	252	2 hrs 41
Brighton, Adelaide	20.3	8.9	382	738	2 hrs 41

Notes

• Notable abuse from passing motorists didn't always make for a pleasant ride despite a great welcome once we were off the bikes.

• Some distances between places meant our ride in Australia was more cycling than touring.

• The coast from Melbourne was the highlight in terms of riding.

• Pleased to have included Australia on our tour, though this is perhaps a country where you can see so much more of all that's on offer if you hire an off-road camper!

The world at 10.2 mph (based on an average of averages).

14.

HOSPITALITY

*"He who believes in Allah and the Last Day should
accommodate his guest according to his right."*

The Koran

There are of course many countries and people that could prompt us to talk about the warmth we were met with during our trip. However, the posters and signs noting 'hosgeldiniz' as we cycled through Turkey were certainly matched with the 'welcome' in reality as well as words.

Islamic society places a huge importance in 'honouring guests' and hospitality has long been considered one of its most significant values. Indeed, the quote given at the start of this chapter is not alone in verses dedicated to this subject throughout the Koran. Whether purely for religious reasons or also matched with the need for tourist income, there was no place we were made to feel more at home than Turkey.

Positioned as the gateway from Europe to Asia Turkey is perhaps an easier introduction to the Islamic World than other countries people travel and cycle through. As the Bosphorus sets apart the two sides of its largest city, Istanbul, we too saw the mix of West and East as we made our way through this fabulous place. We'd both been to Turkey before. I'd visited the Black Sea coast back in 1999 for the solar eclipse and John had travelled here much more extensively given his sister has lived in Turkey for many years. Despite having changed our starting place from Iran to Turkey we'd still mapped out an extensive ride. It was to be our last tour and we planned to cycle back to the UK. There were of course many routes we could take and in truth, given there was no need to book a flight back to the UK, we were pretty much looking at options as we went along. What we did know is that we would start in Trabzon, on the Northeast coast, cycle through Cappadocia, in Central Turkey, make our way to the South coast and the more traditional tourist sites and then head up towards Istanbul, passing through Kusadasi, where John's sister was based.

However, before any of this we had a wedding to attend – in Denmark. While it's certainly not an obvious diversion I didn't want to miss my friend's wedding and it's fair to say, the hospitality there was certainly fitting of this chapter in the book too. I left my ma's place on my bike somewhat overloaded. I'd not really done any of my cycle tour on minimal luggage so by the time I added in a wedding outfit and high heels I'm lucky there was room on the bike for me! We were catching a ferry from Harwich and John and I had arranged that we would meet up the night before. The first few days then would be the solo-ride section of my trip and I certainly missed my navigator and pal. I caught a train from Wolverhampton to Milton Keynes and as luck would have bumped into Geoff Thomas, former footballer, and organiser of the Cure Leukaemia Tour de France fundraiser. It was a great start, though with overhead thunder and lightning storms as I left Cranfield, and my choice of routes through Cambridgeshire I'm not sure I was really made for solo touring. Ordinarily the fields and rough paths would be a joy but with so much gear and gates I couldn't fit through, without removing and reattaching gear, I wished I stuck to more conventional main roads. John would have probably just been able to lift my heavily laden bike. Still, I eventually arrived in Colchester a few hours later than John. Despite having booked our hotel I managed to go to two hotels in the same chain before arriving at the right place. It's all in the detail!

The next morning, and with John and the GPS we found a great route to the ferry port ready to head to Esbjerg. It was an 18-hour journey and with an early morning arrival the day we landed we opted to take in a short tour of local island, Fano. We'd had six weeks off the bikes and while we knew headwind may be challenge in these parts the lack of significant climbing was quite a relief. It's amazing how much fitness you can lose in a few weeks. The wedding would take place in Bording, and we had a few days to make our way to Jackie and Bo's house. It was a great feeling just cycling in and soon our first cold beer was consumed. Bike paths in Denmark were incredible but it was quite something to adapt to having right of way... we're just not used to it. The wedding was amazing and a fabulous opportunity to meet other friends too but four days later we were back on our adventure. We would fly from Copenhagen but first took the chance to ride through Silkeborg, Arhus, Roskilde (via another ferry ride), Koge and Copenhagen, once again taking the chance to meet with Africa cycling friends Gus and Irin first. Other than noting our diversion so the table listed at the end of this chapter makes sense it was a great warmup for the trip that would come next, which by contrast to Demark would be full of hills.

Minor detour complete, we arrived in Trabzon at the beginning of August. The weather in Turkey would be super-hot – as it had been in Denmark – and we were grateful to cool down in the mountains at Sumela Monastery before setting off on what really would be an epic ride home. Trabzon was a great city and the cheap hotel I'd booked had been very accommodating – our bikes were stored in the restaurant (then closed) while Ishmael, the next-door kebab shop owner was incredibly friendly. It was a theme that would continue.

The road out of the city, as they all are, was busy but soon we would find ourselves on quieter roads passing forts, boatyards and thousands of hazelnuts laid out to dry in the sun. While it wasn't always picturesque it was great to be back cycling on the coast. The hospitality continued, this time with Arden, and the chocolate/hazelnut spread and cheese lunch and the riding was relatively easy. It was a great first day. We were heading

East along the Black Sea Coast towards Samsun though the usual up and down nature of coastal roads was diminished given the number of tunnels we ended up having to ride through. On our second ride day, towards Ordu, we counted we had been through a total of five miles of tunnels during a 58-mile stretch and we deserved a cheeky beer. Ordu was a holiday destination after all and so far, was perhaps the most obvious tourist destination on the coast so far.

Much of our route from Trabzon had been on the Dio. The tunnels could be pretty scary and on reflection I wonder if we would have been better taking a more undulating ride. John lost his pannier in one though thankfully another driver highlighted the issue, and it was undamaged and it's fair to say as we saw a 2.5-mile tunnel ahead as we passed through towards Unye we did opt for the longer detour. It was a whole lot safer. We did not need to tick the box of having survived (hopefully) one of Turkey's longest road tunnels.

As it happens it was a great ride, our first bike lane got us out of Ordu and onto the coast road. The roads were much quieter now though we did still have to face a few small tunnels. The sea was never far away and little coves kept appearing through the trees giving tantalising vistas. While we had just over three days following the coast, we were welcomed everywhere we went with more drinks, food, and positivity. It always makes us wonder whether cycle tourists in the UK get the same experience. Sadly, I imagine it can be mixed, much as our trip on the whole.

Having become used to our coastal route we were about to run inland, and boy did it change. We were heading towards Cappadocia in Central turkey. Famed for cave houses carved into soft rock, phallic landscapes, and hundreds of hot air balloons from which to take a view of the incredible land-scapes below, we hadn't quite realised the hill we would need to climb as we headed inland. We climbed just over 1,200 metres to reach Arkkus. Gee whizz. Almost 40 miles uphill.

As if that wasn't hard enough, we had 50kg + of luggage and the temperature just continued to rise as we continued to climb. At one point the road was edged with concrete walls turning the whole scene into a pizza oven and we were crispy! Sweat bubbled on the surface of skin, factor 50 sun cream holding it in place. We were dripping and it's amazing anyone would want to talk to us yet still the hospitality continued. Having been offered tea at the local garage, we were invited to join a family for refreshments at the side of the road. We were so hot and so tired and were not slow to take up their offer. Yet it didn't stop there. Having left this family behind, we stopped in for lunch but there would be no bill to pay. We'd built up quite an appetite for lunch after all that riding and I'm not sure the guys that were treating us were fully aware of our calorie intake. The food was delicious at the farm, come outdoor bar-b-que area and as we washed it down with glasses of ayran (a Turkish yoghurt drink) we were pretty amazed at our ride so far. This was perhaps one of the toughest rides of our full pannier laden touring and it remains a day that we often talk about. People waved and shouted hello as they passed by and the hospitality that day did not end there either. We arrived in Arkkus looking for a place to stay and soon we were pointed towards a schoolhouse - rooms generally used by visiting teachers. Following a much-needed shower we wondered through the town, shared giggles with three Turkish women following a mime led conversation and were invited to stop for yet another cuppa. While we didn't want to be rude, we did need to eat again but on asking for a suggestion we were promptly escorted to the pide salon (Turkish pizza). Tables were cleared and a group gathered round – the local police chiefs daughter joined having been invited as lead interpreter. We'd been on the bikes for around 7 hours that day and while it will always be remembered as an epic cycle day the hospitality would never be forgotten either. According to my diary that day "the scenery was beautiful, but it was the people that really blew us away". We were definitely welcome in Turkey.

The strange thing is that despite this hard riding day it was the following day that was marked as 'hellish'. I woke feeling ill – shivering, aching and with an awful stomach ache. Thankfully, despite some climbing it was mainly a downhill day. I'd eaten little food, really struggled and as we approached Nikkar, we knew we needed a restful place to stay – a posh hotel apparently. Thankfully a good sleep did the trick and our next day to Tokat started with a short but beautiful ride. The perfect way to get back into the rhythm. I was still not feeling 100% and we would have big climb ahead of us. This time it was shorter but steeper, rising 500 metres over the last five miles and heading to the gravel roadworks. We would enjoy our rest day here despite what was now a rather runny bum - to quote the diary again!

Tokat was a surprising find and a place to which I would love to return. History and architecture surround you. Streets are lined with old timber frame ottoman houses and for budding photographers there was always a picture to be taken. We took our time meandering, walking up to the old castle site and playing football with local kids on the way. And I'll always also remember Tokat for the best gozleme (cheese and spinach pancakes) of the whole Turkish ride. I wonder in fact, as I write this, whether the book would have been better name 'the world at 3,000ish calories a day'.

The rest did us well and there was more climbing ahead to Yildezeli before the road would flatten out a bit through Sivas and Sarkisla. Our next stop was Bunyan, and other than the scorching hot weather and consequently challenging riding it was once again the people that made the day and secured a special mention in this memoir. Just over 10 miles from the end of our ride a young lad pulled over on his moped, inviting us to join his family for cold drinks in their garden. I can't tell you how much this was needed and had they offered to let us stay we would have jumped at that too. We probably stayed a good hour but knew we had to just get going again. We needed to find a room for the night and pick up a few provisions. We stopped in at the local kebab shop for yet another drink and to pick up more liquid refreshments for our room. However, we were not allowed to buy anything. The guy refused to charge us and despite our insistence we left with cold cans of fizzy pop all free and gratis.

I think you can see why I called this chapter hospitality though as we moved into more touristic areas this certainly happened much less. Many talk of feeling hassled in busy tourist zones and as you start to understand that these are areas where folk from all over the country often move for the holiday season and the annual income it attracts, it's easy to understand why. We had just a stopover in Kayseri before we would be in the Cappadocia. Despite being the second most Islamic city in Turkey though we were pleased to find a hotel to serve us a couple of cold beers on arrival. We'd had several tough days since riding from the North Coast and certainly felt like we'd deserved them. Kayseri also sits as a key point between old trade routes and is known for its carpets - I took the opportunity to bag a souvenir, trusting that the parcel would arrive back in the UK at some point in the future.

Thankfully the huge thunderstorm that followed my purchase was not an ominous sign - more a welcome relief from the weather of the preceding days.

Our arrival point into the Cappadocia area was Avanos. I thought I'd booked us a treat hotel – the rooms looked lovely and the pool so inviting after the hot weather. It was not to be. We'd taken a hilly, seven-mile diversion to avoid roadworks and then just as we thought we were nearly there we couldn't find the place I'd booked. Sometimes it is just better to wing this accommodation stuff, but we had an expensive room and we had to find it – we were paying now regardless. Five miles further and we were there. It was not worth it. The hotel was new. The pool wasn't working, there were no other guests and, as yet they had not purchased umbrellas for the outdoor tables. No shade. It was away from everything else, and we were stuck. Worse than that, like many tourist bus places the food was drummed down – bland and tasteless.

The following day we were heading to Urgup, and we made our way through the Cappadocian landscape stopping for numerous photos. Cappadocia is famed for its lunar landscapes, phallic shaped chimneys, cave hotels and churches and numerous walking trails. There was always a photo to take and while this was something we would be doing lots of during the next few days we took the opportunity for Kylie and The Captain to get into shot too. It's hard to always do the full tourist thing when the bikes and all our numerous panniers are in tow, so we had decided to make a base in Goreme for the next few days.

Goreme had been the town I'd stayed in back in 1999 but I noticed had changed enormously since I was last here. It had just expanded and with an influx of Oriental visitors the street-based kebab stalls had been replaced with numerous Chinese restaurants. While at first, I was perhaps a little put off – I never like to see a place lose its own heritage – please be reassured. Cappadocia is still a must visit destination.

We booked into our cave room and over the next few days enjoyed a photo tour day (fabulous) and a more traditional sightseeing trip to lhlara valley, Selime monastery and the Kaymakli underground city (rushed). We would take walks through the valleys around Goreme, enjoy meze and wine and took the opportunity to send a wedding present back to our friends in Denmark. With four days off the bike, it was great to take it easy and it seemed we left fired up for a few long days ahead. Sadly, the bike needed some maintenance and as we headed toward Aksaray we thought it would be a good opportunity to get it sorted. Help was at hand and soon a bike angel appeared from nowhere.

Noticing we were looking for something quite specific we were approached by local resident. In need of a bike repair shop, Mustafa led us around the town to a number of possibilities before taking us back to his friends pide salon. Lunch sorted we were invited to join them again later for dinner and we arrived armed with fruit and baklava. We knew they would not let us pay – again! Bike fixed we left Aksaray completely oblivious to the fact that we were about to do our 100- miler - well, 99.7 miles but I'm rounding this one up! We'd planned a two-day journey to Konya but with the first potential stop over too quick in the day and the halfway point being somewhat barren we were forced to continue and just over nine hours later, as dusk had set in, we pulled into Konya at 8pm. Exhausted but pretty proud of ourselves. We'd done these distances while in Africa, but our luggage was not an issue then and heavy panniers is not far off giving someone a backie all the way. Too tired to celebrate we ate in the restaurant opposite the hotel, and took the chance to rest a little, amidst being a whirling dervish and Rumi tourist the following day. My notes recall how hot it was and I struggled to walk around that day. At least on the bike there's often a wee breeze.

Having arrived so late at Konya the hotel we were in was actually rather fancy by our standards and the breakfast buffet I'd eaten the first morning had been fantastic. It was wasted the morning we left. Once again, I had the squits and it made that ride out a struggle. The road was certainly undulating and as the Garmin noted it was low on battery as we got closer to Seydishir I knew exactly how it felt.

We were almost through central Turkey and tomorrow we would arrive in Cide, on the south coast. We knew we had another long ride ahead, but the elevation gains were far less apparent. Over a big distance the ups and downs look like small undulations yet based on this ride day I can only advise that you look more carefully. While our stats at the end of the day noted a 2,572m descent we still also registered 1088 metres of climbing and were on our bike for just under 10 hours that day. In fact, at three hours 45 we'd only managed to reach 22 of our total 91 miles. "Wowsers" – another direct diary quote!

It was also while on this road that I found a welcome that was much too familiar and sadly I guess the reason many women don't enjoy a solo ride. We hit roadworks about 55 miles in -wet tarmac on loose gravel and on a steep hill. As John carried on riding, I needed to push. One of the local workmen approached – friendly at first but then he tried pushing his luck. He blew kisses at me first and I pointed ahead noting John was in front. Undeterred, he continued... 'I fuck you'? I'd been polite initially but knew I had to stand my ground and even started to plan a downhill turn. John would come back for me, and I could get away fast that way if needed. Thankfully, my sharp response did all that was required though I had never been so pleased to reach the top of a hill – this time not just for the sense of achievement. Thankfully, this was the only time on our trip I was made to feel so uneasy.

It made me feel uneasy for a short while after though as the dry hilltop landscapes turned green and we enjoyed miles and miles of rolling downhill I soon had a smile on my face again. It was so brilliant to be in Cide. We were now very much in tourist Turkey and a cold beer was easily available - in fact one or two were consumed that night.

We were on such a high, but it was short lived. With a rest day in Cide and access to Wi-Fi I called my ma. She was doing okay but as my chief financial controller (mom was monitoring my accounts while I was away) she told me I needed to be careful. She said she was quite worried, and I needed to check.

*

"S**t. She was right. Needed to go home".

It was a short extract from my journal that day and of course much more sentiment sat behind writing these words. We needed to plan our return. Perhaps I'd been too complacent. Perhaps I was too much in the moment. Perhaps we should have scrimped a little more? Perhaps, perhaps, perhaps. There were so many questions but alas only one answer.

Our ride had been incredible, but I knew I would not have the funds to ride home as planned. Many tears were shed that evening and while John was understanding I knew he was upset too. Our dream was shattered, and I really felt like I was letting him down again. We'd had the most incredible few years and as we talked through our scenario, we were both happy we'd done the trip the way we wanted. Yes, we could have been on our bikes for many more years, but we would not have had the amazing experiences we'd had so far. We were so grateful for all we had seen and done and as we looked at the options for our return, we were determined to make the most of our time. I can't deny that is wasn't weird riding for the next few days and it certainly put a cloud over our time in Cide to some degree.

As we moved on with our journey there was both a noticeable rise in temperature on the south coast, many more people, much more tourist infrastructure and of course, higher prices. However, it was not hard to understand why Turkey is so popular with foreign visitors and even if some are more drawn to cheaper booze, lying on beaches and large resort complexes there is so much more to enjoy. Historical monuments are everywhere, often seemingly abandoned, the food is amazing and the scenery stunning. We were in for a few brilliant, final weeks.

We followed the coast, calling first at Antalya then onto Olympus. It was so, so hot and as we pushed on (not literally but certainly metaphorically) we could see the hills ahead. Our moments on the bikes felt like welcome breaks from the more commercial and occasionally hassle bound tourist areas, in fact, having left a lunchtime eatery on our way to Olympus the café owner followed us to hand back the tip. Turkey really can be unreal, and it warms the heart while reassuring us of the mostly good nature of humanity.

We had a day off in Olympus, a chance to jump into the sea and feel the sand beneath our toes. It was important to have holiday vibe to our last few weeks. We worked out that we would now cycle to Kusadasi, ending our cycle tour once we reached John's sister's house. It was a family home even if it wasn't quite our ride home. As we headed next towards Demra we knew there was a big hill to climb back up from Olympus and even with the inevitable period I felt pretty good. The route was stunning, the sea bright, bright blue while the road clung to tan coloured cliffs. Noted in my journal as 'the best coastal day in Turkey' it really was a joy to ride and despite the up and down nature of the roads we were loving it. That was, we both were until the ride into Fethiye.

Having stopped in Kalkan, our day to Fethiye had started with a climb again and while it felt hard first thing in the morning that was the easy bit. John was sick – really ill – but having set off and with accommodation booked we decided to continue. Sometimes it's just not a good idea. We had about 25 miles to go but it was clear John may not make it. He was lying on the side of the road, and I was trying to get help – a lift. No success. We'd tried at the garage a little earlier, but no-one was able to help us out. We were pushing our bikes and John was in tears. We would walk a bit, ride a bit, rest a bit. Eventually we had just 10 miles to go but it was so hard. It was time to stick out the thumb again though based on our earlier attempts we weren't sure how it would go. However, as is the nature of travelling this way we saw the possibilities pass by... and then a result. We had a lift to Fethiye. This time I could have cried.

Bikes loaded we were soon dropped off again. We had a short ride to our accommodation but knowing we had just a couple of miles made it all the easier. John went straight to bed where he remained the following day too while I took to planning my return to the UK.

I applied for a job, and it was a very strange feeling. Of course, you only apply for a role you want to do, but to quote the diary - "I am so torn. I really want this break for freedom. This getting off the treadmill. I fear this is a step back on". Given these very mixed emotions I set about mind-mapping and writing down thoughts on my ideal return. I was writing a children's book, thought of selling the Edinburgh flat so I could reduce a mortgage and in essence develop a portfolio career. I was sure I wanted to get a dog and call him Mr George Woofer. But I completed the job application just in case too. As I said, it was all very strange.

Thankfully, John felt better the next day and so I was able to step away from the obsession with what next. For now, we were still in the moment, and we had a day off to explore Fethiye and nearby Oludinez. We headed over the hill for the latter first – by bus! Oludinez is a well-known holiday resort, and the bus was busy, filling up at the resort hotels that say between these two key destinations. Once there, we took a beautiful walk around the lagoon, refusing to pay for expensive loungers and instead resting a towel on the sand for a few minutes. We never stay still for long, and John was also keen to try the paragliding. It was not on my radar – not after the micro-lite experience.

Once more I was left with my thoughts, and my notebook though I was told it would just be for an hour or so. Five hours later John landed on the beach. I'd really started to get worried, but I think in reality they had just sold too many flights to too few instructors. You gotta make your money when you can and while John was away, I supported the local beach bar. Well, I had to sit somewhere!

The next day we were back on the bikes to Dalman and, once showered, we set off to get filthy dirty – at the mud baths. Late into the day, we were the only people there and after we'd paid, they turned off the hot pool. We were not happy though as we expressed our discontent we were rewarded when our hotel owner directed us to a natural hot pool instead. Result.

We had just five more days of riding and decided we needed to book a flight. It had never been the intention but never having now got used to the notion we were going home it felt positive to have a plan. Feelings over the next few days would inevitably waver, for both of us I'm sure but with the weather still roasting and a few hills to climb our minds were once again just on pushing the pedals.

Our last ride day in Turkey went from Soke to Kusadasi and with just 15 miles or so to go we were soon at Reni's door – John's sister. It was so bitter-sweet. Great to see familiar faces, to share stories of our adventure – especially with Bulent, her husband, but our ride had ended. Just like that. We'd not completed a circumnavigation but with around 20,000 miles under our belt we had cycled just over the round the world route. It may not have been the initial trip either of us had signed up for, and ended prematurely, but we had seen the world and had the most incredible two or more years. Turkey had been so friendly and generous, but we knew we were heading to an even warmer welcome on our final return home.

The Stats; UK, Denmark and Turkey
1,642.7 Miles

Destination	Total Distance	Average Speed	Metres Up	Metres Down
Milton Keynes to Cranfield	10	-	-	-
Village Near Cambridge	61.2	10.1	269	251
Harwich Hotel	53.3	9.4	317	422
Ferry Port	16	10.6	129	156
Esjberg Circular (Fano)	26.2	9.1	14	29
Felding	53	10	45	66
Bording	31	10	67	54
Arhus	43.7	10.5	255	393
Roskilde	50.4	11.2	357	437
Koge	17.8	10.6	70	117
Trabzon, Turkey	(Flight)	-	-	-
Trabole	52.5	12	228	307
Ordu	58.2	12.4	116	214
Unye	48.8	10	329	473
Akkus	37.6	5.5	1206	418
Niksar	25.8	7.6	424	1479
Tokat	34.1	8.1	681	557
Yildizeli	38.5	7.1	840	426
Sivas	29.5	10.7	212	349
Sarkisla	51.6	12.4	248	324
Bunyan	54.8	10.7	398	487
Kayseri	30.2	10.7	58	343
Avanos	52.9	10.9	287	512

Destination	Total Distance	Average Speed	Metres Up	Metres Down
Urgup	13.7	6.5	293	243
Goreme	6.1	5	149	175
Aksaray	57.5	10.3	516	811
Konya	99.7	10.7	141	231
Seydishir	58.4	9.6	623	735
Cide	91.1	9.2	1088	2572
Antalya	49.1	12.2	130	144
Olympus	53.8	9.2	538	783
Demra	45.8	8.1	513	654
Kalkan	45.2	7.1	888	1161
Fethiye	45.2	8.9	425	501
Dalman	40.7	9.8	464	572
Akyaka	38.3	10	210	246
Yatagan	33.1	8.1	693	590
Selimiye	33.9	9.4	415	777
Soke	40.4	10.2	298	417
Kusadasi	13.6	8.1	259	329

Notes

• UK ferry ride (140.5 miles); Denmark 222.1 miles); Turkey (1280.1 miles)

• Longest climb – 37.6 miles with 1206 metre gain in height

• Longest ride – Just under 100 miles into Konya.

• Longest decent – 2572 metre drop in elevation. An amazing downhill to the coast at the end of a hard day.

The world at 9.5 mph (based on an average of averages).

15.

HOME

"There's no place like home; there's no place like home; there's no place like home."

L. Frank Baum

(author of The Wizard of Oz)

It's fair to say coming home felt like a bit of a shock. I'd no replacement or new equipment needs, no bike to service and no further trips to talk about. This time the questions were all about 'what next' and there were no quick answers to that one. Perhaps there is a right time to finish? We were on a high – there had not been an argument or accident. Perhaps we could save up and head out again. Perhaps this was it. Perhaps, perhaps, perhaps...

We landed back at Stanstead on the 27th of September. Such a strange feeling knowing that the adventures that had been our lives for the past two or so years were at an end. While I can't speak for John, I'm fairly sure we shared the same vacuous space. Fear, uncertainty, and the sense of a new stage of life were overwhelming.

Easy to reflect and wonder whether we should have wild camped; survived on a tighter budget and stretched out the ride, yet we have no regrets. The decisions we made were right for us. Early on we discussed wanting to see the sites, eat great food, discover different experiences, and indeed share the odd moment of luxury too. They say you can only really regret the things you haven't done, not the things you have, and we were certainly both proud of all we had accomplished.

Friends and family had been following our ride and it was great to know now that we were home that the connections with friends and family would be for more than just a quick hello. There were lots of things to catch up on, with many memories, photos, and stories to share. While many of my friends live miles away from Stansted, John's friends were a little closer to the airport, and we were delighted to be met for the ride back to Stokenchurch. Mentally, this final trip was not easy. In truth, I think we both would have carried on riding as we had forever and so the company of friends was a welcome distraction form all that was on our minds. What would the next stage of life bring?

Neither of us had any specific plans. While we were back in Turkey, I'd started to look at potential jobs for my return, fantasised about a life removed from the rat race and even started writing a few children's books. John had no idea. We were both nervous. Both unsure. Coming home was, in many ways, more daunting than the starting the ride back in Seattle. All very strange.

While travelling I've been renting out my flat in Edinburgh and with such an abrupt end to the trip my flat was still occupied. I would be going back to my ma's house for a while. My tenants would need good notice - life was quickly changing for them too. For the first few weeks I'm not sure the fact the trip had actually ended really sunk in. Having completed our tour in five, five-month blocks, being at my mom's house initially felt similar to our previous drop ins. However, as more friends and family asked 'what now' the notion our journey really was over began to sink inn. What now? It was a good question.

I gave notice to my tenants and in the second week of November returned to the city that I loved, Edinburgh. It was exciting and felt like another new start - catching up with friends, looking for work and unpacking clothes, books and music that had all been boxed away for the past three years. I've always thought of myself as fairly resilient and while disappointed, I continued to find joy and opportunity in whatever came next. One decision I had made was to move on from my much-loved city centre flat. There was no way I could get out of the rat race and continue to live in central Edinburgh.

Cleaning and decorating took hold, and I was busy. John on the other hand was struggling.

It's hard coming to terms with the fact that your, once in a lifetime opportunity has ended. What could ever top this? How do you adjust to normality? What is the impact of the trip on the rest of your life? John and I had gone our separate ways but with him at a complete loss I suggested he join me in Edinburgh-maybe it was a place he too could settle in, at least for a short while. He moved into the spare room, and I began to show him around Edinburgh but whether he just couldn't see himself in the city or whether our time together had ended now the trip was over I wasn't sure. But I knew he wasn't right.

After a few days he left in tears and as I came home from Waverley Station I was also crying. I was so worried about him, nervous about what he would do and how he would move forward. I'd tried to help but hadn't been able. I was so relieved to hear when he finally arrived back in Stokenchurch. I really had been that worried. We continued to speak and as John sought help, I got on with sorting my belongings and decorating the flat. I too would soon be leaving.

It was the first week in December when I took call from my uncle. Mum was not great. She'd been struggling a little before I had left, and it seemed things got worse. I decided to return home to the Midlands (Dudley) early for the Christmas break yet as I loaded computers clothes and sundries into my suitcase, I think I knew I would never be going back.

Nothing had really prepared me for what came next. I don't think anything ever can. Mum had been unsteady on her legs and the doctor was treating her for vertigo. However, it was the cancer that had spread and for the past two days she had been unable to walk at all. The cancer had moved into her spine, and it had been this that had been causing issues with mobility. Frightened, yet also relieved to be home we were awaiting a visit from the Macmillan doctors. It was not great news and less than 24 hours after stepping off the train, we were waiting for an emergency ambulance.

Mum remained in hospital for the next month, and I would visit twice daily. These situations make cycling the Annapurna circuit seem like a cinch. Christmas came and as I joined her at the hospital bed it confirmed that our unconventional, staged approach to cycling the world had been the correct choice. The time between trips was so valuable, providing the time with mom and of course, with other friends and family too.

While back in Dudley, I continued to stay in touch with John. He gone back to his old job though sadly this was just a temporary situation. He was still finding the adjustment just too hard. In a strange way my return had been eased by a situation way out of my control. Given the situation I was now in, I felt a huge sense of relief that there really is a right time to stop. I was so glad to have been back in the UK just as I was most needed. Mom had felt awful when I cancelled the initial trip and I know she would have kept her ill-health from me as long as possible, but some things are just more important. Strange how things work out eh?

It was during December that conversations with John changed the course of events for both of us. Mom was not well, and one day, during a routine visit she suddenly took a turn for the worst. Faced with multiple organ failure doctors were not sure she would make it through the night. Pumped full of steroids we would just have to wait it out. They were awful times and I'll never forget being in the hospital at this time.

I returned to the house and while not alone – I was still looking after her student lodgers, given she hadn't wanted to disrupt their final month or so in the UK – I felt very much on my own. The doctor had promised to monitor mom's stats and when the phone rang around midnight to say she had improved I can't describe the sense of relief. What a roller-coaster.

The next day I called John again to update him and he offered to come and stay for a few weeks. It was a big relief, though still nothing compared to that of knowing that mom had made it through. My family, friends and friends of my ma had been brilliant but after two and a half years in each other's company John had become my rock. A few weeks after that awful night mom was allowed home. A room was set up with a hospital bed and care provision was also at hand. John agreed to stay until a routine was settled. In truth, I think having a new focus and goal was also helping him. We'd developed a huge bond during our time on the road yet we both look back now and say it was cemented during this period that followed. I'd had some tough days while touring but they were generally rare. I don't know whether it was my increased vulnerability, or the chance John may have felt to be part of a team again, that brought us together, but it was clear that our lives were moving forward as one. While still just best of friends, John moved in and as he took on a housekeeper role focusing on cooking and cleaning, I was able to spend time by mom's side.

It was November 2015 when mom passed away. Thankfully, while bed bound, she had remained in good spirits and John and I often joked that we ran a café, constantly making tea and buying cakes for the daily visitors. I'd never thought of this 'stage' of my life and really it was more about a 'stage' in someone else's, but it was a time I will always cherish. It also meant relatively quickly we were faced with another 'what next'?

John had become accustomed to the Midlands yet for me this was an area I had left when I was 18 and headed to university. I just didn't see myself in suburbia. Having left the city, my cycle tour life had put me in a variety of settings – all far removed from a busy social life and built-up areas. Moving was on the cards but we needed to work out where to. For John, his ideal location was somewhere warm – France, Italy, Spain. For me, I loved Scotland and wanted to return. We also of course had to think about work and income.

While the rat race was ruled out, I did still want a challenge and sense of achievement. I could do consultancy work, but I was also really keen to run my own business. John was nervous about heading back into the conventional workplace again and we decided we would look at the options for running self-catering/holiday accommodation. Budgets however were not endless and as we started to visit Scotland it soon became apparent that taking on an existing business was not so straightforward. For many owners, running a business like this was seen as post-retirement work - a hobby business not a full commercial venture. Far from sweating the assets, we found that raising the finance for a business that had tapered down like this was nigh on impossible. We were back to the drawing board.

I'd already started to look at existing businesses with 'add-ons' in mind and was keen to bring creativity and some of our experience from travelling to our plans. Glamping was an obvious links and so properties including farms and houses with land, were all added to the shortlist. Despite several trips to Scotland, we were still struggling to find the perfect place and for a while our search zone extended to Wales too. Maybe we were looking across too wide an area but after viewing a number of damp, derelict and wholly unsuitable places we were almost about to hit the starting blocks again. We kept looking in Wales, but it never really felt right. The Highlands were stunning but a long, long drive from both our families. In the end it was one trip to Dumfries and Galloway that sealed our fate.

We didn't buy the house we went to view near Newton Stewart but as we drove along the A75, passing the water to our left and looking out at the peninsular in front of us, we both knew this was where we wanted to be. Often by-passed and known as the forgotten corner of Scotland. Dumfries and Galloway is a truly stunning part of the country – perhaps as far from the rat race as I could have envisaged. Knowing we had found our place in the world, even if only by location, felt great. A new home was starting to emerge.

We returned to the Midlands knowing where we wanted to be and as mom's house was now on the market we would need to find somewhere fairly soon. My own Edinburgh flat had also been sold in the past year, belongings were in storage and the clock was ticking. Over the next few months, we would make several trips. We put an offer in on a small 10-acre farm but were gazumped. I had all the agents on speed dial, constantly checking web sites, looking for new listings and researching areas that were new to us. We saw an amazing farm but ruled it out on price, visited properties that worked on paper but then didn't seem right on viewing and found suitable land, but the living accommodation was too small. Just as we were about to reconsider the property wish list, we viewed a fabulous house with potential land over in Wigtownshire. We were just discussing a likely offer when the phone rang. The amazing farm had dropped its asking price.

It's funny how you can look for a while and then multiple options come at once – we opted for the farm and soon our offer was accepted. Plans made for sheep, ducks, pigs, and chickens, I was also busy researching glamping pods and local planning guides. Mom's house was sold and in September 2016 we were on the move. The farm was just as I'd remembered. Situated on a Category C, single track road between Gatehouse of Fleet and Lauriston, the 65-acre farmhouse, shed and outbuildings offered so much potential. I was confident we had found the right place for our plans. But it was not to be.

Despite tears of joy from us both after our second visit and my continued enthusiasm, within 24 hours of arrival John had changed. Perhaps the reality of living here had hit home, maybe he was more overwhelmed by what lay ahead but he was soon back as the John who had left my Edinburgh flat in tears at the end of 2014.

I was super excited, and he was an emotional wreck – either way we were not on the same page. I couldn't do this on my own - I would just have to wait to see if he could do it at all. Neighbours arrived to welcome us, we sorted stuff (unpacking again!) and made some early property changes but as I waited to see if John would settle it became obvious that this was not going to happen. We were back as we had been when we first landed at Stanstead. The only difference now being that we were moving forwards together. Two weeks after moving in we agreed to put the property back up for sale. This was not our new home after all.

People often talk about the transition from the adventure of a lifetime back into normal life and so far, we had found it to be a very rocky road. I would have to find my optimism and utilise problem solving skills to my upmost. We would make this work, much as we had when we first set out. Consigned to moving on again, the farm was up for sale and once again, we needed to find another place to live. Thankfully, with the decision now made to move, John did start to feel a little better – just a massive sense of relief, I guess. We showed several people round, always honest about the why. While we didn't want anyone else to have the same experience, we also wouldn't want them to jump to any incorrect assumptions either. The farm and land were brilliant. It really was perfect for all we had planned.

Viewings came and went but when looking at land and property everyone is very fussy - ideas and subsequent needs vary. I guess we were just waiting for someone with the same plans as us. The Hunters arrived during the Easter bank holidays – we were the last property they were looking at before returning home. Like us, they had been searching primarily in Scotland and with a tentative venture into Wales too. Like us, they cried on seeing the farm. The deal was virtually signed and sealed that weekend. Now we really needed to find somewhere to live.

Again, we saw several places – house too small, no room for a polytunnel, too far to walk to the pub. We viewed a variety of places, but nothing seemed quite right, and we needed to get this move right. Having exhausted our initial possibilities, we were left with just one house. The space and garden looked great, and it was in the right location, but it's fair to say it was ugly and while we both had the house saved in our online searches, we had both held back. Yet with nothing else coming on the market we reluctantly went to view.

Despite the off-putting exterior, it did actually tick all the boxes. There was room for my shoes, pianos (yep – plural), books and all our furniture. It offered views over the town and estuary, a back gate into the woods, and the town offered all we were looking for. It's weird how things go and as we walked away that day, we knew this really was it. Home.

Over five years on now and we're still there. We're still just the best of friends but somehow, we know this is us. John works part time at the local builder's merchant and I work in a freelance capacity, supporting impact-led businesses through-out Scotland. We've added new doggy members to the 'family' and we are happy. I still dream of publishing my children's books and John has taken up woodworking. I'm pleased to say the house has also now moved on from its 1970's style and our ugly house is no more.

Perhaps the strangest thing about settling back home is that for both of us, despite loving our tour and riding bikes a lot before then, the bikes have been gathering dust. While busy with dogs and house renovations (still ongoing) I can't really say why we've not been back out on The Captain and Kylie. Maybe cycling just isn't the same anymore but I hope that in finishing this book and remembering all we have achieved that this may just be the encouragement we need to get back out there.

I don't know if we'll ever have the chance to travel like this again or indeed whether I'll be fit enough for quite the same type of adventure but one thing's for sure this trip changed my life and my outlook.

One life. One opportunity.

What will you do with yours?

The Stats; The Last Ride

59.9 Miles

Destination	Total Distance	Average Speed	Metres Up	Metres Down
Stansted	(Flight)	-	-	-
Stokenchurch	59.9	10.7	661	700

Notes

- 5 friends joined us as a few others cheered us in.

- Pints consumed on our final night... I wasn't counting!

Perhaps it's time to admit that the world at 15mph was perhaps a little optimistic. Oh well – why change the habit of a lifetime!

16.

REFLECTIONS

"She who succeeds in gaining the mastery of the bicycle will gain the mastery of life."

Frances E. Willard

Oh, if only that quote were true.

Despite being all fired up to get this book out at the end of our tour we are now some 10 years on. I don't want to finish the book with self-indulgent waffle at the end of the 'pilgrimage'. Of course, I've learnt stuff - about me and about others. I have perspectives on the places I've been and the country to which I've come home. I've always held these interests and will continue to do so. I wanted to end the book with some thoughts that may help others whether planning a cycle tour, a long period of travel, simply finding themselves at a cross-roads in their life and some notes on coming home. If it's indulgent – I apologise. If it helps – brilliant. If you just don't care that's fine too.

1. You don't regret what you do – only what you don't do! One life; one opportunity has long been the motto at The World at 15 mph. Read "The top five regrets of the dying" by Bronnie Ware and apply this to your own life. Be courageous!

2. Post MBA, I had big time career aspirations. Going on this long-term break, being a carer and then choosing to live in Dumfries and Galloway has certainly messed up a career trajectory. Sometimes I do question the price paid from a work perspective but as with the note above – I have no regrets. This trip will always hold the most incredible memories and introduced me to my friend for life.

3. I love a challenge. ... I'm proud of things I've achieved (they were beyond my own expectations) but it's not a competi-tion. Too often adventure and travel seems to be presented in this way. Push yourself but you don't need to complete with others unless that is the key purpose of what you're doing. It's not about cycling the furthest, surviving on the cheapest

budget you can, climbing the biggest hills – it's about what you want to do - not what others are doing.

4. Remain interested in others. This statement is true whether you're travelling or have returned home. I really enjoy doing talks about our tour, but my favourite part is always when others share their experiences too. I've particularly enjoyed doing talks for the WI and other retirement clubs. I love being surprised as the quiet, unassuming, and often older audience participants tell tales of buying a bus and driving to Afghanistan in the 60's and remark on photos that remind them of their own trips and adventures. The best bit about talking of your own stories is hearing people respond and share their own tales. The best bit about travel are the people you meet.

5. Recognise when you've been fortunate (I am very grateful I was able to do the trip the way I did) but also take credit for making things happen. Lots of people dream but not everyone invests time and resources or takes risks to actually do the doing. The first steps are always the hardest and you can always turn around BUT make that a conscious decision. Don't let fear paralyse you.

6. 99.999% of people are good. They are proud of where they live, proud of their roots and just want to live their best life. We often get asked about dangers, robbery, and personal safety. We had few negative experiences on our trip but were overwhelmed by people's good nature and hospitality.

7. Document your trip - Get some camera skills before you leave and keep a diary. Even as I read through my own notes there are huge gaps in data I'd now love to know; there are places and experiences I wish I had better photographs of and

there are comments that while they made sense at the time are less clear now.

8. Reduce your calorie intake when you stop. We ate huge meals while riding each day; we ate cake most days when we could, and I liked to have a beer at the end of each ride where possible. Sadly, when the exercise regime reduces, so too should the intake. I wish I'd thought of this earlier!

9. Your first, second and even third attempt at packing will always include things you don't really need. - though I still hold that my nail polish was a brilliant luxury item and travel essential. There are some items that could have been vital even if you didn't need them (insurance, anti-biotics/ pre travel injections) and some items that just make it easier if you have just in case (enough inner tubes, pumps that work, spare tyre, spokes etc).

10. If you're travelling by bike - Our fold away holdalls were brilliant for plane travel, and we always tried to book airlines where your paid for an extra bag (this included a bike box) rather than extra kilos. We were not worried about using buses, trains, car hire and even planes when in countries where time, visa restrictions and the places we wanted to visit would have not been possible had had a 'bike only' rule. If you're doing the Annapurna circuit – take a mountain bike or walk!

Remember, getting started is the hardest part. After that you can do anything. Perhaps that's the thing to master.

Some thoughts from John

"Naomi has asked me to say a few words and while its actually quite difficult to add anything to the tale, I do have a couple of things to say.

Firstly, I got so lucky finding someone who wants to go travelling with me (or was that the other way round). Better still, meeting someone who really enjoyed the detailed planning that trips required was a godsend.

Secondly, I'm not sure whether I told of mentioned to Nao that I'd never cycle toured yet alone put up a tent before or that I'd been diagnosed as clinically depressed. Either way, Nao accepted me, helped me, and possibly saved my life. It's a bold claim but seriously having the ability to go travelling was amazing but what probably saved me was being housekeeper to her mom.

Thirdly, having just celebrated the ten-year anniversary of our trip ending, I finally proposed to my best friend. Thankfully, she agreed to marry me and it's hard to believe it all started by being brave enough to sign up for an organised cycle event.

Be brave, you never know where it may lead."

Acknowledgements

So many people were amazing and helped to make this happen, not least John. I'm so chuffed he made that initial contact once the organised tour we'd both sign up for had been cancelled. I'm ever grateful for all the support he gave me, when looking after my ma and more recently on losing my dad. He may, by his own admission, be a bit grumpy at times but he really is incredible.

Mark Beaumont inspired the ride, while good friends supported me to sign up for the initial trip (Kim and Jim). My folks, despite being nervous, helped me enormously. Close friends offered support and challenge – it's always good to have both. Then there's the bike shop, the travel agent, help with self-publishing, with web sites and all the food, lifts, and accommodation we received on the way.

Lastly, to those that continue to want to listen to this story and encouraged me to get this book finished. I thank you.

Nao

ABOUT NAOMI

Naomi now lives in Southwest Scotland working as a freelancer for a variety of impact focused businesses and projects.

You can read more about this adventure on the website links given below and if you'd like to **book Naomi as a speaker** for your club or event then do get in touch through the website. As well as sharing details and inspiration from her trip for a general audience, Naomi can also offer business focused presentations, taking lessons from her adventures and enterprise experience.

For more information, please visit: www.bikemind.co.uk or look up John's Cycle Tour (wordpress.com)

Milton Keynes UK
Ingram Content Group UK Ltd.
UKHW010103020923
427886UK00005B/44